# After You Marry

*101 Questions and Answers on a Lasting Marriage Relationship*

**Ben Adewuyi**

The House of Scribes, Inc.
Nashville, Tennessee

THOS

The House of Scribes, Inc.
P. O. Box 293334
Nashville, Tennessee, TN 37229
Www.myhouseofscribes.com



Unless otherwise indicated, scriptural quotations are taken from the King James Version (KJV) and New International Version (NIV) of the Bible.

ISBN 978-1-946740-06-9

First edition, November 2017

Printed in the United States of America on acid free paper

For counselling and trade enquiries, contact the author,
Pastor Ben Adewuyi
Tel: (615) 668-5801
Email: ben_adewuyi@yahoo.com

# Dedication

I dedicate this book to my sweetheart,
my confidant, my wife
Pastor Toro Adewuyi,
for joining me on this marital journey
since October 18, 1997.
To God Be the Glory!

# Acknowledgment

I am grateful to God for saving me on December 24$^{th}$, 1984 and for calling me into the ministry on May 27$^{th}$, 1994. As written in 1 Timothy 1:12 "*And I thank Christ Jesus our Lord, who hath enabled me, for that he counted me faithful, putting me into the ministry.*" Most importantly, I thank God for the wisdom and grace to write this book.

This book would not have been completed successfully without the support of some wonderful people whom God has placed in my life. Neither words nor money can ever be enough to thank everyone for their unparalleled support, efforts and sacrifices. Some of you have gone beyond and above measure to ensure the success of this project from start to completion. Some of you provided questions asked by your members. Some of you assisted with the editing, proof-reading and critiquing of the manuscript. And some of you just encouraged. My sincere appreciation is extended to all of you: Pastor Tunde Adenola, Pastor Yinka Adeyemo, Pastor Philip Ajayi , Pastor Isaac Aladeniyi, Pastor Owupele Bamson , Pastor Gboyega Esan, Mrs. Temitope Falana, Evangelist Clara B. Gifford, Dr. Moses Ochonu, Pastor Tony Odugunwa, Dr. Adebayo Oyebade, Pastor Brown Oyitso, and Pastor Francis Tekobo . I greatly appreciate each one of you.

My special thanks and gratitude are extended to the most precious people in my life: My family, the people who supported, encouraged and cheered me on from start to completion of this project. They are the nucleus, the people to whom I return home daily, who love, honor and respect me, despite my state of mind and being. I am eternally grateful to my wife, the woman who although has witnessed my shortcomings, imperfections, errors and insensitivities, yet has endured gracefully and remained by my side, showing me her unequivocal love and support through it all. My children, the daughters who bore my frustrations, forfeited some of their benefits, and assumed my household chores to enable me to complete this book.

# Foreword

The initial thought I had after reading Pastor Ben Adewuyi's first book - *Before You Marry* - was everyone should read this book before dating or getting married. This sequel by far exceeds that.

*After You Marry* is a manual that every couple should own. It is a practical and sensible guide, not only for days when answers to questions are sought, but a tool to aid in understanding and managing the major scenarios that arise in marriage. The book makes godly marriages simple to understand, follow and more workable. The book details principles of marriage in such a simple way that it can be taught in churches and seminars. I also recommend this book to pastors, teachers and marriage counselors.

Marriage is an institution established by God, the union of a man and a woman, to positively influence their environment, and to be the back bone of every community in society. With the current rise in divorce cases, even in churches, it is apparent that we need to return to the foundation; understanding what marriage is. The importance of wisdom and understanding in marriage cannot be overemphasized. Proverbs 4:7 states *"Wisdom is the principal thing; therefore, get wisdom. And in all your getting, get understanding."*

Just as ***Before You Marry*** answers over a hundred questions that should not be ignored before marriage, this book, ***After You Marry***, is an insight into the challenges of marriage and how to understand, address, overcome and defeat them. It makes distinctions between godly and ungodly marriages. It explains the impact of in-laws and families upon marriage. And it addresses the sometime difficult issues of money, sex, abuse and other prevalent matters in marriage.

Pastor Ben Adewuyi, a Zonal Coordinator of the Redeemed Christian Church of God, North America, armed with over 20 years' experience in marriage counselling, provides a compendium of godly answers to the most common questions that couples face in the most complicated moments of everyday life and existence. While I appreciate the fact that the questions and answers are not equivalent to being in the scenario first hand, they do however provide insight into the godly knowledge necessary for such moments. I cannot think of a better guide to accompany couples while on their journey to marital bliss.

This invaluable book is a must read for all those who want to experience marital bliss and make a success of their marriages.

Pastor Brown Oyitso
Special Assistant to the General Overseer, Missions
Pastor in Charge of Region 19
The Redeemed Christian Church of God

# Table of Contents

# List of Questions

Chapter 1
**Marriage Principles and Faith**

1. What are the principles of marriage in Genesis Chapter 1?
2. What are the principles of marriage in Genesis Chapter 2?
3. What are the principles of marriage in Genesis chapter 3?
4. What are the principles of secular marriage?
5. What is the nature of the heart of man in marriage?
6. What is the condition of the heart of man in marriage?
7. How can a heart of stone become a heart of flesh, or a cold heart become a burning heart?
8. What are the classifications of married couples?
9. Why does the Bible describe wives as the weaker vessels?
10. Should couples belong to different churches?
11. How can the church help couples live peacefully?

Chapter 2
**Roles and Responsibilities**

12. What are the roles and responsibilities of a woman in marriage?
13. What are the roles and responsibilities of a man in marriage?
14. What is the importance of love and respect in marriage?
15. What are the ways a wife can express respect to her husband?
16. What are the ways a husband can express love to his wife?
17. What is the ultimate responsibility of a husband?
18. What are the differences between a virtuous and a foolish wife?
19. What are the differences between a wise and a foolish husband?
20. What are the deadly sins or behaviors in a marriage?

# Introduction

I write this book for three reasons, the first of which is to fulfill the purpose of my first book. My first book on marriage and relationships, ***"Before You Marry"*** was written for three distinct reasons: my sincere passion for marriage, the need to address numerous unanswered questions facing young men and women in their quests to get married, and the need to provide godly counsel to Christian men and women both young and old. These reasons have not diminished or changed, but have become stronger and broader. The flame of my passion for marriage is still fervently burning and intensifies daily. I find it difficult to hold my peace when proper attention is not given to marriage seekers and the questions raised by singles and couples alike remain unanswered. I am emotionally disturbed and spiritually dismayed when godly counselors and spiritual mentors are unavailable to singles and couples who seek valid answers to genuine questions and situations that arise, prior to and after marriage

The second reason is to meet the request for a book suitable to couples in marriage. My first book, ***"Before You Marry",*** highlights principles and truths of God's word and focuses on the single men and women who are preparing for marriage. I am grateful to God that this book has fulfilled its purpose and has been a catalyst in drawing people closer to God in the areas of relationship and marriage.

Many people who read the book did not only give positive reviews but have shared their personal testimonies of how God has used the book to enlighten them. For lack of space, the following are three excerpts from some reviews and testimonies.

- *"Without the lessons I learned from this book, I would probably not be where I am today..."*
- *"Masterfully crafted and grounded in divine wisdom of God through the Holy Bible, Pastor Ben Adewuyi's book offers to its readers God's blueprint for a blissful marital union."*
- *"Congrats for this wonderful and timely book. I received it a few days ago and I was reading it inside a plane yesterday. To say the least, the materials are excellent. By His grace, I am a family based clinician who has practiced in US for about 10 Years and currently the CEO of an agency that organizes seminar and training on marriage and relational issues. It contains so many questions they asked me during seminar on marriage. This book has become my dictionary. It is a blessing. I give you my kudos for a job well done."*

Many, and especially marriage counselors and couples, have requested a book that will mainly focus on those who are already married. That is what this book "***After You Marry***" addresses. It answers practical questions raised by couples in marriage based on the word of God. It is important to emphasize that most of these questions were asked during marriage counselling sessions, seminars, and couples' programs.

Finally, this book is borne out of my strong desire to obey the leading of the Holy Spirit in my life. There is absolutely no doubt that I have wept, and fasted and prayed because of difficult marriages of many people, trusting God for intervention to hold these marriages together. Now, I believe the Lord is prompting me to extend my pastoral ministry to include marriage ministry. This book, I believe, affords me a platform to explain these godly principles to many couples that I would not be able to reach personally and physically.

In conclusion, I need to make a confession here, the same as the one I made in my first book: I am not an authority on this subject, but I am only a vessel in God's hands. The content and context of this book are a product of over 33 years of service to the Lord and learning the word of God. If there is any part of this book you do not understand, please consult your pastor and teachers for clarification. For speaking engagements, you may invite me or request your pastor to invite me to come to speak to your groups, fellowships and churches during your marriage and relationship programs. Also, if you wish to contact me personally, you may write via email (ben_adewuyi@yahoo.com) or leave a comment on my Facebook page and I will be more than happy to respond. I strongly hope and pray that this book blesses you and your marriage.

Chapter 1

# Marriage Principles And Faith

*Faith in God* is a means of gaining access to God. It is the belief and trust we have in God that He is what He says He is and can do what He says He can do. Without faith, it is impossible to please God. We are saved and live righteously by faith. Faith is the foundation of joy, peace, blessing, happiness, and blissfulness. Jesus Christ is the epitome of faith and the source of faith is the word of God. Physical senses measure a thing by how it looks, smells, tastes, sounds and feels; but, on the contrary, faith measures a thing by what God says and the principles of the word of God. According to Romans 10:17, *"So then faith cometh by hearing, and hearing by the word of God.* The first couple (Adam and Eve) lost it because they listened to a different voice and deviated from faith, but the couples of today should learn how to practice and stay in faith by obeying the word of God. Couples should maintain faith in their marriages by trusting God and following His principles.

1. **What are the principles of marriage in Genesis Chapter 1?**

The main issue of marriage is, "the heart of man," and "how marriage should be from the beginning." By "beginning," I mean, the principle, truth and revelation detailed for us in Genesis Chapters one, two and three. Apart from marriage, there are many secrets and principles of success in career, faith, business, and life embedded in these three chapters of the scriptures. The response to this question will highlight seven principles of creation as related to marriage from Genesis, Chapter One. Dr. Mensa Otabil, of the International Central Gospel Church, identified four of these principles in his message about "Creating Order in Life".

- **Principle of Light** - The first thing God created was light.

> "***In the beginning God created the heavens and the earth. Now the earth was formless and empty, darkness was over the surface of the deep, and the Spirit of God was hovering over the waters. And God said, "Let there be light," and there was light.*** Genesis 1:1-3 (NIV)

The absence of light leads to confusion, crisis and conflict. As a car without light is heading for an accident, a marriage without light is heading for failure. Light brings illumination, success and speed. Light not only exposes darkness, but it establishes peace and order through its removal. Literally, light is knowledge, and spiritually light is Jesus Christ. There is no premium too high for knowledge, and its alternative is destruction. Jesus Christ is the Light, and accepting Him as Savior guarantees light and life.

> ***"My people are destroyed for lack of knowledge..."*** Hosea 4:8

> ***"... He said, "I am the light of the world. Whoever follows me will never walk in darkness, but will have the light of life."*** John 8:12

The couple in a peaceful and lasting marriage will not only have Christ as their Lord and Savior, they will also seek the knowledge of God for their life and marriage.

- **Principle of Separation** - God was so excellent in creation that He did not commingle what He created. He separated, differentiated, and distinguished between everything He created.

> ***"God saw that the light was good, and he separated the light from the darkness. God called the light "day," and the darkness he called "night." And there was evening, and there was morning--the first day."*** Genesis 1:4-5 (NIV)

He made a division between light and darkness, night and day, heaven and earth, sun and moon, male and female, man and woman, and the list continues. The God of creation applied the same principles throughout the Bible - heaven and hell, believers and unbelievers, but Christians today don't want to be different. Same-sex marriage cannot be of God. Christian marriage should be, and is quite different from, the non-Christian marriage.

> ***"That be far from thee to do after this manner, to slay the righteous with the wicked: and that the righteous should be as the wicked that be far from thee: Shall not the Judge of all the earth do right?"*** Genesis 18:35 (KJV)

- **Principle of Boundary** - God set boundaries and limitations in everything He created.

> ***"And God said, let the waters under the heaven be gathered together unto one place, and let the dry land appear: and it was so. And God called the dry***

> ***land Earth; and the gathering together of the waters called He Seas: and God saw that it was good."*** Genesis 1:9-10 (KJV)

The water and land were restricted to specific spaces, the Sun was restricted to day, the moon was constrained to night, fish were made for water, Adam and Eve were made for one another and were restricted from eating certain fruit. Any violation of boundary will lead to crisis and ultimately death. Every person has their own boundary. If a person plans to enjoy marriage, it is necessary to understand and respect spousal boundaries.

- **Principle of Growth** - God made room for growth in creation. He created and allowed all things to develop from infancy to maturity, smallness to greatness, and a little to an abundance.

> ***"And God said, Let the earth bring forth grass, the herb yielding seed, and the fruit tree yielding fruit after his kind, whose seed is in itself, upon the earth: and it was so. And the earth brought forth grass, and herb yielding seed after his kind, and the tree yielding fruit, whose seed was in itself, after his kind: and God saw that it was good.*** Genesis 1:11-12 (KJV)

God created the earth and out of the earth came the land, out of the land came the garden, and out of the garden came the forest. He created the light, and out of the light came the sun, moon, and stars. He created water, and out of the water He created the ponds, streams, seas, oceans, and rivers. Even Christ, the Savior came as a child. Luke 1:80 (KJV) reads, *"And the child grew, and waxed strong in spirit ..."* Couples should grow to varying levels of maturity in their marriage - by not repeating past mistakes, rendering forgiveness to one another, being mutual in decision making, and not taking advantage of one another's weaknesses.

- **Principle of Seed** - God created once and empowered each creature to produce after its kind. He embedded seed within everything He created.

  ***"And God said, Let the earth bring forth grass, the herb yielding seed, and the fruit tree yielding fruit after his kind, whose seed is in itself, upon the earth: and it was so. And the earth brought forth grass, and herb yielding seed after his kind, and the tree yielding fruit, whose seed was in itself, after his kind: and God saw that it was good.*** Genesis 1:11-12 (KJV)

  A good marriage is most likely to birth good children who may produce more good marriages. An abusive or failed marriage will most likely produce more abusive and failed marriages. God's intent was to make man and woman a manufacturer, decider, and creator of their kind.

- **Principle of Time** - God created time and season for a reason.

  ***"And God said, Let there be lights in the firmament of the heaven to divide the day from the night; and let them be for signs, and for seasons, and for days, and years."*** Genesis 1:14 (KJV)

  He has predestined accomplishments for each day. Couples should have an understanding and respect for time. The intention of God is that couples will correctly appropriate their time to satisfy themselves, their spouse, and Him. Right things should be done at the right time. There is a problem when work, business, career and friends will not allow one to care for spouse and family.

- **Principle of Leadership** – God created the earth to have a leader. Leadership is important for the success of any venture or organization.

  ***"And God said, Let us make man in our image, after our likeness: and let them have dominion over the fish of the sea, and over the fowl of the air, and over the cattle, and over all the earth, and over every creeping thing that creepeth upon the earth. So God created man in his own image, in the image of God created he him; male and female created he them."*** Genesis 1:26-27 (KJV)

  ***"Surely the Lord GOD will do nothing, but he revealeth his secret unto his servants the prophet."*** Amos 3:7

  Leadership is responsibility, management and accountability. God will not start a project, venture, or purpose, without first appointing a leader. He created man to rule and lead the world. He called Moses to lead the Israelites. He chose Jesus to save the world. Likewise, he chose the man to be the leader in marriage. To enjoy a lasting marriage, the man, that is the husband, should head and lead his wife, marriage, and family.

2. **What are the principles of marriage in Genesis Chapter 2?**

Marriage is the union between a man and a woman orchestrated for the glory of God and the fulfillment of life's purposes. Marriage allows for friendship, procreation, and recreation. It cures loneliness and inadequacies. It ensures complement and completeness. Marriage unites two people from different backgrounds, families, philosophies, and interests and makes them one. There are three types of marriages: Genesis Chapter 2 Marriage, Genesis Chapter 3 marriage, and Secular Marriage. The Genesis Chapter 2 Marriage exhibits the perfect will of God.

The Genesis Chapter 3 Marriage is a product of the permissive will of God, while the Secular marriage is the fulfillment of the perverse will of God. When Jesus said in Matthew 18:8 that, "... from the beginning it was not so..." he was referring to principles under which God instituted marriage in Genesis Chapter 2 before man fell into sin. The principles in Genesis Chapter 2 are many but for the purpose of this question, seven principles will be identified.

- **Principle of Composition** – This principle explains how many people or parties are in marriage. It establishes the truth that marriage consists not of two parties (man and woman), but three, namely, God, man and woman.

  > "***Then the LORD God made a woman from the rib he had taken out of the man, and he brought her to the man.***" Genesis 2:22

  Marriage is a tripartite covenant that involves God, man and woman. Marriage composition is as a triangle with the base angles as man and woman, and the head angle as God. God establishes and joins the couple in marriage. The inability to recognize this composition of marriage is the cause of failure and abuse in marriage. Godly marriage is not a marriage of two men or two women in a same-sex marriage. A perfect marriage is not a polygamous relationship of one man who is married to multiple women, nor one woman married to multiple men. In the beginning, God was a part of marriage, and today He should still be the most intricate part of it.

- **Principle of Leaving** – This principle explains who qualifies to marry. It establishes two very important requirements of marriage: maturity and independence.

***"Therefore shall a man leave his father and his mother and shall cleave unto his wife and they shall be one flesh."*** Matthew 2:24

Physical, emotional, financial, and spiritual maturity is expected from the married couple. A husband without emotional maturity may verbally abuse his wife because the food is not ready on time, while a wife that lacks emotional maturity may run to her mother at the slightest disagreement with her husband. The other part of this principle emphasizes that a couple is to be independent of their parents. The words of parents are no longer rules and laws binding on their married sons and daughters, but their words are mere advice to be considered or rejected. The couples should make their own decisions.

- **Principle of Cleaving** – This principle explains the need to know, woo and unite with a spouse. The word cleave implies adherence firmly, closely or loyally and unwavering. In essence, to stick together. It is called dating, courtship and romance with regard to marriage. Dating is a process of going out and doing things together, becoming familiar with one another, spending quality time. This does not end at the wedding but should be the beginning. Couples should continue to date each other, spend time with each other, go out to dinner, to movies, and concerts with one another. Married couples are also encouraged to exhibit public displays of endearment such as holding hands and walk through the mall or park. Courtship is a process of becoming acquainted with each other. There is a pre- and post-marriage courtship. Pre-marriage courtship ends at the wedding as it allows the couple to know each other with the confidence of marriage. Post marriage courtship allows unity with each other physically, financially, emotionally, and spiritually and promotes cohesiveness. Couples who cannot put their incomes together are not cleaving. A husband who does not support his wife's interests and career, or harnesses the couple's interests together is far from cleaving. A couple who hates to pray and worship together are not cleaving. Another part of cleaving is romance. This is accomplished through the process of creating excitement, fun, and enthusiasm with a spouse. The climax of an effective romance leads to meaningful, satisfying and fulfilling sexual intercourse.

- **Principle of Joining** - This principle explains the oneness and unity of the couple in marriage. Marriage starts from the wedding and does not end until the death of one of the spouses. In the beginning, the intention of God was to make them one flesh with no room for separation. This oneness allows the couple to defend each other from internal and external aggression and predators. A husband who cannot protect and defend his wife from the harassment of his family is not working within God's principle of marriage.

- **Principle of Suitability** - This principle presupposes and/or assumes that a couple is only fit for each other. Marriage is between a man and a woman and it is neither between the man's or woman's entire family. The support of both families is crucial and should be sought, but marriage is not for the family but rather for the couple. In the beginning, marriage was based on this principle, not on the culture of satisfying parental interests.

***"And Adam said, this is now bone of my bones, and flesh of my flesh: she shall be called Woman, because she was taken out of Man."*** Genesis 2:23

Because of this principle, the couple, especially the husband, has enormous work on his hand to stand and defend his wife from the ridicule of his family members who do not like her. She is made for and given to the husband, not the family. The husband should encourage his family to accept his choice without issue or questions.

- **Principle of Transparency** - This principle explains and expresses the need for openness, truthfulness, and sincerity in marriage.

  ***"And they were both naked, the man and his wife, and were not ashamed."*** Genesis 2:25

  In the beginning, there were no lies, half-truths, manipulations, pretenses, or deceptions between Adam and Eve. They were willing to expose their weaknesses, vulnerabilities, and strengths to each other. They celebrated each other's successes and accomplishments. They did not expose or attack each other's inadequacies, and neither were they ashamed of themselves. They were not afraid of having sex with each other and did not use it as a weapon to get even.

- **Principle of Completion** - This principle explains that the divine destiny of a man and woman is completed in marriage. It explains that man and woman are different, and marriage is a vehicle to cure and complement their differences. A man's rib (or his completeness) is also in a woman.

  ***"And the Lord God Said, It is not good for man to be alone, I will make a help meet for him."*** Genesis 2: 18

  Husbands and wives are brought into marriages to help, support, and complement each other. They marry for friendship, partnership, companionship, and fellowship. It is important to realize that the position a wife holds in marriage cannot be substituted with work, business, parents, sports, entertainment, or travel. In the beginning, there was an understanding of the composition of the family unit and it consisted of the husband, wife, and children.

3. **What are the principles of marriage in Genesis Chapter 3?**

The key to a lasting marriage is to apply the principles of marriage established in the beginning with a right heart. These principles spread across Genesis Chapters 1 through 3. The principles in Chapter 3 are a combination of the original intentions before the fall of man and remedial intentions after man sinned. Before the fall, man was under the influence of God and Satan, but after his fall, he came under God, nature, and Satan. The fall of man gave birth to nature and the senses. These principles in Genesis Chapter 3 are the basis of the permissive will or Genesis Chapter 3 type of marriage. The Genesis Chapter 3 concept of marriage reveals that marriage can be sweet, pleasant, beautiful, and blissful sometimes; and can be sour, painful, ugly, and bad at other times. This kind of marriage creates the cycle of matrimony that runs from honeymoon, to the reality of marriage, to old wine, and finally to new or no wine. The cycle of marriage was well discussed in the question 6 of my book, *Before You Marry*. The principles in Genesis Chapter 3 are numerous, but this question will only address seven principles.

- **The principle of Worship** - This principle explains that man and woman were created to worship and have fellowship with God. Their marriage was to glorify and honor God.

  ***"Then the man and his wife heard the sound of the Lord God as he was walking in the garden in the***

> ***cool of the day, and they hid from the Lord God among the trees of the garden.*"** Genesis 3:8

They were not only in the garden to dress or care for the garden; they were there to represent God. Their failure to recognize this led to their disobedience. They ate the forbidden fruit and ran away to escape from the presence of God. A marriage that has no room for faith and worship of God, is a time bomb waiting to explode. Attendance of worship services and Bible study gatherings, as well as service to God and fellowship with other believers, constitute God's plan for life and marriage.

- **Principle of Individualism** - This principle identifies husband and wife as separate entities rather than a single unit. This is the aftermath of the fall of man and woman.

  > ***"The man said, "The woman you put here with me— she gave me some fruit from the tree, and I ate it. Then the Lord God said to the woman, what is this you have done? The woman said, the serpent deceived me, and I ate."*** Genesis 3: 12-13

  The man that called the woman the bone of his bone and flesh of his flesh passed the blame of his error to the woman. The woman refused to assume responsibility, and allowed the blame to stick with her. She passed the errors to their neighbors, children, the serpent, work, and anything else that was associated with them. The original plan of God was to create togetherness and unity, not the individualism to which men and women have since resorted. To have a lasting marriage, a couple should shun individualism and independence and embrace unity, togetherness and interdependence.

- **Principle of Warfare** - This principle raises the inevitability of conflict and warfare in marriage. There will be conflict among all parties related to a marriage; that includes husband, wife, in-laws, and any other faceless people. The conflict may be physical, psychological, or spiritual. The intention of God was that marriage would be without conflict. However due to the fall of man, consequence of sin created warfare in life and marriage. To identify this conflict, Christ added a statement to the word in Genesis 2:24 as now stated in Matthew 19:5-6 that reads, ***"and said, 'For this reason a man shall leave his father and mother and be joined to his wife, and the two shall become one flesh'? So then, they are no longer two but one flesh. Therefore what God has joined together, let no man separate.*** *"* Marriage is facing assault from all sides because of various forces militating against it. As part of that warfare, the earth was cursed, work became laborious, living became sweaty, childbirth became painful, death became part of nature, the woman became subjected to the man, and spiritual enmity between man and Satan began.

- **Principle of Leadership** - This principle explains who has responsibility for leadership in a marriage. This was not an issue before the fall of man, because in creation God made them equally as male and female. However, following the blame game that ensued after the fall, God had to assign the final responsibility of marriage to man and subject woman to man in marriage. The campaign of gender equality is a good initiative that is workable outside of marriage, but a woman who wants to succeed in marriage must respect this leadership principle.

***"To the woman he said, I will make your pains in childbearing very severe; with painful labor you will give birth to children. Your desire will be for your husband, and he will rule over you."*** Genesis 3:16

***"For the husband is the head of the wife as Christ is the head of the church, his body, of which he is the Savior."*** Ephesians 5:23

The man, as head of the family, is expected to cultivate and to nourish his wife and bring out the very best in her. Not only that, among other responsibilities, he is also to protect her, and provide direction and guidance to her, as her pastor.

**Principle of Communication** - Since communication is vital to the success of any marriage, this principle emphasizes the need for couples to express themselves freely and to share and exchange their thoughts, opinions, and information.

***"When the woman saw that the fruit of the tree was good for food and pleasing to the eye, and also desirable for gaining wisdom, she took some and ate it. She also gave some to her husband, who was with her, and he ate it."*** Genesis 3:6

The communication between the woman and the serpent seemed attractive, but communication between the woman and the man was dysfunctional. The man did not stop the outsider, the serpent, from communicating with the woman. Their communication resorted to being a blame game, finger pointing, regretful, and an ignorant experience. This was not what God intended. God's intention was that the man and his wife could engage in good communication with each other, and that both of them would involve each other in communication that involved outsiders. A couple is discouraged from criticizing, complaining and condemning their spouse publicly. A couple is encouraged to speak positively and to support each other, not only in private, but publicly as well.

- **Principle of Forgiveness** - This principle explains the importance of forgiveness in marriage. God gave the example of forgiveness that marriage requires. Man and woman sinned against God, and instead of asking for forgiveness, they blamed God, each other, and other creations of God. Instead of staying in the place of appointment of worship and fellowship, they ran away into hiding. Because the wages of sin is death, they lost the glory of God and were sent out of the garden. God would have been unjust if they had not been punished, but He showed them mercy. He covered their nakedness by killing and shedding the blood of animals, and He arranged for the seed of the woman (Jesus Christ) to crush the head of Satan.

  ***"The Lord God made garments of skin for Adam and his wife and clothed them."*** Genesis 3:21

  Forgiveness is divine and helps to restore the offender. It is meaningful when it is done for unforgivable offenses. For couples to enjoy a lasting marriage, forgiveness cannot be in short supply.

- **Principle of Sexuality** - This principle explains the sexual attractiveness of married couples to each other. In the beginning, before the fruit was good for food, pleasing to the eye, and desirable for wisdom, it was all about the glory of God. The man and the woman were physically naked, but not ashamed, because they were clothed with the glory of God. The man and woman walked and worked in the garden naked, the woman spoke to the serpent naked, they both attended worship in the garden naked, and the glory of God was there to cover them. The first thing Satan did was to open the eyes of man and woman to see their sex life and their nakedness. Before they had sex, there was no complaint, but now complaints abound such as not being sexually satisfied, sexually active, and sexually compatible. Now sex is commercialized, abused, and violated. Sex is now the norm, even outside of marriage. Satan has opened wide the creative eyes of men and women to commit and approve fornication, adultery, pornography, homosexuality, lesbianism, open marriage and polygamy. The intention of God was for man and woman to enjoy sex within the coverage of His glory, but having lost the coverage, God made garments of skin to cover them.

***"Your beauty should not come from outward adornment, such as elaborate hairstyles and the wearing of gold jewelry or fine clothes. Rather, it should be that of your inner self, the unfading beauty of a gentle and quiet spirit, which is of great worth in God's sight."*** 1 Peter 3:3-4

4. **What are the principles of secular marriage?**

Secular marriage is one that differs from the marriages of Genesis Chapters 2 and 3. This marriage has as its basis, principles that differ from the Bible, the word of God. Secular marriage could be based on other religious books, norms, and practices. It could also be based on culture, customs, community, state constitutions and statutes. There are many principles paramount and evident in secular marriage, but this question addresses only seven of them.

- **Humanity** - Humanity is the condition and quality of human beings. It is the art of survival, maintenance, and acquisition of the quality of life by human beings. Humanity is both man and nature. It is the principles, ideas, and truths that man initiates, develops, and practices. It is also the products and deliveries of natural phenomenon. For instance, through humanity, man developed medicines to give good health and long life; transportation to move around safer and faster; money and commerce to produce wealth and prosperity; governments to exercise control and leadership; marriage and relationship to become friendly and social beings. The challenge in the practice of humanity varies from one place to another, and some may violate the principles of God. Humanity also allows for man to recognize things that can and cannot change about nature, and modernizes or explores those that can change and works around those that cannot change.

> ***"As long as the earth endures, seedtime and harvest, cold and heat, summer and winter, day and night will never cease."*** Genesis 8:22

Everyone, including couples, should enjoy humanity except when it contradicts the word of God.

- **Logic** - Logic determines how to evaluate or analyze situations, arguments, or events that enable us to reach conclusions. It allows the application of the human senses of sight, taste, touch, hear, and smell. These senses determine how humans think, feel, act, and react. A secular marriage is based on human senses. Although there is nothing wrong with human senses and critical thinking, however, the covenant of marriage is more than human logic.

- **Happiness Syndrome** - Happiness is based on what happens or does not happen. This syndrome has nothing to do with the joy of knowing God or doing His will. This makes people enter into marriage for predetermined benefits and to end it or to get out when the benefits are no longer available. The happiness syndrome may include economic, financial, political, and imagined benefits. For example, you are in a secular marriage when you marry to legalize your immigration status with the pre-conceived notion or intention of divorce after attaining the desired status. It is a secular marriage when problems ensue because your spouse is no longer able to make as much money as they use to make. It is a secular marriage when your goal is to please and satisfy yourself rather than caring for your spouse and honoring God.

- **Public Opinion** – Public opinion is the viewpoint or idea of the majority that becomes the view or idea of everyone, or can influence the idea of everyone. Public opinion is sharpened by the press and the ballot. The press, by their own agenda, may initiate or promote a cause by giving more coverage to it. There are liberal and conservative, communist and capitalist, and socialist and fascist news organizations. Ballots and elections which are bases of public opinion are sometimes bought and rigged. Secular marriage takes its cue and operates, based on public opinion. In today's world, public opinion supports open marriage relationship, same-sex marriage, separation, divorce, and remarriage, even when God is against it.

- **Courts, Laws and Governments** – The government, through its agencies, may redefine marriage. The government may enact, implement and interpret laws that are against the word and will of God. Secular marriage is based on the courts, laws and governments. The United States of America and few of the countries in Europe have legalized same-sex marriage, which is illegal in the word of God. The courts have no problem in marrying couples today and divorcing them tomorrow. Pre-nuptial and post-nuptial agreements are legal, but contrary to marriage and contradict the word of God.

- **Culture and Tradition** - Secular marriage follows the culture and traditions of a people that may not be congruent to God's will. Culture is the accepted norm and way of life of a people in a society or community. It may allow ideas and principles that are detrimental to godly marriage. For instance, while a godly marriage makes husband and wife one, there are cultures that treat wives as acquisition, property, or products, and do not see them as part of marriage.

- **Satan** - Satan, formerly called Lucifer, was one of the anointed Cherubs. He was in the same class of Arch-Angels like Michael and Gabriel. Given an enormous power and authority that he perverted, Lucifer wanted to exalt himself above God, instead of just being an Arch-Angel of God. He was cast out of heaven along with one-third of all angels.

  ***"Therefore rejoice, you heavens and you who dwell in them! But woe to the earth and the sea, because the devil has gone down to you! He is filled with fury, because he knows that his time is short."*** Revelation 12:12

  Due to the fall, Lucifer became Satan, and all the fallen angels became Demons. Satan, though limited in power, time, and location, yet captures non-believers and fights Christians to undermine their relationship with God. Also, Satan hinders and takes away the word of God, deceives and accuses believers, blinds the eyes or hardens the hearts of people, ruins marriages and families without any premonition, and takes captives of both believers and non-believers. Secular marriage satisfies and glorifies Satan. Unfortunately, many Christians are powerless to resist the devil but instead have accepted all his popular gimmicks, tricks and schemes about marriage.

5. **What is the nature of the heart of man in marriage?**

Man is a triune being comprised of spirit, soul, and body. The spirit is the real man, the life that comes from God and the energy that makes the body and soul function. The soul is the invincible nature, traits, and attributes of man that involves his mental, emotional, and intellectual capacity. The soul consists of the will, the emotion, and the mind. The mind consists of faculties of reasoning, memory, and imagination. The body is made up of physical organs and parts that include hands, legs, head, heart, kidneys, liver, and brains. The body with spirit and soul produces numerous senses including smell, taste, sight, touch, and feeling. Ordinarily, the heart is the organ that is covered by the rib cage and pumps blood to different parts of the body. It supplies nutrients and oxygen, and removes carbon-dioxide and waste from the body. Figuratively, the heart is the spirit of man, and the controller of the body and soul. Sometimes the heart is described as a combination of spirit and soul, and other times as spirit.

> ***"Don't you understand either?" he asked. "Can't you see that the food you put into your body cannot defile you? Food doesn't go into your heart, but only passes through the stomach and then goes into the sewer." (By saying this, he declared that every kind of food is acceptable in God's eyes.) And then he added, "It is what comes from inside that defiles you. For from within, out of a person's heart, come evil thoughts, sexual immorality, theft, murder, adultery, greed, wickedness, deceit, lustful desires, envy, slander, pride, and foolishness. All these vile things come from within; they are what defile you."*** Luke 7:18-23 (NLT)

For the purpose of this questions and book, the heart is considered figuratively.

The heart is important in marriage for the following reasons:

- **It determines the Person** - The identity of a person is not only determined by the name and where the person comes from, but by the personality and character of the person.

  "***The hearts of the wise make their mouths prudent and their lips promote instruction.***" Proverbs 16:23

  A man who abuses his wife is a wicked man. A wife who lies and cheats on her husband is a liar or an adulterous woman.

- **It determines the Action** - What a spouse will do in marriage is a function of the heart. A husband that loves his wife has a good heart, and a wife that respects her husband possesses a great heart.

  ***"So we rebuilt the wall till all of it reached half its height, for the people worked with all their heart."*** Nehemiah 4:6 (NIV)

  What really matters is not the mouth, but the heart. In order to do what we say we will do, our hearts should align with our words.

- **It determines faith and the belief system** - The condition of the heart is the condition of faith.

  ***"He hath blinded their eyes, and hardened their heart; that they should not see with their eyes, nor understand with their heart, and be converted, and I should heal them."*** John 12:40

  Whether or not a spouse is born again, or has a personal relationship with God, is a function of the heart. It is also a function of the heart as to whether or not a spouse listens and obeys the word of God.

- **It determines marriage** - A marriage that will glorify God, raise godly children, and enjoy a lasting and blissful relationship is one where couples have good hearts.

***"Jesus replied, Moses permitted you to divorce your wives because your hearts were hard. But it was not this way from the beginning."*** Matthew 19:8

The remedy for bad behavior and attitudes in marriage is a good heart, and the cure for divorce is a soft heart.

6. **What is the condition of the heart of man in marriage?**

The success and failure of a marriage depend on the conditions or types of heart the couple possesses. Couples with good hearts will produce a happy and blissful marriage, while couples with bad hearts produce marriages full of fighting, problems, abuses, and ultimately divorce. There are different ways to categorize the heart, but consideration will be given to three categories:

Hearts based on the law; nature, and on a relationship with Christ.

- **The heart based on the law** - In the Old Testament of the Holy Bible, the relationship was based on the law. The law was either obeyed or disobeyed. Those that observed the law were regarded as having the hearts of flesh, and those that rejected the law were beings with hearts of stone. A heart of stone was a stubborn, obstinate, hardened heart; while a heart of flesh was a tender, pure, and undivided heart.

***"I will sprinkle clean water on you, and you will be clean; I will cleanse you from all your impurities and from all your idols. I will give you a new heart and put a new spirit in you; I will remove from you your heart of stone and give you a heart of flesh. And I will put my Spirit in you and move you to follow my decrees and be careful to keep my laws."*** Ezekiel 36:25-27

Couples who desired success in their marriage would imbibe the heart of flesh.

- **The hearts based on nature**: This heart is modeled after the parable of the sower. These hearts were categorized as four kinds: the road side heart; the rocky heart; the thorny heart; and the good or fruitful heart.

  ***"...A farmer went out to sow his seed. As he was scattering the seed, some fell along the path ... some fell on rocky places ... other seed fell among thorns ...still other seed fell on good soil..."*** Matthew 13:3-8 (NIV)

  - **The Road Side hearts** - These are hearts of unbelief where Satan rules. These hearts are void of God's words and Spirit, and are led by the world. The road side hearts are associated with the following:

    - Many exits. This means there are many ideas, opinions, and philosophies that are placed above or override the word of God.

    - Many stop signs, detours, traffics: These cause delays, distractions, and diversions from the word of God.

    - Many contradictory billboards and signs competing for attention: These billboards display stores, malls, restaurants, hotels, motels, casinos and other organizations that may create a negative impact and bring confusion to marriage.

    - Many trash, dust, dirt and noise: These create sin, pollution, and curse.

    - Different accidents, injuries and death: These lead to complications, miscarriage, and termination of vision and relationship with God.

- **The Rocky hearts** - These are hearts of a nominal Christian who walk by sight rather than by faith. They lean towards humanity, logic, reasoning and philosophy, but lack the basic principle of God.

  > ***"For therein is the righteousness of God revealed from faith to faith: as it is written, the just shall live by faith."*** Romans 1:17 (KJV)

  Rocky hearts are not good for planting. They are fallow ground, amusement and sight-seeing centers. They are hearts with wrong and faulty foundations. Couples with rocky hearts have no depth in the word of God and their relationship with God is based on convenience. Couples with these hearts start well, but because of their wrong foundation and lack of in-depth relationship with God, fail in marital relationships.

- **The Thorny hearts** - These are hearts that pretend to be repentant, converted, and regenerated, although they are not. These hearts are strongly influenced by the affairs of the world - the desire of the flesh, the lust of the eyes, and the pride of life. These hearts have the form of godliness, but deny the power of faith. Couples with thorny hearts chase after and prefer a Hollywood marriage over a Bible-based marriage.

- **Good Hearts** - These are hearts that believe and are rooted in the word of God. These hearts may have zero knowledge of God's word, but quickly learn and adapt to new truths learned in the word of God.

  > ***"But the path of the just is as the shining light, that shines more and more unto the perfect day."*** Proverbs 4:18 (KJV)

These hearts grow in faith and godly virtues, from zero to thirty- fold, from thirty to sixty-fold, and from sixty to hundred-fold. These hearts worship and glorify God, and are ruled by the word of God. Couples with good hearts experience a blissful and lasting marriage.

- **Hearts based on the relationship with Christ** - These are burning hearts, cold hearts and lukewarm hearts. These three categories are explained in question #67 of my book, ***"Before You Marry".*** Couples with cold hearts follow the world and endure their marriage; couples with lukewarm hearts have a pendulum marriage, with one leg in God and the other leg in the world; but couples with burning hearts glorify God through their marriage and enjoy joyful lasting marriage.

7. **How can a heart of stone become a heart of flesh, or a cold heart become a burning heart?**

Let's not forget that one of Jesus' solutions to the issue of marriage is the conditions of the heart; such that couples with good hearts will have a good marriage and couples with wicked hearts will experience a terrible marriage. But there are few challenges in dealing with the condition of man's heart.
Firstly, the heart or spirit of man is not visible like the outward appearance of man. A husband may have a handsome and robust physical outlook but harbors a wicked or hardened heart. Likewise, a wife with an angelic face and a model-like body may hide a road-side heart in her chest.

> ***"But the LORD said unto Samuel, Look not on his countenance, or on the height of his stature; because I have refused him: for the LORD seeth not as man seeth; for man looketh on the outward appearance, but the LORD looketh on the heart."*** 1 Samuel 16:7

Secondly, the heart of man is naturally wicked.

> "***And GOD saw that the wickedness of man was great in the earth, and that every imagination of the thoughts of his heart was only evil continually.***" Genesis 6:5

Despite the many factors that shape man, including parents, education, culture, belief systems and environment, the heart of man is still unpredictably wicked. A man will kill another man for money, a spouse kills the other spouse for business or career, husbands abuse the wife for power, the wife poisons the husband for status and positions. The list goes on.

Thirdly, it is difficult to determine the condition of the heart.

> ***"The heart is deceitful above all things, and desperately wicked: who can know it?"*** Jeremiah 17:9

This difficulty leads to pretense, secrecy, and manipulation in marriage. This explains the frustrations and disappointments of many spouses as they claim this is not the man or woman they married.

Fourthly, transformation of heart is divine. The condition of the heart is either that it is righteous or wicked, good or bad, wise or foolish, stony or fleshy, rocky or thorny, and cold or lukewarm. The transformation of the heart from wicked to righteous, or from stony to fleshy is possible through divine intervention.

- It was promised. It is available in abundant supply.

> ***"I will give you a new heart and put a new spirit in you; I will remove from you your heart of stone and give you a heart of flesh."*** Ezekiel 36:26 (KJV)

- It was asked for. It is not automatic, but those that want it will have to ask for it.

  ***"Create in me a clean heart, O God; and renew a right spirit within me."*** Psalm 51:10 (KJV)

- It was given. God will touch and change heart, if and when asked.

  ***"And Saul also went home to Gibeah; and there went with him a band of men, whose hearts God had touched."*** 1 Samuel 10:26 (KJV)

There is a process for obtaining a new heart or experiencing a transformation of heart.

> Ezekiel 36:25-27 reads, ***"I will sprinkle clean water on you, and you will be clean; I will cleanse you from all your impurities and from all your idols. I will give you a new heart and put a new spirit in you; I will remove from you your heart of stone and give you a heart of flesh. And I will put my Spirit in you and move you to follow my decrees and be careful to keep my laws."***

These scriptures highlight five major ways of experiencing transformation of heart: Clean water, representing the word of God; a new heart, representing the new birth; God's Spirit, representing the Holy Spirit of God; art of following, representing worship and fellowship; and art of carefulness, representing willpower.

- **New Birth** - Salvation brings a transformation of heart. The old nature is removed and is replaced with the new nature. New birth is not about religion, church going, water baptism, confirmation or sacrament; it is more of accepting Christ as Savior and Lord.

***"Who hath delivered us from the power of darkness, and hath translated us into the kingdom of his dear Son."*** Colossians 1:13 (KJV)

Being "Born Again" is not rotational or stretching; it is a change of heart that is transformational.

- **Word of God** - We hear and speak words. We speak from the abundance of the words we hear and store in our hearts. Our word is our world and character. What we hear, and the sources of such, matter. We change our hearts by changing what we hear. We renew our mind and hearts by reading, studying, and meditating on the word of God.

  ***"How can a young person stay pure? By obeying your word."*** *Psalm 119:9 (NLT)*

- **Holy Spirit of God** - The Holy Spirit is the power of God, the enabler, the comforter, the teacher, the energizer, the reminder and the helper. In the beginning, God breathed on man and man became a living soul. Man's heart came alive through the Holy Spirit, and his heart can only be transformed through the same Holy Spirit.

  ***"But there is a spirit in man: and the inspiration of the Almighty giveth them understanding."*** Job 32:8 (KJV)

- **Worship and Fellowship** - Attending and participating in worship services are important factors in the transformation of a heart of stone to a heart of flesh. Couples should not ignore the presence of God when they appear in God's house if they wish to go from strength to strength, wisdom to wisdom, and glory to glory. Couples should not forsake the assembly of the saints.

> ***"As iron sharpens iron, so one person sharpens another."*** Proverbs 27:17 (NIV)

- **Willpower** - Man is made of spirit, soul and body. The soul of man consists of the will, the emotion and the mind. The will is the unique part of man that allows him to make choices. Man's willpower is his ability to choose rightly or wrongly. The will of man can range from weak to strong; but through the blood of Christ, the word of God, and Holy Spirit, man can have a renewed will. A roadside heart can become a fruitful one when we exercise our renewed will.

> ***"And be not conformed to this world: but be ye transformed by the renewing of your mind, that ye may prove what is that good, and acceptable, and perfect, will of God."*** Romans 12:2 (KJV)

8. **What are the classifications of married couples?**

The word "couple" can mean different things. In marriage, it is used to describe two people who are joined together as husband and wife in holy matrimony.

These are a few terminologies related to married couples:

- **Unmarried Couples** - Married spouses should be referred to as couples, but today men and women who are co-habiting are also referred to as couples. Since the world has infiltrated marriage, it's important to establish that any man living with another woman (or vice-versa) without the oath or vow of marriage is unmarried, and such can only be referred to as an unmarried couple. Unmarried couples, though engaged and who are cohabitating, are acting contrary to God's will, especially if they are engaging in sex. The cure is to get married. If they refuse to marry but live as a couple because they don't believe in marriage, it means they are not Christians, and they are not born again. The common law may permit them, but God does not approve.

- **Married Couples** – These are men and women who are married by way of traditional, court, or church wedding, and who live together as couples. Although, a married couple may have their share of marital crisis, they are proud of the marriage relationship because they have honored God's requirement of matrimony.
- **Married Singles** – The married singles may fall under two categories; couples who live apart due to distance, and those who give a false impression about their marital status. Distance, employment, businesses, academics and other logistics can cause people to live apart, yet present themselves as a married couple. For instance, due to an immigration restriction, my wife and I lived apart for about 5 years before we eventually started living together. During this period, I was not ashamed to tell people that I was married. The second category concerns those who give a perception of being single even though they are married. As a pastor, I cannot comprehend why someone who is married does not want the world to know that he or she is married. In such situations, there is a possibility of sinful living, or someone is ashamed of his or her partner. I once heard an excuse that one should not advertise oneself to the world. I disagree. Marriage is a wonderful state of existence when couples live as God has designed it to be.
- **Married Separated** – Married couples sometimes face crisis that causes them separation. Because of such crisis, couples may live apart or separately before finally terminating the marriage. Christians should seek counseling before their marriage problems reach this point.

- **Widows or Widowers** - Sometimes, bad things happen to good people. When a spouse passes away, the living spouse becomes a widow or widower. The living spouse should take as much time as needed to mourn his or her departed spouse. However, the living spouse is permitted by God to remarry if he or she desires.
- **Divorcees** - A divorcee is someone who has married and terminated the marriage. The institution of marriage is under attack as divorce is very popular in the world, as well as in the church. Both believers and unbelievers are now called divorcees.

9. **Why does the Bible describe wives as the weaker vessels?**

God created man and woman as male and female in His image and likeness. God is neither masculine or feminine as human knowledge may suggest, and non-discriminatory to either man or woman. The make-up of both genders differs so does their interests, needs, desires, and functions. Two of such differences have been highlighted from the beginning.

> ***"Then he said to the woman, "I will sharpen the pain of your pregnancy, and in pain you will give birth. And you will desire to control your husband, but he will rule over you.*** *And to the man he said,* ***"Since you listened to your wife and ate from the tree whose fruit I commanded you not to eat, the ground is cursed because of you. All your life you will struggle to scratch a living from it."*** Genesis 3:16-17 (NLT)

- A man is created with a physique to do hard labor.
- A man is created to provide for his family.
- A woman is created to conceive and give birth to children in marriage.
- A woman is created to submit herself to the leadership of her husband in marriage.

In our world today, only some of these standards are adhered to. The complexity of the modern world has changed the roles of a man and a woman in marriage. The wickedness in the heart of men makes them abuse their wives instead of loving them. Likewise, the Feminist Movement propagates equality and superiority of a woman over a man. Unfortunately, these issues account for why some marriages are in trouble. The created cannot ignore the good and stable plan of the Creator and still expect stability. Christians will have to return to the basics of the Bible and its principles if they truly expect to serve God accordingly.

> "***Likewise, ye husbands, dwell with them according to knowledge, giving honor unto the wife, as unto the weaker vessel, and as being heirs together of the grace of life; that your prayers be not hindered.***" 1 Peter 3:7 (KJV)

The question of wives described as weaker vessels is a powerful mystery that every husband should understand for the success of his marriage. This matter requires great wisdom, and the best advice to husbands is to seek the guidance of the Lord. The fact that wives are weaker vessels should teach the husband to love their wives when there is a tendency to hate them, and to be patient with them when anger is visible. The term "***as weaker vessel***" is not about women; but rather about wives, so this is within the context of marriage. A woman who is against this description probably does not understand the mystery of marriage. The same scripture describes both husband and wife as heirs together of the grace of life, which emphasizes their equality before God and outside the institution of marriage. But in marriage, the husband should understand that he has more responsibilities than his wife. The reasons that wives are described as the weaker vessels can be summarized from the physical, psychological and spiritual perspectives.

- **Physical Reasons** - A man and a woman are different in their physiological makeup. The husbands' physical muscles should not be used to abuse his wife, but rather to protect her. Domestic violence and lack of responsibilities should not occur among believers if husbands recognize that their wives are the weaker vessels. In marriage, God made husbands the head of the wives, and thereby expects men to take more responsibilities. To ensure peace in the home, husbands sometimes must accept responsibility for everything; they may need to take responsibility instead of shifting them to wives, even when they are not to blame. The reason for the occurrence of single-motherhood is the refusal by some men to take responsibilities.

- **Psychological Reasons** - Women are more emotional than men. They display their emotions more and have more feelings than most men. They get scared easily, cry easily, and express happiness easily. Sometimes the emotional nature of wives may not allow them to consider all factors outside the family before making decisions. This is not true for every woman, but most women think about themselves and family only, and may not deeply concern themselves with others outside their immediate family. How many wives will put all their resources in the joint account with their husbands, especially when some financial decisions are not in their favor? Husbands are not expected to quit the marriage just because they are upset. Rather, the scriptures encourage them to honor and love their wives even when they behave weakly. Also, husbands proposed to their wives, therefore they occupy a more comparative advantage position.

- **Spiritual Reasons** - Men were created first, and the first woman, Eve, was brought to the first man, Adam. This contradicts the theory of evolution that humanity has given us. Also, the scriptures highlight the fact that a woman can be easily persuaded, just as the first woman was deceived and became the first sinner. God made husbands to be the head of the wives, and encourages wives to be submissive to their husbands.

> ***"And Adam was not the one deceived; it was the woman who was deceived and became a sinner."*** I Timothy 2:14 (NIV)
>
> ***"For the husband is the head of the wife, even as Christ is the head of the church: and he is the savior of the body"*** Ephesians 5:23 (KJV)

God expects the husband to lead and pastor their children and their wife. They should encourage them and pray for them as Isaac prayed for Rebecca, his wife. They should offer themselves to their wives as Jesus, the Savior, did for the church. The headship of a family unit is important because the scripture says in Matthew 26:31 *"Strike the shepherd and the sheep will scatter."* If the head is removed, there is little or nothing the body can do. Husbands should be intensely mindful of their leadership roles and responsibilities in their homes.

10. **Should couples belong to different churches?**

Marriage makes a husband and wife one. This indicates unity. Unity brings power and success and couples should be united both in words and deeds. Couples are also encouraged to belong to and attend the same church. The husband is considered as the covering for his wife. Therefore, the church should not stand against the way of God.

> ***""Look!" he said. "The people are united, and they all speak the same language. After this, nothing they set out to do will be impossible for them!"*** *Genesis 11:6 (NLT)*

> ***"And said, for this cause shall a man leave father and mother, and shall cleave to his wife: and they twain shall be one flesh? Wherefore they are no more twain, but one flesh. What therefore God hath joined together, let not man put asunder."*** Matthew 19:5-6 (KJV)

In an ideal situation, husband and wife should attend the same church. However, here are some scenarios that may permit couples to belong to different churches:

- **When a spouse is not a believer**: A believer is someone who has accepted Christ as Lord and Savior. The spouse who is a believer will desire a bible believing church, while the unbelieving spouse does not care about the type of church he or she attends. The unbelieving spouse may even be from a different faith or religion. A believing wife may not be able to convince her unbelieving husband but may strike a compromise and obtain permission to attend a different church.

- **When a spouse does not attend church regularly**: Sometimes both spouses may be believers and one may not attend church regularly due to his or her nature of work. The other spouse may not like to attend church alone and may seek the permission of the working spouse to attend the church he or she likes.

- **When a spouse lives in a different city, state or country**: Circumstances such as business, career and immigration may compel a couple to live separately in two different locations. While it is advisable for couples to live together, in unavoidable circumstances, different home address may mean different church memberships.

In any of the situations described above, it is the responsibility of the pastor and the church leaders to ensure that couples are united in church membership. They should encourage the husbands to convince their wives to go with them to church, and wives to join the membership of their husbands' church. The pastor and church leaders should encourage submissiveness of wives and unity of marriage.

11. **How can the church help couples live peacefully?**

The church is a place of worship. It is a meeting place between God and man, but it also means an individual, a group of believers congregating together, and the entire body of believers in Christ. An individual connects with the church when he or she accepts Christ as Lord and Savior, and lives according to the principles of the Bible, the word of God. The church is established to provide a conducive environment to worship God, teach people about the Word of God, encourage believers to be the light of the world, and prepare believers for the kingdom of God. Rick Warren, in his book *Purpose Driven Church,* identified five basic purposes of the church; worship, evangelism, fellowship, ministry and mission. It is one of the responsibilities of the church to encourage the believing couples to live together in peace and harmony. Consequently, the church can help couples to live in harmony and fulfill their important responsibilities through:

- **Regular marriage education**. The church should create educational opportunities and curricula for couples to learn about godly marriage. This can be done through organized marriage courses, Bible study and sermons devoted to marriage topics.
- **Marriage enrichment programs.** The church should make conscious efforts and investments in the marriages of their members. The church should not only have a budget for this, but should promote it. This can be done through organizing couple's day or night-out, dinner, retreat, vacation, picnics and games.

- **Counseling and Conflict Resolution**. The church should have marriage or couple's counseling teams, young couples' mentors and regular counseling sessions for its members. This will not only prevent or reduce marital conflicts, it will also resolve it.
- **Marriage policy education**. The church should have marriage policies that stipulate God's principles on marriage and how believers in Christ should conduct themselves in marriage.
- **Prayers.** The church should create time to pray for marriages, couples, and families. Couples should be encouraged to pray together as a family, and attend church prayers for the family.

While it is pertinent for the church of Christ to help couples live peacefully, it is more important for them to want to be helped. Many couples pass through the church, but the church does not pass through them. Such couples listen to the world more than the church. They believe they know more than the church, so their beliefs and principles are different from what Christ teaches. Unfortunately, the leadership and doctrines of some church denominations are closer to the world than to Christ. Many pastors, elders, reverends, and bishops that lead the church are not good examples of godly living and marriage, and therefore cannot provide needed help to the church members.

The church of Christ is expected to be different. The church must be where people find solutions to their marital problems. Regrettably, it has become part of the problem instead of the solution. Man may pollute and fail the church, but Christ, the owner and builder of the church, will not fail. The leadership of the church may fail but the Bible, on which the church was built, will never fail. The word of God transcends genders, generations, and governments.

Chapter 2

# Roles and Responsibilities

*Source* is defined as the origin or foundation of a thing. It determines the validity and success of a thing. We list sources to give credibility to our words, writing, research and actions. God was interested in the source of actions and responses when He asked Adam in the garden *"Who told you?"* Today, the question remains the same: Who told you to do what you do in all matters of your life? The source or voice you listen to is what shapes your life's values, principles, and beliefs. There are three voices that speak to us; the voice of man, the voice of Satan, and the voice of God. The voice of man is your voice or conscience and it is influenced by many things including your upbringing, culture, the world, Satan, and God. Conscience gives approval or disapproval to an action. The voice of Satan or God is heard by man through various means such as conscience, family, friends, people, entertainment and the world. The voice of Satan is influenced by the evil spirits while the voice of

God is influenced by the Holy Spirit. Isaiah 30:21 reads that *"Whether you turn to the right or to the left, your ears will hear a voice behind you, saying, "This is the way; walk in it."* Couples should examine their source of action. Who told them to be angry, hateful, and unforgiving to their spouse? Couples need to ask themselves who told them cheating and unfaithfulness to their spouse are acceptable and normal. The source of our action matters to God.

12. **What are the roles and responsibilities of a woman in marriage?**

Among other things, marriage is necessary for mutual fellowship, prevention of sexual sin, procreation of children, and the fulfillment of God's will. As ordained by God, marriage consists of God the joiner, man the husband, and woman the wife. Each occupies a unique position and performs specific roles and responsibilities. The following are the position, roles, and responsibilities of a woman:

- **She is a wife** - God created and planted a woman in marriage to be a wife, the female partner or a spouse, in a marital relationship. She is the better half of a husband and the need for her is that a man alone cannot fulfill God's plan in marriage. A wife completes a husband in marriage.

  ***"In this same way, husbands ought to love their wives as their own bodies. He who loves his wife loves himself."*** Ephesians 5:28 (NIV)

  As a wife, a woman should engage in a good relationship and sexual activities with her husband. Communication, laughter and sex should not be in short supply if a woman is to fulfill her role as a wife. She becomes his sweetheart, dearest, honey, and lover. This role also requires a wife to be submissive to her husband.

- **She is a mother** - Except for delay in childbirth, reproduction problems and the decision of couples not to have children, a married woman is expected to have children after a few years of marriage. A married woman with children is not just a wife, but also a mother and a role model. Jointly, she and her husband care, train, and nurture the children. This is a huge responsibility and involves an enormous investment of time, energy, finances, and skills for both spouses. Oftentimes this scenario causes a wife to give up or change her dreams and aspirations for the sake of becoming a mother to their children.

> ***"Train up a child in the way he should go: and when he is old, he will not depart from it."*** Proverb 22:6 (KJV)

This responsibility is a shared one between wife and husband, but today many women solely bear the entire responsibility both in and outside of marriage. Some cultures make a wife to regard herself as her husband's mother. Such cultural practices contradict the word of God. Except for romantic gesture, a woman who sees herself as a mother to her husband is working against a lasting marriage relationship. A wife is a mother to her children and wife or better half to her husband.

- **She is a helper** - Although there is an on-going argument whether a woman is a helper or mate of her husband, in a Christian marriage, a woman is a helper to her husband. The intention of God in marriage is to make the woman a helper that will complement her husband, and not a mate that will compete with her husband. Also, it is not the will of God that a husband should shift all the responsibilities on the wife. She is brought in to help the man and not for the man to push all responsibilities to her.

> ***"The LORD God said, "It is not good for the man to be alone. I will make a helper suitable for him."*** Genesis 2:18 (NIV)

As a helper, a woman is her husband's primary supporter and cheerleader. She is his confidant, friend, and companion.

- **She is a family woman** - In a marriage, a woman becomes a family woman. Therefore, she cannot behave as a single and unmarried lady who can go out or do things any time she likes. As a family woman, she should be accommodating and friendly to her immediate family, blended family, extended family including the in-laws, and her friends and those of her husband.

  > ***"Houses and wealth are inherited from parents, but a prudent wife is from the LORD."*** *Proverbs 19:14 (NIV)*

  This responsibility shows the kindness, wisdom, and hospitality of the woman. One of the reasons many married women have unpleasant relationships with their in-laws is because they fail in their responsibility as family women.

- **She is a home maker** - This is an important responsibility of a married woman. As a home maker, she takes responsibility of the home by ensuring that everything needed in the home including food, clothing, and other home necessities are available. She ensures house chores are done, engaging children and husband to help out as needed.

  > ***"The wise woman builds her house, but with her own hands the foolish one tears hers' down.*** Proverb 14:1 (NIV)

Today, the involvement of women in the economic market place demands homemaking to be a shared responsibility between couples. A wise woman would not reverse gender roles; rather, she would recognize that home making is one of her specialized areas of responsibility.

13. **What are the roles and responsibilities of a man in marriage?**

Marriage establishes family and requires work. Marriage is not for the lazy and slothful. Living life and taking care of ones' self is enough work already, much more adding spouse and children. A married man should recognize and perform his responsibilities in marriage. These are some of a man's roles and responsibilities:

- **He is a husband** - A husband is the male partner or a spouse in the marital relationship. He is the raw material for the creation of his wife. The better the man, the better his wife. The wife is made for him alone and not for the taste and expectations of his friends and family.

  ***"Then the LORD God made a woman from the rib he had taken out of the man, and he brought her to the man. The man said, "This is now bone of my bones and flesh of my flesh; she shall be called 'woman,' for she was taken out of man."*** Genesis 2:22-23 (NIV)

The responsibility of a husband is to provide an exciting relationship, sexual partnership, and love to his wife. Relation-ship cures loneliness and allows for talking, sharing, and giving. A good husband will not allow his wife to feel or be lonely emotionally and physically. The sexual needs of a wife should be met by the husband. A good husband will not defile his marital bed by cheating on his wife. Love is one of the needs of a wife, and a husband should shower his wife with an unconditional love such as that of God.

- **He is a father** - This is the responsibility that differentiates men from boys. There is a saying that *"all men can birth children but not all men can father children."* A father is a role model, trainer, mentor, teacher, counselor, provider and the world to his children. He sacrificially works to instruct, train, lead, discipline, guide, protect, and provide for his children.

  ***"The father of a righteous child has great joy; a man who fathers a wise son rejoices in him."*** Proverbs 23:24

  Many of society's vices are attributed to the absence of fathers in homes and the lack of fatherly guidance and counsel in their children's lives. Fathers need to invest in their children's lives failure to do so will cause regret.

- **He is a leader** - A man is called to lead the marriage, his family and his home. He is the head of the wife, the guardian of his children and he leads by example, influence and sacrifice. His leadership is not in control and power, but rather it's in responsibilities and accountability. He sees to the welfare of his wife and children.

  ***"For the husband is the head of the wife as Christ is the head of the church, his body, of which he is the Savior."*** Ephesians 5:24 (NIV)

  The contest of leadership in marriage between a husband and wife should not exist for believers in Christ. The husband's headship is not for mistreatment and abuse of his wife, rather it is for service and sacrifice for his wife.

- **He is a family man** - A married man is called to be a family man. A family man deals with a variety of issues from the immediate family, blended family, extended family, friends and community. He is mature, strong, tolerant, patient and wise. He comforts, encourages, resolves disputes, and does whatever it takes to maintain peace and the welfare of the family. A family man does not make decisions without bringing other stakeholders in the family to the table and considering the effects of such decisions on his faith, family, and future.
- **He is a cultivator** - A married man is called to bring out the best of his wife and family. He should nurture, motivate, and pamper his wife to make her shine and fulfill her dreams. He should be her best friend, confidant and soul mate. A cultivator is not an abuser or a victimizer but an encourager and a supporter. A cultivator removes weeds and tares that can hinder the growth of plants. Likewise, a married man is expected to help remove, and not reinforce, the undesirable traits in his wife, through prayer and supplication.

14. **What is the importance of love and respect in marriage?**

In my other book, *Before You Marry,* I explained the needs of wives in marriage especially from their husbands to include love, leadership, romance, security, affirmation, fear of God and success. I also explained the needs of husbands in marriage to include sex, respect, homemaking, beauty, fear of God, and submission. Love and respect are the two major needs of couples in marriage. Both spouses want love and respect but man's major need from his wife is respect, while the woman's major need from her husband is love.

> ***"However, each one of you also must love his wife as he loves himself, and the wife must respect her husband."*** Ephesians 5:33 (NIV)

Most husbands may not be concerned about whether or not their wives love them; but they will cry foul when they perceive that their wives do not respect them. Likewise, most women want respect from their husband, but they are more desirous of his love. These wives believe that their husbands cannot love them without respecting them. The implication of this is that, to ensure a lasting marriage, a husband must give his wife the love she wants, and a wife must give to her husband the respect he desires.

Literally, most husbands love their wives and most wives respect their husbands. The basis of this love and respect is what creates contention. There are three bases to this - Neighbor, Self, and the Lord.

- **Neighbor-Based** - The least favorable of the bases is how we demonstrate love and respect towards our neighbors. We hold our neighbors and the public in less esteem. We desire to be better than, and outshine, them. When there is a problem in the neighborhood, we wish that it affects other people and not us. We worry about a speck in our neighbor's eye when we have a log in our own. We use phrases like *"blood is thicker than water"* to exonerate ourselves. To address the maltreatment of neighbors, God commanded us to love our neighbors as ourselves.

  > ***"Do not defraud or rob your neighbor. Do not hold back the wages of a hired worker overnight."*** Leviticus 19:13 (NIV)

  Husbands cannot love their wives the way they love their neighbors and expect their marriages to last. Wives don't treat their husbands as they treat just any other man in the neighborhood if they expect their marriages to last.

- **Self-Based** – Under the second basis, the world teaches us to love and respect ourselves by using phrases or statements such as "*treat others as you want to be treated*" and "*respect is reciprocal*". I like the Discover Credit Card logo or commercial which expresses the message: "*We treat you like you treat you.*" Here, you are the basis. You only love to the extent that it cannot hurt you. It is about your happiness and comfort. There is no sacrifice, no overlook of errors, and no forgiveness. When marriage is measured by a couple's personal standards, separation and divorce are inevitable, and lasting marriages only happen by miracle.
- **The Lord-Based** – The third basis is expression of love and respect based on the injunction, "*as unto the Lord.*" It's our new order as believers. If you want your life and marriage to give glory to God, you must love and respect your wife not as you do to your neighbors or to yourself, but as you will do unto the Lord.

> ***"And whatsoever ye do, do it heartily, as to the Lord, and not unto men."*** Colossians 3:23 (KJV)
>
> ***"This is my commandment, that ye love one another, as I have loved you."*** John 15:12 (KJV)
>
> ***"A new commandment I give unto you, that ye love one another; as I have loved you, that ye also love one another."*** John 13:34

The Lord loves us, not on the basis of what we have done, but on the basis of the abundance of His grace. A couple that desires a lasting marriage relationship should love each other as Christ has loved them.

15. **What are the ways a wife can express respect to her husband?**

The major need of a husband from his wife is respect. This is respect based on the act of service to the Lord, not because the husband demands or deserves it. This is not an earned respect, but one that gives honor and glory to God. Examples of the ways a wife can respect her husband are:

- **Allow the husband to lead.** Every woman in a marriage should recognize and accept that her husband is the head of the marriage. This is not about sex equality, male supremacy, women's liberation or feminism, but rather it is about the will of God. A ship may have a co-captain, but it cannot have two chief captains; neither can a plane with a co-pilot have two chief pilots. It is the chief captain or pilot that calls the shots, the co-captain or co-pilot assists or takes over if the chief captain or pilot becomes incapacitated or diseased.

  ***"Wives, in the same way submit yourselves to your own husbands so that, if any of them do not believe the word, they may be won over without words by the behavior of their wives. When they see the purity and reverence of your lives.*** 1 Peter 3:1-2 (NIV)

  A wife that wants to engage in a lasting marriage should be ready to yield the leadership of the marriage to her husband. It is a hallmark of respect for a wife to let her husband lead the marriage. This is done through submission, acceptance, and respect.

- **Provide positive public perception of your husband.** The manner that a wife talks about her husband to her family, friends, neighbors, and the general public determines whether she respects him or not. A wife can disagree with her husband at home or in secret, but she will be dishonoring or disrespecting him if she verbally abuses or disagrees with him in public.

> ***"If a house is divided against itself, that house cannot stand,"*** Mark 3:25 (NIV)

Wives should be aware of people they think are their friends and helpers but who are there only to mock them. Thus, they are not to complain about their husband's job, career or profession to others.

- **Accept the In-law**. Most husbands are in good terms with their in-laws, while most wives have challenges with their in-laws. Husbands face a dilemma of how to deal with their parent vis-à-vis the position and role of their wives. A husband will feel honored and respected when there is a good relationship between his wife and his parents.

  > ***"The wise woman builds her house, but with her own hands the foolish one tears hers down."*** *Proverb 14:1*

  A wise wife will appreciate her husband's desire for her to respect and accept her in-laws. A wife with relationship challenges should not take her frustration out with her own parents or her husband's parents.

16. **What are the ways a husband can express love to his wife?**

As already established, respect is the major need of a husband while love is the major need of a wife in marriage. Christ is the basis of how love and respect should be expressed between husband and wife. Some of the ways husbands can express love for their wives are:

- **Pray for her**. Prayer is very important to the success or failure of the marriage relationship. Husbands should not only play with their wives, they should also pray for them. They should pray, fast, intercede and prophesy over them.

> ***"Isaac prayed to the LORD on behalf of his wife, because she was childless. The LORD answered his prayer, and his wife Rebekah became pregnant."*** Genesis 25:21 (NIV)

You should pray for what you cherish, and if you cherish your wife, you must pray for her. Prayer is an important way to show love.

- **Apply the love language**. In his book, *The Five Languages of Love*, Dr. Gary Chapman provided a detailed explanation of 5 ways that people want to be loved. These 5 languages of love are: Words of Affirmation, quality time, receiving gifts, Acts of service, and physical touch. Some wives want bonding time of meaningful conversations and activities and some others prefer gifts. It's romantic to a wife when her husband expresses her love language. A husband should understand how his wife wants to be loved and he should express it to her.

- **Engage the Agape principles**. "Agape" is the Greek word for unconditional love as detailed in 1 Corinthians 13. This type of love exhibits kindness, patience, selflessness, humility, forgiveness, decency and faith. Agape love is not envious, proud, or provocative.

> ***"Love is patient, love is kind. It does not envy, it does not boast, it is not proud. It does not dishonor others, it is not self-seeking, it is not easily angered, it keeps no record of wrongs. Love does not delight in evil but rejoices with the truth. It always protects, always trusts, always hopes, always perseveres."*** 1 Corinthians 13:4-7 (NIV)

There will be times in a marriage when the endurance of each of these attributes will be tested. Husbands should be willing to love their wives no matter the situations and circumstances. A Christian husband should grow in godly virtues so that he will have an abundance to draw upon in time of need. In his book, *"How to get what you want... and want what you get"*, Willard Tate explained the acronym of LOVE as Listen, Overlook, Value and Encourage. Husbands, you cannot love your wives without engaging in these four attributes: listening to her, overlooking her errors, valuing everything about her including her opinion, and encouraging and motivating her to achieve great things.

17. **What is the ultimate responsibility of a husband?**

There is no organization that can succeed without leadership. Absence of leadership marks the beginning of disorder and chaos. Leadership is inevitable as God is a God of order. Every assignment given to man by God begins with the appointment of a leader. For instance, God created Adam to lead the earth. He chose Gideon to lead Israel out of Midianites. When God decided to save man, He appointed the leadership of Jesus Christ. In general terms, the position of leadership is not limited to the male, but to both male and female. However, leadership in a marriage and in the home, is entrusted to man, the husband. The ultimate responsibility of a husband is to lead his marriage and home. The reason for manly leadership is to ensure that marriage and home are protected from predators and parasites, and secured it from failing and falling. Husbands cannot blame their wives for the collapse of their marriage. It is the responsibility of the husband to hold it together. The husband's responsibility is not based on whether the marriage relationship is sweet or sour, or whether the wife cooperates or not, but it is about doing all it takes to keep the marriage and family functional and intact. This ultimate role is made clear through the following:

- **Man should leave his parents:** Man is commanded to leave everything, including his parents, and cleave to his wife.

  ***"And said, 'For this reason a man will leave his father and mother and be united to his wife, and the two will become one flesh'? So, they are no longer two, but one flesh. Therefore, what God has joined together, let no one separate."*** Matthew 19:5-6 (NIV)

  One reason why God commanded man to "leave" is to recognize the importance of the marriage and to become inseparable from his wife. Marriage is not child's play. It is not for boys but for mature men. It is not a part-time responsibility but one that demands a full-time mandate. Husbands, do whatever it takes to make marriage work effectively.

- **A man finds his wife**: Many husbands tend to forget that they proposed to their wives. They forget all their efforts to win a date with their spouses. This sometimes happens after a lot of teasing, chasing, dating and conversation.

  ***"He who finds a wife finds what is good and receives favor from the LORD."*** Proverb 18:22 (NIV)

  What attracted you to her? What made you say "I love you"? Husbands, it is too late to back out or change your mind or forget your first love. If something is missing, it is your duty and responsibility to search, find, and repair it.

- **A husband should honor his wife**: Men and women are created equally in the image and likeness of God.

However, in the context of marriage, wives are the weaker vessels.

***"Likewise, ye husbands, dwell with them according to knowledge, giving honor unto the wife, as unto the weaker vessel, and as being heirs together of the grace of life; that your prayers be not hindered."*** 1 Peter 3:7 (KJV)

This allows the husband to serve, protect and sacrifice for his wife. Husbands need not win an argument or prove a point at all cost with their wives. The wise husband will win or lose an argument to the satisfaction of his wife. He will seek peace with his wife rather than assuming a chauvinistic position.

- **Man should behave like the prodigal son's father**: The parable of the prodigal son in Luke 15 not only reveals the behaviors of the two brothers; it highlights the responsibility of their father.

***"And the son said unto him, Father, I have sinned against heaven, and in thy sight, and am no more worthy to be called thy son. But the father said to his servants, Bring forth the best robe, and put it on him; and put a ring on his hand, and shoes on his feet: And bring hither the fatted calf, and kill it; and let us eat, and be merry: For this my son was dead, and is alive again; he was lost, and is found. And they began to be merry. Now his elder son was in the field: and as he came and drew nigh to the house, he heard music and dancing. And he called one of the servants, and asked what these things meant. And he said unto him, Thy brother is come; and thy father hath killed the fatted calf, because he hath received him safe and sound. And he was angry, and would not go in: therefore came his father out, and entreated him."*** Luke 15:21-28 (KJV)

The younger son expected his father to treat him like a servant, instead the father celebrated him. The father also went out to plead with the angry older son to come home. That is the responsibility of man in a home. He has to forgive before forgiveness is asked for, and he has to do whatever it takes to keep the family together. Relationship is not about the right of the husband; instead, it focuses on his role as husband and father.

18. **What are the differences between a virtuous and a foolish wife?**

Two scriptures establish this question:

> ***"House and riches are the inheritance of fathers: and a prudent wife is from the LORD."*** Proverbs 19:14
>
> ***"A wise woman builds her home, but a foolish woman tears it down with her own hands."*** Proverbs 14:1 (NLT)

It is safe to say that a wise or prudent woman is a virtuous wife, and a foolish woman makes a contentious wife. This question will highlight the attributes of both types of wives.

Proverbs 31:10-31 (NIV) describes the attributes of a virtuous wife; some of which are:

- **She is valuable** - A virtuous wife is highly esteemed by her husband. Her likeness and worth is not based on just being a wife, but on what she has rightly earned by her faith in God, and character and attitude towards her husband and family. Proverbs 31:10, 31 reads, *"A wife of noble character who can find? She is worth far more than rubies. Give her the reward she has earned, and let her works bring her praise at the city gate"*

- **She is trustworthy** - She is reliable and dependable, and her husband has confidence in her. She is transparent and truthful, and is not a deceiver or a covenant-breaker. Proverbs 31:11-12 reads that, *"Her husband has full confidence in her and lacks nothing of value. She brings him good, not harm, all the days of her life."*

- **She is diligent** - She is not lazy, but initiates, develops, executes and concludes ideas, actions, and ventures. She gets things done in and outside of the home. She is a headliner, rainmaker, and profit maker. Proverbs 31:13-14, 17-18, 24 read *that, "She selects wool and flax and works with eager hands. She is like the merchant ships, bringing her food from afar. She sets about her work vigorously; her arms are strong for her tasks. She sees that her trading is profitable, and her lamp does not go out at night. She makes linen garments and sells them, and supplies the merchants with sashes."*

- **She is a homemaker** - She does not neglect her home and family - husband and children. She does not excuse her responsibilities as homemaker and family woman; on the contrary, she creates a conducive atmosphere of peace for her family and guests. She feeds her children and husband and does not replace them with her job or career. Proverbs 31:15-16, 27-28 read *"She gets up while it is still night; she provides food for her family and portions for her female servants. She considers a field and buys it; out of her earnings she plants a vineyard. She watches over the affairs of her household and does not eat the bread of idleness. Her children arise and call her blessed her husband also, and he praises her."*

- **She is generous** - She is opened to the needs of her family, friends and community. She is generous to her immediate, blended, extended and spiritual family, and her neighbors both known and unknown. Proverbs 31:19-21 reads, *"In her hand she holds the distaff and grasps the spindle with her fingers. She opens her arms to the poor and extends her hands to the needy. When it snows, she has no fear for her household; for all of them are clothed in scarlet."*

- **She is a lover** - She does not starve her husband sexually, but offers him her body as he offers his body to her. Thus, she does not give the excuse of tiredness and work when it comes to the time of intimacy. Proverbs 31:22 reads *"She makes coverings for her bed; she is clothed in fine linen and purple."*

- **She is reputable** - She is respected and gives respect to her husband. She demonstrates good character and earns good reputation. She does not bring shame and disgrace to her husband and family. Proverbs 31:23, 25 reads, *"Her husband is respected at the city gate, where he takes his seat among the elders of the land. She is clothed with strength and dignity; she can laugh at the days to come."*

- **She is prudent** - A virtuous wife is prudent and wise. Her wisdom comes from her relationship with and the fear of the Lord. She is faithful to her husband and to God. She is not just a noble woman, but also a wise wife. She knows and serves God faithfully, and has work ethics, good character, and a husband. Proverbs 31:26, 29-30 reads, *"She speaks with wisdom, and faithful instruction is on her tongue. Many women do noble things, but you surpass them all. Charm is deceptive, and beauty is fleeting; but a woman who fears the LORD is to be praised."*

Some of the attributes of a foolish wife are identified as follows:

- **She lacks wisdom** - She does not respect her marriage, home, and husband. She leaves home whenever she likes and she disrespects her husband both in private and in public. Proverbs 24:3-4 reads, *"By wisdom a house is built, and through understanding it is established, through knowledge its rooms are filled with rare and beautiful treasures."*

- **She is contentious**. She is combative, inconsiderate, and quarrelsome and turns every issue into a quarrel. She is suspect of every move of her husband and ignores her responsibility and sometimes becomes a bully. Proverbs 21:19 (KJV) *reads "It is better to dwell in the wilderness, than with a contentious and an angry woman."*

- **She is nagging** - She is difficult to please. She complains and criticizes her husband. She finds fault and does not see anything good in her husband. Instead of cheerleading him, she discourages and harasses him. Proverbs 27:15 (NLT) reads *"A quarrelsome wife is as annoying as constant dripping on a rainy day."*

- **She is noisy and angry** - She lacks meekness and humility. She yells, backbites, and broadcasts family matters to other people. This has nothing to do with being an extrovert or introvert, but a foolish wife lacks the discretion to know when to be quiet and calm and show respect. 1 Peter 3:4-5 *reads, "But let it be the hidden man of the heart, in that which is not corruptible, even the ornament of a meek and quiet spirit, which is in the sight of God of great price. For after this manner in the old time the holy women also, who trusted in God, adorned themselves, being in subjection unto their own husbands."*

19. **What are the differences between a wise husband and a foolish husband?**

Marriage relationship turns a man into a husband, and a woman into a wife. Marriage is a blessing when the relationship is between a wise husband and a wise wife, and it is a pain when both husband and wife are foolish. Marriage is enjoyable only when the husband is wise and the wife is virtuous; but it is unbearable and problematic when the husband is foolish. A wise husband displays knowledge, understanding, discretion, intelligence, imagination, and decisiveness, while a foolish husband displays lack of trust and irresponsibility. A wise husband fears and obeys God and His words while a foolish husband does what he likes without being accountable to God, wife, and family. A wise husband sees the light and makes adjustment to align his ways to the light, while a foolish husband sees the light but wants the light to adjust and align to him.

> ***"Therefore everyone who hears these words of mine and puts them into practice is like a wise man who built his house on the rock. The rain came down, the streams rose, and the winds blew and beat against that house; yet it did not fall, because it had its foundation on the rock. But everyone who hears these words of mine and does not put them into practice is like a foolish man who built his house on sand. The rain came down, the streams rose, and the winds blew and beat against that house, and it fell with a great crash."*** Matthews 7:24-27

The characteristics of a wise husband are many, but here are a few:

- **He is a righteous husband** - A righteous husband is a God-fearing man who is born again, obedient to the word of God and accepts the personality, principles, and power of Christ. His righteousness is not based on his personal work and achievement, but on the finished work of grace through Christ. A righteous husband recognizes Christ in his wife and serves his wife as a service to the Lord. He does not criticize or complain about his wife. He does not shame his wife, rather he covers up her weaknesses and strengthens and celebrates her.

- **He is a loving husband** - He loves his wife and family in word and in action. The wife can testify to his love for her and their children. He cares and bears the burden of his wife. He protects and defends his wife from external aggression or harassment. He cultivates and endears his wife to shine.

- **He is a good leader** - He is a responsible and honest husband who seeks and works for the wellbeing of his wife and family. He is trustworthy, reliable, and friendly to his wife. He does what it takes to make his wife and family happy. He accepts responsibility for the management of thc home and gives deserving credits to his wife.

- **He is a husband of one wife** - A righteous husband is not a cheat, an adulterer, or a polygamist. He honors his wife with his body and possessions and does not engage in extra-marital activities. He has no hidden agenda outside of his marriage.

- **He is not a quitter** - A wise husband keeps his marriage covenant. He is courageous and able to handle the storms of marriage. He does not run out of town because of disagreement. He does not ask for a divorce because of a crisis. He tries to prevent storms and crises from happening, and if they do happen, he uses them as an impetus for growth and maturity in the marriage relationship.

The characteristics of a foolish husband are many, but here are a few:

- **He is a wicked husband** - A wicked husband ignores God and His words. He may claim to know God and be born again and religious, but he is not because he does not obey and follow His words. A wicked husband may hear the words of God but he does not serve or worship God. A wicked husband may sound morally good to his wife but such goodness is temporal.

- **He is an abusive husband** - A foolish husband abuses his wife. He may abuse her verbally, emotionally, financially, and physically. He may not only hit her with objects, kick her with his leg, or slap her with his hand, but additionally may insult her or deprive her of necessary provisions. He may nag her, criticize her and be too controlling. He may reduce her to a slave or maid and make her feel inferior to him.

- **He is a cheater**- A foolish man is a deceiver; an untrustworthy and unreliable husband. He will cheat on his wife and keep secret love affairs from his wife. A foolish husband engages in adultery, fornication, and polygamy. He leaves his wife and children and runs after other women. A foolish husband patronizes prostitutes.

- **He is a dangerous husband** - A foolish husband is a dangerous spouse who does not love his wife and family. He exposes them to problems and predators. He does not care but creates crisis for his wife and family. A dangerous husband is an absent and irresponsible husband. A foolish husband does not appreciate marriage and he is not willing to make required sacrifices. He is not a leader that holds the family during the time of the storm.

20. **What are the deadly sins or behaviors in a marriage?**

Like any other institutions, concepts and initiatives, there are factors that promote or destroy the marriage institution. Even God reveals certain sins and behaviors that are deadly to His relationship with man.

> ***"There are six things the LORD hates, seven that are detestable to him: haughty eyes, a lying tongue, hands that shed innocent blood, a heart that devises wicked schemes, feet that are quick to rush into evil, a false witness who pours out lies and a person who stirs up conflict in the community."*** Proverbs 6:16-19 (NIV)

The focus of this question is to highlight the factors and behaviors that are deadly to marriage? Here are seven of many factors:

- **Infidelity/ Unfaithfulness** - This is one of the most serious issues in marriage. Couples are expected to be faithful to their spouses. They are expected to keep their marriage vows and promises of not sharing their body with anyone else. An unfaithful spouse disrespects the other spouse, violates the trust, dishonors the marriage, and disgraces himself before God. This character is deadly to marriage, and except for repentance and forgiveness, the marriage is rocking the bottom.

- **Abuse** - This is another serious issue. Abusive behavior is the harmful treatment of another person in order to control the person. These treatments may be physical, emotional, and verbal. Some abusive behaviors are criminal offenses and may lead to legal struggles, fees, health issues, and imprisonment. Abuse is a major factor leading to the demise of marriages.

- **Money** - The love of money is said to be the root of all evil. Relationships are battered because of the love of money, and lives are lost as well. Spouses kill each other because of life insurance money and children of the same parents drag themselves to courts because of their love of money. Even Jesus was called upon to settle rifts over money and inheritance between two brothers. Couples should be transparent and sincere about money and financial issues. Failure of one, or both spouses, to treat and handle money correctly, is the beginning of strife and danger in a marriage.

- **Communication** - Communication is everything in marriage. Couples express their feelings, thoughts, desires, concerns, and requests through communication. Communication can be direct and indirect, verbal and non-verbal, and traditional and technological. Relationship falters where there is no communication. Couples will have to learn how to communicate with each other in a respectful and honorable manner. Criticism, complaints, nagging, and comparison create a negative atmosphere of communication.

- **The In-laws** - The excessive influences of in-laws on marriage is another issue that cannot be ignored. Marriage requires the couple to be physically, emotionally, and financially independent and separate from their parents. Failure of independence and separation is an undeniable factor in the demise of a marriage.

- **Sex** - Couple should endeavor to fulfill marital rites and sexual responsibility to each other. Starving each other of sex is the beginning of problems. On the other hand, using sex as reward or punishment is bad in marriage. Couples should help each other to enjoy and fulfill their sexuality.
- **Spiritual Ignorance** - The fear of the Lord is the beginning of wisdom. And except the Lord builds the house, the laborers work in vain. Making God the foundation of marriage is not enough; it should entail continuing in Him and living day by day on the principles of His words. When a couple likes what God likes and hates what He hates, that couple is building and strengthening their marriage.

Chapter 3

# Finance and Home Management

Fear is a feeling of agitation and anxiety caused by the presence of danger, otherwise known as "False Evidence Appearing Real" or "Forget Everything And Run." It is also a reverence and trust toward a supreme power. The fear of the Lord is the beginning of wisdom and a foundation of righteousness. Fear is faith in reverse. It gives birth to worry, doubt, and negativity, and may be a sign of mental illness. Fear holds people from taking steps and actions. For example, many fail to request a favor because of fear of rejection; fail to act because of fear of failure; or fail to travel because of fear of height or water. Fear is universal, and a reminder of our human limitations and frailties. Fear, though not real, can be dangerous if it is not dealt with. Fear has robbed many people of joy and great experiences. Job 3:25 reads that *"What I feared has come upon me; what I dreaded has happened to me."* Couples should learn to be vulnerable to one another and not allow fear to steal their joy. They should face and overcome their fears through self-examination, self-ability, godly counsel, and engagement with God.

## 21. How should couples handle money in marriage?

Money is a sensitive issue in marriage. If it is not well managed it can cause frequent conflict. Apart from life, money is next to the air we breathe. Money, whose purposes are to serve as a medium of exchange, measure of unit, store of value, and standard for deferred payment, has become an object of excitement, power, love, and conflict. As an example, many have assumed immense authority and power because of their fate with money. Many brothers and sisters have parted ways because of disagreement over money. Today, many marriages are destroyed because of money. To ensure a lasting marriage relationship, the subject of money should address the following: underlying principles, sources, control, security and the spending of money. This question will only address the underlying principles that husbands and wives should consider when handling money.

- **Love and Unity**: Money should be used by the couple to express unity and love to each other. Marriage seems to be synonymous with love. You cannot talk about marriage without talking about love. A husband and wife are in marriage because they love each other. They demonstrate this love in words, behavior, appearance and actions. For instance, some wear a ring band, and some buy flowers, gifts, hold hands and kiss in public to tell the world they are in love. The aspect of unity seems hard but is important to the sustainability of marriage. Couples will have to seek to consolidate their resources to foster unity in marriage.

- **Transparency and Trust** - Couples should be transparent and honest in their dealings with money. Trust will be hard to achieve where there is secrecy and non-disclosure. Depending on the couples' agreement, husbands and wives should have clear knowledge and understanding of the money available to the family. A wife should be ready to answer all money related questions from the husband and vice-versa.

- **Goals and Vision** - Money should be utilized for the fulfillment and realization of the goals and vision of the couple or family. Goals are the objectives and ambitions that the couple wants to accomplish or achieve. A couple's goals may include: owning a home in an affluent area, sending children to an Ivy League college, owning a luxury car, traveling on vacation once or twice a year, starting a business, retiring at a particular age or supporting the orphanage. The couple should discuss and agree on these goals, otherwise each spouse may be running his or her own goals, or the couple's relationship with money may negate their dreams.

- **Security** - One reason why there is disagreement in the handling of money is when one spouse realizes financial vulnerability in the future. A wife will be willing to give all her money to her husband for the welfare of the family when she believes that her financial future is secured based on the financial decisions in the marriage. Couples should manage money in such a way that everyone in the family will feel secure about the future. For instance, no one wants to engage in a white elephant project that the spouse does not believe in, as it can raise questions of financial security.

- **Personality and Value** - Couples should handle money in such a way that individual personalities and values can still flourish. There is a need for compromise, but money should not be over regimented and structured to the extent that the initiative and creativity of each spouse is not considered. Life becomes boring when one cannot pleasurably enjoy his/her money. The difference in personality is what makes one spouse a saver and the other a spender, one frugal and the other a spendthrift, one who believes in now and the other in retirement.

- **Financial Health** - Couples should handle money in such a way that it will foster financial health and prosperity. Good management of money should avoid uncontrolled debts, bad credit, and bankruptcy. Couples should ensure their spending habits and tastes are congruent with their income. Couples who engage in business and investments should ensure that their business and investments are structured in such a way that their marriage and family will be protected in the event of business or economic downturn.

- **Glorify God** - Couples should manage their finances in a way that will give honor to God.

  > ***"For the love of money is a root of all kinds of evil. Some people, eager for money, have wandered from the faith and pierced themselves with many griefs."*** 1 Timothy 6:10

  Couples should not only have a relationship with God but should also seek to please God with their money. Couples should not bury the worship of God because of their search for, or acquisition of, money.

Money is not the answer to every issue of life. Money can buy good healthcare but it cannot buy happiness. Money cannot buy a family's happiness; therefore, one should not exchange one's spouse for money. It cannot buy faith in Christ, because it is a free gift from God. Couples should not treat money as if they cannot have a decent living without plenty of it. Couples should manage money to foster their relationship with God and their family.

22. **What are the couple's sources of income and its implication on marriage?**

Money is described as anything generally accepted as a medium of exchange, a measure of value, or a means of payment for goods and services and repayment of debt. Examples of items that serve as money are paper currency, coins, money orders, traveler's checks or gold. Money allows couples to buy goods and services, pay debts, and store wealth for their current and future needs. There are many sources of money available to couples:

- **Employment Incomes**: Couples can offer their skills, ability, and knowledge to individuals, companies, churches, and other organizations for employment. Employment incomes are regarded as earned income. These incomes are earned by working for someone else. Examples of employment incomes are wages, salaries, gratuity, honoraria, bonuses and commissions. Examples of employments available to couples are many but here are a few: working as accountant, doctor, attorney, engineer, pastor/minister, secretary, nurse, technician, sales clerk, bank teller, electrician, plumber, painter, manager, director, chauffeur, stylist, administrator, office assistant and receptionist. This list is not all inclusive but is continuous and varied.
- **Business Incomes**: Couples can offer their own skills, abilities and knowledge to work for themselves. Business Incomes are also considered as earned income. These incomes are earned by exerting one's skills and energy to create and sell value to others. Couples may form and organize a business as a sole proprietorship, partnership or corporation. Business incomes may include wages, salaries, fees, rents and profits, after an offset of business expenses and losses. Examples of businesses available to

couples are many but here are a few: Real Estate agency, Child Care service, Home or Elder care service, Car dealership, Medical & Clinical practice, Law Firm, Accounting & Bookkeeping firm, Shipping service, Consulting & Counseling practice, Publicity practice, Photography & Recording and entertainment.

- **Investment Incomes**: Instead of working for money, couples may let their money work for them. Investment incomes are considered as passive income. These are returns obtained from putting money into any investment account. For instance, there are interests from savings, dividends from the sharing of company profit, gain from sales of stocks, securities, assets or business. Examples of investment vehicles are many but here are a few: investing in real estate, stocks, bonds and commodities.

- **Inheritance Incomes**: Couples may obtain incomes as a bequest from parents or anyone who had passed away. These incomes are considered as gifts, donations, legal settlements, endowment or returns from the sale of estate of the deceased.

- **Other Incomes**: There are other incomes available to couples in marriage that do not fall in one of the income categories above. These are the following: royalty, severance payment, insurance claims, alimony, child support, unemployment income, social security income, and other support from government.

The effects of identifying various income categories are:

- **To determine the total amount of money available to couples in marriage**: All incomes should be pulled together in the couple's coffers. The source of money is different from the management or usage of money. The management of money depends on how the couple has agreed to control their money, but couples must have the knowledge of its sources. Failure to identify all incomes is a deception to the marriage. The skimming of a spouse to hide sources of income is the beginning of marital problem. Transparency and trust are important ingredients for the success of a marriage.

- **determining a couple's quality of life**: The couple should know what they can or can't do, buy or can't buy and where they can or can't go. For instance, a reasonable spouse who knows all the sources of income will not demand something far beyond the financial reach of the couple.
- **planning for marriage and family**: Couples may want to seek a change of career, take up other employment, go to school or invest in the children. Knowing what you have helps you to know what to do to get what you want.

23. **How should a couple address their financial worries?**

In partnership arrangements, each partner wants security of his or her investment. As a result of this, some partners become general partners to ensure they control the operations of the partnership. Others become limited partners to limit their losses from their initial contributions or investments. In marriage, not only do couples become one but also each spouse has an equal stake in the affairs and resources of the marriage. The Common Law injunctions and Property (Relationship) Acts in the Western world permit an equal sharing of marital property. The nasty divorce battles we have witnessed are often due to disagreements about each partner's share of the marriage estate. It is important for couples to understand the feelings of the other spouse with respect to security. Such feelings may include but are not limited to the following questions:

- Will my spouse and I have enough money to live a decent life?
- Will my children be able to go on vacation, to college, and live a normal life?
- In case of emergency, will my family be able to continue to live well?
- In case there is problem with my spouse, will I be able to obtain an equitable portion of resources to sustain myself?
- As a stay-at-home mom or dad, will the sharing of resources compensate for loss of income and sacrifice?
- Will my spouse and I be able to have a decent retirement?
- What are the stakes of the in-laws?

These, and other financial questions are legitimate concerns and couples who seek lasting marriage relationships should not ignore them whether the other spouse expresses them vocally or not. These concerns influence the behaviors and actions of your spouse.

On one hand, in order to address these concerns, prenuptial or postnuptial agreements are not the answer for Christians who want to please God. As stated in my book, ***Before You Marry***, prenuptial agreements redefine and remove God from marriage and envisage its failure even before it commences.

On the other hand, these concerns can be alleviated through insurance, savings, and financial planning.

The first way to address these concerns is through Insurance. There are various insurance plans that couples may engage in including the following:

- **Auto Insurance** - Couples that own cars should have auto insurance on their cars. These may range from limited to collision or compressive insurance. The fact that you have no loan on the cars and no statutory requirement from the bank or government is not an excuse to ignore auto insurance. Auto insurance saves you from going into debt and other psychological stress in case of a vehicular accident.

- **Homeowner Insurance** - Couples that own homes should have homeowner's insurance on their dwellings. These may range from flood damage, fire damage, to theft insurance. These types of insurance save your family from becoming homeless, bankrupt and subjected to other physical and emotional distress in case of emergency even if you have no mortgage on the home.

- **Liability Insurance** - If you have a business from which you derive part of your living income, then you need to have liability insurance for your business. This is not only to save your business from collapsing but it saves your family income and the trauma of the litigation or law suit against your business.

- **Health Insurance** - Health is wealth. Couples should have comprehensive health insurance for their family. Couples who live in a country where there is no public health insurance should obtain private health insurance for their families. Spouses who work for companies that offer health insurance should participate in the company's health insurance to cover themselves and their family. Spouses who own business should obtain health insurance through the business. Couples who live in a country and work for companies where there is no health insurance should save money for health purposes.

- **Life Insurance** - There is the reality of death, except we don't know the time. Since death brings pain, sorrow and agony, it is important for couples to have life insurance protection to reduce the pain, suffering, loss and confusion that exist after the death of a loved one. Life Insurance may cover funeral and living expenses for the living spouse and children. There is nothing unscriptural about Christians having life insurance. It protects your spouse and children, and allows them to give you a befitting burial.

The second way couples may address the concerns of financial security is through savings. There are various saving mechanisms such as:

- **Rainy Day Saving** - Incomes can be spent, invested or saved. It is important for couples to have at least three months of income saving in a liquid asset account such as cash, bank deposit, certificates of deposit, traveler's or cashier's checks. These savings come in handy and are quite useful in case of emergency situations such as loss of wages, fees or unemployment.
- **Children Education Fund** - Couples are encouraged to invest in their children through good education. Because of skyrocketing college tuitions and high interest rates in student loans, many children who cannot obtain scholarships are ignoring a college education. In the United States, parents can take advantage of tax-exempt Coverdell Education Saving Account and 529 College Saving Plan in paying for their children's college tuition.
- **Retirement Plan** - In developed countries, the elderly can enjoy social security benefits that depend on what they paid in during their working days and the goodwill of the government. Experience shows that these benefits might not be adequate or available when needed due to incessant changes in public policy. Couples are encouraged to plan for the future when they will not have enough strength to work. Most retirement plan policies of the government have tax deferment benefits. In the United States, there are retirement plan vehicles such as 401k, 457B and 403B

to name a few. These accounts are provided by organizations and governments such as companies, schools, religious bodies, hospitals local, state and federal governments. There are also retirement vehicles with tax benefits for individuals through Individual retirement plans (IRA) both Traditional and ROTH.

Apart from insurance and savings, the third technique couples may adopt to allay the important concerns of financial security is financial planning. This is described as:

- **Establishing a Trust**: A trust is a fiduciary arrangement that allows a trustee or third party to hold assets for a person that will be distributed to the person or the beneficiaries of the person. A Trust has tax benefits and excuses assets from going through the probate process. Trust may be revocable and irrevocable, depending on who benefits from the assets. Couples should plan their estate and establish a trust to provide financial security for the living party after the death of a loving spouse.

- **Writing a Will**: A will is a device that allows you to tell the world who you have chosen as the beneficiary of your assets. If you die without one, the State will decide who gets what, without regards to your wishes or the needs of your heirs. Couples are encouraged to have a will to detail their wishes and desires (backed by their assets) for their family after one or both spouses have passed on.

### 24. How does a couple address the control of money?

There are many questions a couple should answer when it comes to the control of money in marriage. Some of these questions are: who should control money in marriage? Should couples put their money in a single or separate purse? Who should provide the money in marriage? There are many more questions.

The control of money in marriage without debate is the role of the husband as the head of the home. However, a husband who controls the fund to the detriments of the wife commits a sin. Also, it is the responsibility of the husband to provide the money in marriage while it is the responsibility of the wife to care for the children and husband as homemaker.

> ***"Husbands, love your wives, just as Christ loved the church and gave himself up for her".*** Ephesians 5:25
>
> ***"But if any provide not for his own, and especially for those of his own house, he hath denied the faith, and is worse than an infidel"*** 1 Timothy 5:8

Interestingly, the complexity of the modern world has turned these traditional individual responsibilities to shared responsibilities. At least Proverbs 31:11-31 show that a virtuous wife or woman provides for her home, and Ephesians 5:25 implies that a loving husband gives himself to his wife even in derisory situations. Men and women are now active in the marketplace sourcing for money for the family, and in the kitchen caring for the family. The fact that tasks like payment of bills, transportation of children to and from schools, mowing of the lawn, buying of groceries, investing of money and the like, have become shared responsibility. This has made the control of money in marriage equally a shared responsibility.

The control of money in marriage is physically expressed in how funds are being kept in bank accounts and utilized. There are three options for how a couple can control their money.

- **Individual Bank Account** - This is when each spouse has his or her own separate bank account. The total income each spouse earns from employment, business, investment, or inheritance is deposited in their own account without full disclosure to the other spouse. Couples that have individual bank accounts divide the household and marriage expenses between each other. For instances, the husband may agree to pay the house rent or mortgage, the children's school fees, his own car loan, phone bill, and tithes, while his wife may agree to be responsible for utility bills such as electricity, cable and internet, gas, groceries, her own personal phone bill, car loan, and tithes. The benefit of an individual bank account is that each spouse has independence and creativity on how to spend his or her money, while the detriments are that it encourages secrecy and distrust, and creates surprises and suspicion, especially when one spouse forgets to or fails to fulfill his or her agreed upon responsibility. As an example, the wife who pays the water bill may be angry because the husband bathing with too much water; or he does not have enough money to pay the rent or mortgage. The husband may also complain when the wife who is supposed to buy food for the house is not bothered when there is no food in the house. Individual Bank Accounts are operated by immature couples.

- **Joint Bank Accounts** - This is when the couple operates one bank account that has either or both the husband and wife as signatories. The total incomes earned by both spouses from all sources are deposited into this one account and all household and marriage expenses are paid. Either of the spouses may withdraw or write checks at any time and for any purpose with or without limit from the account. Depending on the couple, they may place a limit that requires signatures of both parties for payment or withdrawal above a certain amount. The advantage of a joint bank account is that it fosters transparency, disclosure and trust. Besides, there is no financial secrecy. The disadvantages of this account are that it creates excessive focus on money, and may kill creativity and individual taste. It also raises questions such as should a partner spend money for personal effects without notice to the spouse? Should a partner send to or spend money on his or her relatives without the approval of the other spouse? Should a non-working spouse have a say in the financial decisions? And many more questions.

- **Hybrid Bank Account** - This is when a couple operates a combination of individual and joint bank accounts. In this scenario, there are three official bank accounts - one Joint account and two individual accounts for each spouse. Depending on the agreement by a couple, all incomes are deposited into the joint account where all household and marriage expenses are paid, and each individual account receives monthly or periodic transfers from the joint account for personal use. The couple may agree that certain sources of income will go to the joint account, and other sources of income will fund the spouse's individual accounts. It is the prerogative decision of the couple to decide how this should work. The benefits of hybrid Bank Accounts are that it enjoys all the benefits of both individual and joint bank accounts, and removes the challenges associated with individual and joint bank accounts. The disadvantage is that couples may not be transparent to each other in money matters. Full incomes may not be disclosed.

## 25. How should couples spend money in a marriage?

Money plays an important role in building a lasting marriage. Five important elements drive finance in a marriage, and these must do with how money is sourced, secured, controlled, spent and the underlying principles of money. This question addresses the process of spending money. It is simply the identification of what the couple's finances are expended for. Financial expenditures are usually expressed in a document called a budget.

What is a budget? *The American Heritage Dictionary* defines a budget as "an itemized summary of estimated or intended expenditures for a given period along with proposals for financing them." Like an individual, the couple's budget may have categories such as tithes or offerings, housing, food, transportation, education, insurance, debt repayment, entertainment or recreation, childcare and personal grooming. A Budget can be short term, medium, or long-term in nature. The following are the factors that determine budgetary items:

- **Spouse's Personal Needs** - Marriage brings two people of different backgrounds, interests, tastes, and values to live together as one. Differences in individual taste may be vast or non-existent depending on the level of maturity of the couple. Individual tastes determine what each spouse will buy. Couples should accommodate each individual's tastes when assessing marriage finance otherwise there may be frequent disagreement on the spending levels of each spouse. The budget should consider each spouse's individual interest and taste. In most cases, couples with widely varying tastes find it difficult to operate joint accounts

- **Couple's Vision** - Irrespective of the couple's income, their goals, vision, and agendas should influence the budget. The more the couple's income, the higher their purchasing power. A visionless couple, however, will be wasteful, emotionally stressed and unhappy. Vision allows the couple to harness their individual interests for the success of the marriage. Couples with a vision can operate hybrid bank accounts that unify the couple's goals on one hand, and allow individual creativity and interests to shine, on the other.

- **Household Needs** - expenditures made on the couple and their children to maintain and sustain their family can be classified under household needs. These needs go beyond food, shelter and housing. They should also include social and psychological needs, and are detailed in a budget.
- **Parental Care** - Couples can also spend money to take care of their extended family including their parents and in-laws. Caring for aged parents may not be a generally accepted practice in some cultures and countries, but there is nothing wrong with couple's caring for their parents. The money to be spent, or the attention to be given to the couple's parents at a point in time may or may not be of equal value, but it should be proportional to their needs. Parental needs should be included in the budget.
- **Expectations of friends and relatives** - Though not mandatory, expenditures can also be made to help friends and relatives. This type of spending should also be provided for in the budget. Siblings and other close relatives of the couple usually have very high expectations that their monetary needs will be met whenever they make requests. This category includes budget spending on friends and associates as well as money expended on individuals, organizations and communities as charitable giving.
- **Government Obligations** - taxes are legal obligations imposed on citizens by government. Tax is a mandatory part of a couple's budget, and failure to pay required

taxes usually attracts interest and penalties. Examples of taxes are income tax, sales tax, excise tax, business tax, export tax, import tax, corporate tax, capital gain tax, gas tax, property tax, death tax and inheritance tax. Couples are advised to comply with tax laws and regulations as stipulated by the government. Most governments are very strict when it comes to taxation, and typically impose stiff penalties like property seizure or imprisonment.

- **Spiritual Obligations** – As Born-Again children of God, we are expected to be faithful stewards. Faithfulness requires us to worship God, support the work of God, and expand the kingdom of God with our finances. Faith requires us to pay tithes, give offerings and redeem our vows.

  ***"Honor the LORD with your wealth, with the first fruits of all your crops;"*** Proverb 3:9

  ***"Bring the whole tithe into the storehouse, that there may be food in my house. Test me in this," says the LORD Almighty, "and see if I will not throw open the floodgates of heaven and pour out so much blessing that there will not be room enough to store it."*** Malachi 3:10

Tithes and offerings should have a place in a couples' budget as failure to make these obligations is akin to robbing God. The Bible requires believers to give to God what is God's, and to Caesar what is Caesar's.

26. **When is it acceptable for an individual to hide something from his/her spouse, especially regarding giving financial assistance to his or her extended family?**

The ideal is for a couple to be fully transparent and share information with each other. Even the most devoted couples deliberately or inadvertently, make arrangements that encourage hiding information from each other. There is nothing wrong in a spouse supporting his or her family financially. The issue is when such support is not a joint effort of the couple, or it is not disclosed to the other spouse. The answer to this question will focus on four issues: why couples hide information; the information they hide; the degree of information they conceal or disclose; and how secrecy is encouraged.

The reasons spouses hide information from the other spouse are many but here are a few:

- **Individualistic Couple** - Marriage turns two independent people into interdependent people. The language changes from "I" and "me," to "we" and "our." Spouses may no longer claim personal privacy and space. Couples that maintain individualistic lives are prone to secrecy.

- **Different Goals and Visions** - Marriage unites and harnesses the goals and visions of a couple. When spouses cannot agree to speak with one voice or on decisions and direction, they create room to hide information. Differences in vision encourage each spouse to plan, pursue, and protect his or her own visions secretly or openly.

- **Foundation of Marriage** - People enter marriage for different reasons. Some marriages are not based on godly principles but on deception, desperation, and other reasons. These are recipes for non-disclosure of information.

- **Condition of the couple's heart** - Some people have wicked hearts and are pre-disposed to disappointing and failing others. They are like a leopard that cannot change its spots.

***"Can an Ethiopian change his skin or a leopard its spots? Neither can you do good who are accustomed to doing evil."*** Jeremiah 13:23.

A spouse can love, be submissive, sacrificial, friendly, and communicate well, yet the other spouse's heart remains wicked. A spouse with a wicked heart works in secret.

The information couples hide - Financial information is not the only type of information couples hide from each other. Information couples hide may include:

- Support for extended family.
- Infidelity or extra-marital affairs.
- Secret family or children born out of wedlock.
- Secret bank or investment accounts.
- Purchase or building of property.
- Secret business.

The degree of information that couples conceal or disclose - There are three view points to the degree of information couples conceal or disclose.

- **Shares no information unless asked** - This is when a spouse is not willing to freely release information unless the other spouse asks. The idea is to let sleeping dogs lie. This is common among couples that have trust and communication issues.

- **Shares some, but not all, information**- This is when a spouse is selective in the sharing and releasing of information to the other spouse. Some information is shared freely without asking, but some information is deliberately concealed. This is common with a spouse that is not fully committed.

- **Shares all information** - Couple shares information freely and willingly without deliberately hiding any fact. Sometimes, not all information is shared because of a memory loss but such forgotten information is shared as soon as it is recalled. This is common among couples in a successful marriage.

  The way couples encourage secrecy: Interestingly, the couple may deliberately or inadvertently encourage the concealment of information.

- Couples who operate individual bank accounts are likely to hide information from each other more than couples with joint or hybrid bank accounts. Couples who engage in long distance marriage relationship are likely to hide information from each other.

- Couples who deprive each other of sex are likely to hide information from one another.

- Couples who frequently disagree or have a communication problem are likely to hide information from one another more than couples who are less argumentative and who enjoy good communication.

- In the United States where there are different filing statuses at tax time, couples who file separate tax returns are likely to hide information from one another than couples who file jointly.

The question of when it is acceptable for couples to hide information from each other depends on mutual understanding. For instance, couples who have separate bank accounts are not accountable to each other as to how they spend their money. The argument that couples can be transparent when they deliberately create an atmosphere of secrecy is unfounded.

Chapter 4

# Family and In-Laws

*Environment* is everything about our surrounding; the place we live, where we attend school, work, and the stores we shop. It is the people we live with, work with, socialize with, the things, events or activities that motivate and inspire us like music, sports and entertainment. Environments are different from one another as they are shaped by culture, public opinion, politics and governments. Globalization encourages us to learn and adapt to certain environments. History, Religious Studies and Languages are taught in schools to promote adaptation to select environments. Couples should understand that their environment will influence them first before they can influence their environment. There is a saying that *if you are in Rome, you should behave like a Roman.* This is not true for Christians. Couples who are children of God should seek to be like Jesus and set good examples for the world. 1 Corinthians 15:33 reads that *"Do not be misled: "Bad company corrupts good character."* Couples should beware of bad company and peer pressure especially with those that align more to the environment. Couples should keep company with people who fear God and are willing to make marriage work.

27. **How can a husband ensure a good relationship between his wife and his family?**

Everyone is born into a family. This family is classified as immediate, blended, and extended. The immediate family consists of the husband, wife, and children. The blended family consists of children from a prior marriage i.e., there is a step-mother or step-father. The extended family consists of blood relations other than the immediate and blended family members and includes mother, father, brothers, sisters, uncles, aunts, nephews, nieces, cousins, grandparents and in-laws. There are different kinds of relationships: brother and sister, father and son, friends, business partners, producer and consumer, husband and wife, church and member, Creator and creature, and creditor and debtor. All relationships are good for the purposes for which they are formed but none except an individual relationship with God is superior to the marriage relationship. This implies that husbands should have relationship with his parents and members of his extended family, but he should recognize that the relationship he has with his wife is more important than the relationship he has with his mother and father. Likewise, the wife should understand her marriage relationship with her husband supersedes the relationship she has with her mother, father, and even her job.

Because of the numerous family relationships, we engage in, there may be a need to ensure that a good relationship exists between a wife and her in-laws to address or avoid disagreements, crisis, jealousy and confusion. To ensure a good relationship, these three approaches should be considered:

- **The Husband's Responsibilities** - Cultivating a good relationship between a wife and her in-laws depends on the husband. He is the head of the home and should take responsibility for everything in the home. These are a few suggestions as to how a husband can achieve this:
    - The husband should wean himself from parental control and influence. Unless he can stand on his own without his parents telling him what to do, he will not be able to ensure a good relationship with his wife.
    - The husband should set the tone of the marriage and communicate boundaries to parties outside the marriage including his parents. He should be able to tell his parents, siblings, and relatives what behaviors are acceptable in his home and with his wife. He should denounce disrespectful comments about his wife and speak well of her to his parents. He cannot castigate or complain about her to his parents and expect the parents to treat her well.
    - The husband should encourage his parents to love and accept his wife. Sometimes parents think their sons should marry woman they personally like, not the woman their son likes. It is his responsibility to convince and encourage his parent to like, love, and respect his wife.
- **The Wife's Responsibilities** - The wife is the copartner in a marriage, and she has the responsibility to ensure peace and harmony in the home. It may be a challenge to have no or bad relationship with her mother in-law and expect to have a good relationship with her husband. These are some suggestions as to how a wife can get along well with her in-laws.
    - The wife should accept, respect, and treat her husband's parents as her own parents. The wife should evaluate

and compare her relationship with her own parents and her in-laws. If they are not similar, she should know she has work to do. The ancient golden rule is “treat others the way you want to be treated.” Treat your parents-in-law the way you want your husband to treat your own parents. The starting point is to accept and respect them.

- The wife should recognize and appreciate her in-laws’ investment in the life of her husband. No husband falls from heaven. Some people birthed, bathed, clothed and fed him. They spent on him, took him to doctors when sick, gave him education, and supported him in various ways. Some wives erroneously think that marriage gives them the ownership of their husbands, and that the husband needs permission from them before he can even greet his parents. Wives should understand that marriage allows a man to be independent of his parents, but it does not allow him to disown them. A wise wife should recognize that these parents have made an enormous sacrifice and reared such a wonderful man for her to marry, and they deserve her respect and appreciation.

- The wife should have a good relationship with them. Some women who do not have good relationship with their own parents may want to turn their husbands against his parents. Other women with character flaws may deliberately want to turn their parents- in-law to wicked mothers, fathers, predators, obstructers or invaders of their home. These are against the health of the marriage. One sign of a healthy marriage is good relationship between spouses and their in-laws.

> ***"Honour thy father and thy mother: that thy days may be long upon the land which the LORD thy God giveth thee."*** Exodus 20:12 (KJV)
>
> ***"For Moses said, Honour thy father and thy mother; and, Who so curseth father or mother, let him die the death."*** Mark 7:10 (KJV)

The longevity of ones' marriage relationship is somehow tied to the relationship they have with both parents. Wives would do themselves a lot of good when they have good relationship with their -in-laws. If they cannot make them their own parents, at least make them their friends which allows them to communicate with them, visit them, send gifts and pray for them.

- **The Couple's Responsibilities** - Good relationship between a wife and her in-laws does not just happen. The couple has collective and individual responsibilities. These are the suggestions for their collective responsibilities.
    - Couples should always be in agreement. A tone should be set and boundaries established, with the husband seeking the opinions and interests of his wife, considering them, and, together with his wife, would reach a conclusion on issues before communicating them to the parents. Husbands and wives should not offer their differing opinions to their in-laws otherwise they will present two different sides. It is important for the husband to support his wife in front of his parents even when he does not agree with her. They should later sort out the differences in private and not in the presence of their parents.
    - Couples should provide for their parents wherever and whenever possible. Children should care for their aged parents. It is the responsibility of the parent to care for their children when they are young and can't work. And

it is the responsibility of the children to care for their parents when they are aged and can't work.

> ***"Children are a crown to the aged, and parents are the pride of their children."*** **Proverbs 17:6**

Children should be proud of their parents at all times whether the parents can provide for themselves or not. In developing countries, older parents heavily depend on their children for their care. While in the developed world, most parents plan and save for retirement, healthcare, funeral expenses and may also receive social security benefits in old age. There is nothing wrong with government assistance and retirement planning, but the children should be there for their parents in their old age, if not financially then physically and emotionally. Relationships between wives and in-laws are strengthened when couples care for their parents.

- Couples should engage their parents. Such actions can cultivate a good relationship with their parents. This can be done when couples visit their parents, seek counsel from them, celebrate them, welcome them to their home for short visits, buy them gifts, send the grandchildren to them for short vacations.

28. **How long should in-laws and guests be allowed to stay on a visit, especially when they are causing conflicts between spouses and the children?**

No human being fell from the sky. Everyone is born into a family. Each has parents, siblings and other relatives. To address this question, we must consider four categories of people who can live with a married couple at any point in time.

- **Parents and In-laws** - These are the mothers and fathers of the husband and wife. They birthed, raised, and trained their children to become fit for marriage. They may be in-laws but without their investments in the lives of the couple marriage may not have been possible. They are special persons and deserve to be treated as such. Parents and in-laws are the first category of people who can live with a married couple.

- **Siblings and Other Relatives** - These are blood brothers and sisters and step brothers and sisters, as well as sisters' in-law and brothers' in-law. A spouse's extended family such as uncles, aunts, nephews, nieces and cousins should also be considered. Siblings and relatives are immediate family and those who become family through marriage; in-laws. They usurp benefits because of blood and marital ties. They can request to live with the couple for short or long periods.

- **Friends and Colleagues** - These are acquaintances or people the couple or individual spouse has established a cordial relationship with throughout the years. They are the people with whom the spouses went to school, church, stores, parties and other places. They are people the couple work or do business with. They are your friends and children or family of your friends. These friends may need some assistance from the couple, which may involve living with the couple for a short or long period.

- **Strangers and Passersby** - These are people who are not parents-in-law siblings, relatives, or friends and colleagues. They are people both you and your spouse care for, or give assistance to, as Good Samaritans. You do not expect anything in return from the strangers and passersby, and many of them may not even have the means to compensate you. A stranger or passersby can be a needy college student who has his/her fees paid by the couple, a new arrival to the city or country that the couple has provided accommodations, or an orphaned child the couple rears without receiving foster child care fees or payments. These strangers and passersby, because of the couple's benevolence and magnanimity, may gain access to live with the couple for a short or long period.

For simplicity and purpose of this question, we will group the people who can live with the couple into three groups, namely in-laws, relatives, and friends. The in-laws are parents of the husband and wife. The relatives are the couple's siblings and extended family. The friend category consists of friends, colleagues, strangers and passersby. Sometimes, we may group the parents and in-laws and siblings and relatives as "in-laws", and the friends, colleagues, strangers and passersby as "guests or friends".

The question of how long in-laws and guests can stay in the couple's home will vary, dependent upon the group being considered.

- **In-laws** - When a couple allows their parents to live with them, it will be difficult to send them away even when they are causing problems. Parents know their children and children know their parents. A spouse that knows that his or her parent is a trouble maker or is too demanding should advise the other spouse before the parent makes the visit or begins to live with them. This will help to prepare the couple to determine the duration of the visit before the visitor arrives. Couples need to communicate and agree on how long the parents will stay, before they come.
- **The Relatives** - The couple's relatives can live with the couple if they both agree and such relative is well behaved. However, as soon as he or she is about to disrupt the marriage or cause problems, he or she should be removed from the couple's residence. A relative cannot impose on the couple or cause any hardships.
- **Friends** - Friends, colleagues, strangers and passersby, as the relatives, can only live with the couple as long as they are

peaceful. The interest and welfare of the marriage is of most importance and should not become work or drudgery. Couples should not hesitate to evict any friend creating problems in their matrimonial home. The peace and harmony of the marriage supersedes the harmony of any other familial relationship.

29. **How should a couple handle the decision to allow in-laws and guests to stay with them?**

The ideal situation is for the in-laws and other guests not to stay or live with the couple, but the reality is the opposite. There are times and occasions that necessitate these groups of people to live or stay with the couple. For the purpose of this question, the in-laws are the couple's parents and relatives, while other guests are the couple's friends, colleagues and strangers. To avoid problems due to live-in situations involving in-laws and guests, the couples should engage the following:

- **Agreement with Spouse and In-laws or Guests** - The first step is to remove the assumption that it is alright for my parents, relatives or friends to come and live with us. The scenario may be okay when one is not married, but after marriage, there is a need to seek the input and agreement from one's spouse before it is acted upon. The couple should communicate and reach an agreement concerning in-laws and/or guest. The agreement may at least focus on the following:
    - The Purpose of allowing persons to live -in - The purpose may include:
        - Visitation - to see, socialize and enjoy the family;
        - Nanny - to help nurse the babies or babysit the children;

- Medical needs – to receive treatment for illness or sickness;
- Retirement – to rest or cure loneliness due to the death of an aged partner;
- Relocation – to settle down in the city, state or country in which the couple lives;
- Immigration – to obtain immigration benefits;
- Business – to stay temporarily while transacting business;
- School – to assist until the completion of school program;
- Others – to live in while transitioning to another city, state or country.

Except the purpose is known, understood and communicated, problems cannot be ruled out.

- **Duration** – Apart from establishing the purpose of the living arrangement, the couple should communicate and agree as to the length of stay of the in-laws or guests. One cannot just assume that she is my mother, aunt or friend so she can stay with us as long as she wants. NO. Except the couple agrees and extends an invitation, this will not work. Of course, the duration can be extended but the in-laws and guests should know how long they will be allowed to stay.

- **Responsibilities, Rights and Limitations** – Couples should establish the responsibilities, rights and limitations of the in-laws and guests depending on their relationship and the purpose of their stay. Parents and in-laws have the highest level of relationship and should enjoy many rights and privileges with less limitation, while strangers have the lowest level of relationship. As an example, there was a disagreement about a mother in-law who was living with a couple, the wife was expecting her mother in-law to cook and perform numerous household chores, but the husband believed his mother was around to rest and babysit the kids. This created division within the marriage. There was another mother in-law who wanted to sleep on the couples' master bedroom or matrimonial bed.

- **Finance and Maintenance** - The couple should agree with the in-laws and guests regarding their expectations when it comes to personal maintenance expenses, utility bills, and medical bills. Obviously, it is the responsibility of the couple to take care of all expenses incurred in their household, however, they should establish an agreement if the parent, in-laws and guests require special diets, care, and time. They are working and earning income while living in their household.

- **Implementation of Agreement** - The purpose of an agreement is to harness the expectations of the couple and the in-laws or guest living with the couple. Such an agreement, thereby, eliminates or reduces the incidents of conflict, issues and problems. For this to be achieved, the agreement must be implemented and adhered to. This is where the maturity and leadership of the husband are tested. The husband should ensure that such agreements are respected and not breached. The implementation will depend on the level of relationship with the parties. For parents and in laws with the highest level of relationship, the implementation should be handled with care. For example, there was a husband who had to obtain an apartment for his mother after her agreed period of stay with the couple expired. The situation worked well because the mother in question became self-sufficient and was able to maintain herself. This was not the case initially. For others such as siblings, relatives, friends, colleagues, strangers and passersby, the implementation of agreements should be done thoroughly without hesitation.

- **Treatments of In-laws and Guests** - living with a family member or friends involves enormous work, and sometimes creates headaches and conflicts. Experience has taught some people not to accommodate other people in their home. Consequently, situations and circumstances beyond human control may necessitate the reality of hosting parents, in-laws and friends for a short or long period. At any time, when hosting a relative, friend, colleague or stranger becomes a burden or creates a problem, one can release themselves from the obligation by letting him or her go. However, husbands and wives should not treat their parents and in-laws like that. They deserve the respect, love and sacrifice of the couple. Each spouse should take his or her in-laws as his or her parents. Love should always be shown to them. Any attention paid to them at a particular time may or may not be equal but should be proportional to their needs.

- **The Superiority of the marriage relationship** - It is important to reiterate the superiority of the marriage over mother/father and daughter/son relationship. The first condition of marriage is to leave one's father and mother and cleave to one's spouse. This is not to disown mother and father but to separate oneself from them and to be joined to one's spouse. This should create empathy for your spouse and to see yourself in their position and to prefer him or her to your parent. A spouse should seek the peace, unity and welfare of their marriage and family in time of conflict between their spouse and their in-laws. There should be no hesitation with regard to revoking an agreement with relatives, friends and strangers in time of conflict between spouses and any relative.

30. **How should a couple handle the decision not to allow in-laws and guests to live with them?**

Parents and in-laws are special to their children and fulfill many important roles in the couple's lives. The parent will always be a parent. The parent shows equal if not more concerns to their adult married children than when they were just kids. They want to be with their married daughter when she delivers babies, their grandchildren. They want to be present when their married son has major celebrations and breakthroughs. Depending on the culture, customs and economic status, many of these parents want their married children to buy them cars and houses, and to give them a good retirement. In situations where parents and their married children live in different cities, states and countries, the parents want to visit, stay or live with their sons and daughters- in-law for the purpose of vacation, babysitting, medical needs, retirement, and immigration benefits.

The couple's main responsibility is to protect their marriage and immediate family. Sometimes the couple may want the parents and in-laws to come for a short visit but may not want a long visit or a permanent stay with them. In African cultures, it is a big issue when the parent or in-laws want to come and live with the couple and the couple refuses, or the couple shortens the period of time they can stay with them. The couple should understand that marriage is a divine institution established by God and it is not based on Western, African, European or Asian culture or tradition. The couple may respectfully refuse the parent or in-laws from imposing their desire upon them, especially if such decisions will create challenges to the couple. Neither husband nor wife should allow anything or anyone that will create unnecessary problems with their spouse and children. This does not mean parents and in-laws should not be welcomed to the couple's home at all. They should be welcomed but for a specified period of time, and if they want to stay longer, other arrangements should be provided.

Another arrangement would be to provide them with external accommodations where feasible. Most couples will want their parents or in-laws to stay and live with them for as long as they are:

- Not causing problems between the couple and children;
- Not too demanding or too difficult to please;
- Not too expensive;
- Not strong and healthy enough to live on their own.

When there is a concern from the other spouse about the long stay of your parents,

- It is time to renegotiate and agree on a new period of stay, or
- Move the parent outside the marital home.

If you cherish your marriage, don't assume the concern will go away. Depending on the situation of your parent or in-laws and the financial status of the couple,

- The couple can extend their stay,
- Ask them to return home to their family,
- Rent an apartment for them, or
- Move them to live with another relative or sibling.

Irrespective to where the parent or in-laws live, the couple should support them.

> ***"Children's children are a crown to the aged, and parents are the pride of their children."*** Proverbs 17:6 (NIV)

The parent or in-law loves their children and grand-children. They are their joy and glory. They are their retirement and financial security. In the Western culture, parents have few children as they compare them to "Consumer Goods" - they spend and spend on them without a plan of getting back later. On the contrary, in the African culture, parents have many children as they compare them to "Capital Goods" – they spend on the children now with a plan that the children will take care of them in their old age. Children are the Social Security, Medicare and Retirement plans for African parents. Couples should support their parents and in-laws physically, psychologically and financially. The fact that they cannot live with the couple does not mean they cannot be supported. Couples are also encouraged to treat their parents and in-laws with love and respect. They did not reject and were not ashamed of their children while they were young; it is not the time for couples to reject or be ashamed of them. They cannot be homeless while you are living in an elegant home. They cannot be naked where you have many clothes to spare.

31. **How should parents treat the spouse of their married son or daughter?**

Parents are a blessing to children. Apart from being fathers and mothers, they are also their guardians, mentors, trainers, providers and protectors, to mention a few. They make huge investments in the children toward their adulthood. Many parents make sacrifices to provide pleasures to their children. Many parents sacrifice their careers for their children's careers. There is an adage that says, "charity begins at home" parents are the home. They create conducive homes so that they and their children can have a great life. What a child becomes is a function of the home. If the home is good, the child is likely to be good; and if the home is bad it will take great efforts to make the child good. Studies have shown that the parental support system is a major factor on how a child performs in school and life. A young, good-looking man with an excellent job cannot help but appreciate his parent who gave him the opportunity to thrive. A smart, beautiful lady with a good education cannot claim she did it all alone without the sacrifice of her parents who gave her education. As I am writing this, I can relate to what it means to be a parent. I travel from pole to pole to ensure that my children have a good education. The point is that parents are important to their children.

Interestingly, marriage makes couples independent of their parents.

> ***"And said, 'For this reason a man will leave his father and mother and be united to his wife, and the two will become one flesh'?"*** Matthew 19:5 (NIV)

This does not make life easy for the parents. Many parents, because of their love for and closeness to their children, will not mind their adult sons and daughters bringing their spouses to live with them. Also, many parents will not mind visiting regularly or moving in permanently with their married sons and daughters. Other parents are happy to let their married sons and daughters become themselves and live independently. Whatever the scenario, marriage establishes a relationship between the couple and their individual and extended families. It is important for the parent or in-laws to relate to the son or daughter, son in-law or daughter in-law in the following manner:

- **Love and Respect** - Parents should not see their son in-law or daughter in-law as someone who has come to remove their daughter or son from them. The mother of the groom should treat her daughter in-law with love and respect as if she were her own daughter. She should use her age and maturity to establish a good relationship with her daughter in-law. Many studies have shown that the couples' male parents have less division with their in-laws than female parents. A Mother in-law who loves her daughter in-law will express cordiality, friendship, forgiveness, kindness and peace with her. Parents and in-laws who respect their son in-law will honor, admire, appreciate and project a positive image of him.

- **Adults, Not Children** - Parents should treat their married sons and daughters as adults. Parents do not need to watch over their married children any more like they used to. They do not need to make decisions for their married adult children as they used to. These children are no longer attached to them and their apron strings. The married couple is no longer children and adolescents that can be punished and locked in as time out.

- **Independent Not Dependent** - Parents should treat their married sons and daughters as independent entities. The United States tax system allows parents who provide more than half of the total support for their children and young adults during the year to claim them as dependents on their tax returns. Apart from their age, income, and relationship qualifications of dependency under the US tax code. A married dependent cannot file a joint return with his or her spouse. A married son or daughter should not subject themselves to being claimed by their parents. Parents should allow their married children to make their own decisions. They should recognize that their counsel to the married children is advisory and not mandatory.

- **Support Not Oppose** - Parents should support their married sons and daughters, and their spouses. It is not parents' responsibility to choose spouses for their adult children. They should accept whomever their children choose to love. Sons and daughters-in-law will commend, approve and defend parents who support their children's marriages. Parents who support their children's marriages give gifts, pray for and assist them whenever they request help. On the other hand, parents who oppose their children's marriages will be angry, confrontational, critical and fight the decisions of their children in marriage.

- **Parents Not Spouses** - Parents should be parents to their married sons and daughters, not their spouses. Some parents still want to cook for their married children as if they are still young children. They want to live with them or visit them on a weekly basis as if their married children are still in kindergarten or boarding school. There is nothing wrong with visiting them, but it should be seldom and by invitation only.
- **Parents as Mentors** - Parents should be good mentors to their married children. Their responsibility is to train the child in the way he or she should go before adulthood. This responsibility is limited to childhood and not transferrable to adulthood. During adulthood, parents become mentors to their married children. Their recommendations are merely advisory and not mandatory. The married children learn more from their parents' character and life than from their words.

Chapter 5

# Vision and Communication

*Selective hearing* by a Christian, is contrary to accepting the will of God, a way of ignoring the message one does not want to hear and concentrating on what one wants to hear. This may sound good when the message does not align with one's values, but bad when it is used as a way to cherry pick and ignore the fact or truth. Selective hearing also allows for a person to hear from people that conform to what a person wants to hear but inhibits a person to hear from people that will tell it the way it is. Selective hearing encourages a person to welcome conforming conditions and to reject challenging circum-stances. The danger of selective hearing is that what we don't want to hear is generally what we need to hear; who we don't want to hear from is generally who we need to hear most, and the situations we run away from are what will grow and benefit us. The people that love us are the people who tell us the naked truth and demand commitment from us. Proverbs 19:20 reads that *"Listen to advice and accept discipline, and at the end you will be counted among the wise."* Couples should learn to listen and hear from each other. They should learn to hear from God, mentors, and the servants of God.

32. **How should couples handle communication in a marriage?**

Communication is the expression of ideas, opinions, thoughts and information in a way that is easily understood. The American Heritage Dictionary defines communication as the "exchange of thoughts, messages or information, by speech, signals, writing or behavior." Communication is the most critical thing in a relationship. Marriage relationships cannot survive without effective communication. How many conflicts have been caused due to miscommunication, misunderstanding and misinterpretation of words? Somebody said communication "*is the first thing we learn as a child, but as we grow older, it becomes the hardest thing to do.*" For couples to handle communication well, there is a need for understanding the principles, components, barriers, and importance of communication. This question will focus on the principles of communication.

- **Communication is important to marriage**. It is one of the make or break ingredients of a marital relationship. There will be conflict and crisis where there is a breakdown in communication. Though there are times and situations when silence is the answer, it does not help the marriage when spouses go mute and refuse to communicate with one another.

- **Communication ensures that the message or information that needs to be conveyed is understood**. Parties may or may not agree or take action on the information, but communication takes place when the message is understood. Couples should ensure their communication is understood and has produced positive reactions. While there is nothing wrong with disagreement, couples should always be considerate of their partners' feelings.

- **Communication should create feedback.** Communication is not complete or effective without feedback, whether favorable or unfavorable. If feedback is ignored, there has not been successful nor effective communication. Feedback is the response, feelings, emotions, impact, or actions created as a result of communication. If words result in a negative response or action from a spouse frequently, one may need to work on their communication skill.

- **Communication can be a complex matter**. Spouses have differing and varying viewpoints, thoughts and backgrounds; therefore, they process, analyze and filter messages and information differently. Communication is not always easy, but one cannot run away from it. It is a course in college and a career from which many make their living. Sometimes, persons may need to present information in different ways or apply multiple techniques of communication with one's spouse to discover the best way and technique to reach them.

- **Communicate to express love.** If a person wants someone to listen and understand what is being said, they should be courteous and polite to the recipient. Communication is not just about hearing, reading or seeing, but also about understanding. Marriage does not provide a license to be abusive, apprehensive or aggressive when communicating with a spouse. Colossians 4:6 says *"Let your speech be always with grace, seasoned with salt, that ye may know how ye ought to answer every man."* Couples should communicate to cherish, appreciate and love each other even in the face of disagreement. In essence, agree to disagree.

- **Communicate to glorify God** – It is important for couples to realize that God is the third party in the marriage relationship. A husband and wife must individually and jointly seek to worship and please God. Matthew 12:36 *says "And I tell you this, you must give an account on judgment* *day for every idle word you speak."* A couple should endeavor to uplift, edify, encourage, motivate and bless each other in words, speech and in writing.

33. **What are the components of communication in marriage?**

Communication is a process through which a person conveys a message to another person or group. The components of communication are the sender of information, the message or information, the medium of communication and the recipient(s) of the information. It is important to understand these components to grasp and practice effective communication.

- **The Sender** - The sender is the initiator of the message. He or she sends out the message with the intent that the recipient will understand and react to it. The sender must have characteristics such as desires, beliefs, and backgrounds. Sometimes such characteristics are different from those of the recipient's, and they can influence the message. The sender should recognize that their condition and state of mind are important to the message. If the message is not understood or ineffective, the sender should see himself or herself as part of the reason for the lack of understanding. For example, if a person is angry when a message is communicated, they shouldn't expect a good reaction or positive response from the recipient.
- **The Message or Information** - The message, information, thought and idea to be conveyed, discussed, shared or communicated is an important part of communication. This information may be categorized as important or unimportant, urgent or non-urgent, frequent or infrequent. The level of importance of the message should determine how and when the message is communicated.

- **Methods of Communication** - This is the medium through which information is communicated or delivered. There are four methods of communication. They are:

  - Verbal communication - This is oral communication. It is expressed through speech, words, and face to face discussions.
  - Non-verbal communication - This type of communication is expressed through gesture. That is body language, eye contact, posture, and facial expression.
  - Visual Communication - This is expressed through signs, signals, drawings, or pictures.
  - Written Communication - This type of communication is expressed through letters, newspapers, cards, and emails.

  Couples should know the best method or technique that will effectively convey their message to the recipients.

- **Receiver** - This is the recipient of the message - the person or group that is expected to understand the message being conveyed and give responses or feedback. Like the sender of the message, the receiver's condition and state of mind are pertinent to the understanding of the message. The first responsibility of the receiver is to listen. One cannot achieve effective communication when a spouse is talking and the other one walks away or hangs up the phone.

34. **How can couples ensure effective communication?**

The importance of communication in marriage cannot be over emphasized. Most conflicts in marriage are attributed to miscommunication. So, to ensure lasting marriage relationship couples should learn how to communicate effectively. Communication skills can be learned, developed and improved upon. To communicate effectively, couples should take note of the following:

- **Right Timing** - Communication should take place at the right time to be effective. Spouses should be considerate of each other in communication. Each spouse has some special and personal habits, interests and hobbies that should be respected. Respecting your spouse's interest does not make you second best or not loved. For example, some men are sports addicted and some women are soap opera addicted. Except for emergencies it will be difficult for effective communication with such spouses during a football, soccer or basketball game.

  > ***"To everything there is a season, and a time to every purpose under the heaven."*** **Ecclesiastes 3:1**

- **Right Environment** - Effective communication must take place in a favorable environment, conditions and circumstances. Communication will not thrive in a contentious environment. Couples should identify these conditions before they initiate important discussion and conversation with one another. A noisy environment is not a place for spouses to bring up a conversation about their finances.

- **Right Topic** - Sometimes a spouse fails to communicate or enjoy effective communication because of the topic of discussion. Couples should be able to express their minds, ideas or thoughts and exchange information freely with their spouse about any situation, but wisdom demands that a husband or wife should not raise an issue or a topic if the other spouse does not want to discuss it at a particular time either because the issue or topic has been a bone of contention in the past, or the topic is brought up to taunt or embarrass the other spouse. Spouses should derive joy in making their partners happy, and avoid any topic that can cause discord or create a crisis. Some issues can definitely be delayed but not totally ignored.

- **Right signal** - It is generally said that what we communicate non-verbally is more than what we express in words or speech. We communicate through the signal we make during conversation with our spouse. Using gestures or a body language like posture, eye contact, facial expressions, or sounds are as important as the words we speak. A spouse, who hisses, laughs to scorn, moves their hands in disagreement, or rolls their eyes, is hindering effective communication.

- **Right Tonality** - There is a saying that *"It's not what you say but how you say it"*. Spouses should consider the tone of their voice as part of what they want to say. Tone of voice is vitally important when expressing feelings or moods like anger, disappointment, excitement, love, empathy, consideration, and calmness. If one raises their voice in anger, a spouse may perceive it as yelling.

- **Right Listening** - The goal of communication is the understanding of the message by the receiver. In verbal communication, there is no way the message can be understood without listening. A spouse should listen, and pay close attention to, and an interest in what the other spouse is saying or wants to say. There are bad and good ways of listening. Couples should engage in good listening. One must be very attentive to the speaker and ask questions for clarification and clarity.

- **Right Assumptions** - Communication takes place when speech occurs as an exchange of information with the person we want to receive it. There is a saying that implies "silence means consent", silence is communication. We make assumptions in communication especially when someone communicates in silence. A wife nags about something she thinks that her husband should know or do. A husband may assume that his wife is behaving negatively because of the visit of her mother in-law. Since couples are not mind readers, they should not make assumptions. However, if they do, it should be the right assumption about their spouse.

- **Right Response** - Effective communication requires the receiver to give right response. Two wrongs cannot make a right. Therefore, the fact that a spouse raises an embarrassing issue or asks a negative question does not give anyone a license to respond with a derogatory answer.

  ***"A gentle answer turns away wrath, but a harsh word stirs up anger."*** Proverbs 15:1

- **Right Spirit** - For effective communication to occur, couples need the right spirit which is the Holy Spirit of God. A spouse filled with the Holy Spirit of God will speak through communication that edifies, encourages and blesses his or her spouse. But a spouse who is void of the Holy Spirit of God will breed fire, contempt, confusion, curse and verbal abuse against his or her spouse.

  ***"Let no corrupt communication proceed out of your mouth, but that which is edifying, that it may minister grace unto the hearers.***
  Ephesians 4:29

35. **What is considered "good" and "bad" listening in a marriage?**

Listening is a very important part of communication. One cannot respond, learn or comprehend information and messages without listening. Listening is the process of decoding, translating and interpreting information, messages, signs and signals, for the understanding of such messages. Listening determines both the quantity and quality of communication that exist within the marriage relationship. A spouse may stop or reduce communication if he/she thinks the spouse is not listening and their communication or lack thereof, only leads to frequent misunderstandings, arguments and conflicts. Couples should therefore improve their listening skills in order to enjoy a lasting relationship.

Bad listening constitutes ineffective communication and includes:

- **Selective Listeners** - Selective listeners filter out some of the messages and concentrate on the part they like. The challenge with a selective listening spouse is that he or she may ignore the most important part of the message.

- **Distracted Listeners** - These listeners concentrate on other matters while communication is ongoing, but interjects or interrupts periodically to show they are still listening. The challenge with a distracted spouse is the possibility of missing the most important part of the message.

- **Deflecting Listeners** - Deflecting listeners change the topics of conversation to suit what they want to hear and not what the sender seeks to communicate. They monopolize and change the focus of the communication from the sender to themselves. The challenge with a deflecting listening spouse is that he or she kills communication.

- **Defensive Listeners** - These listeners ignore the message the moment there is perception of personal attacks or criticism in the message. The challenge with a defensive listening spouse is that the objective, intention and value of the message will not be heard or understood and there will be no communication.

Good listening contributes to effective communication and includes:

- **Active Listening** - Active listening is a deliberate activity to receive and understand conveyed messages without distractions. Active listening involves paying attention by showing interest and being mentally prepared for the message, removing distractions, and noise. It also involves providing feedback by asking questions, paraphrasing or repeating what has been heard. Couples should learn active listening skills to ensure good communication in their marriage relationship.

- **Empathetic Listening** - Empathetic listening is when a listener encourages a speaker to communicate freely without criticizing and attacking him or her. The empathetic listener recognizes and appreciates the speakers' feelings, values, and interests expressed through the message, thereby allowing the receiver to clearly understand the message from the speaker's perspectives. Couples should empathize with one another to enjoy quality communication.

- **Postural Listening** - Communication is generally said to consist of about 10% of what we say, about 40% of how we say it, and 50% of the body language we express when saying it. Postural listening is the non-verbal understanding of a message received. It includes information expressed through body language, facial expression, hands or legs or eye contact or movement, cough and laughter. Couples are encouraged to focus on both the verbal and non-verbal aspects of communication to ensure lasting relationships.

- **Response Listening** - The listening method allows receivers to be honest in their responses, while having consideration for the feeling of the senders. Response listeners do not attack, interrupt or judge the senders or give advice when it is not solicited, but rather the messages are understood for appropriate responses. Couples should be respectful, accommodating, and considerate with their responses.

36. **What communication methods are "bad" and "good" in a marriage?**

Communication is the body and soul of a marriage relationship. It is one of the reasons that couples claim or disclaim compatibility and chemistry. It is in the top list of rationales for cessation of marriage. Failure of communication is the beginning of crisis in marriage while its success leads to marital bliss and an enduring marriage.

Below is a list of words, attitudes and characteristics that constitute bad communication in a marriage relationship:

- Criticizing or opposing one's spouse in public.
- Confronting one's spouse in their children's presence.
- Hanging up the phone or walking out during conversation with one's spouse.
- Yelling in anger, becoming hysterical and resorting to name-calling with one's spouse
- Speaking condescendingly to one's spouse.
- Accusing one's spouse in the presence of their in-laws.

Below is a list of words, attitudes and characteristics that constitute good communication in a marriage relationship:

- Praying, reading and speaking the word of God to one's spouse
- Speaking words of affection to one's spouse - for example: "I love you," and "You look great."
- Praising, commending and appreciating one's spouse - for example: "Thank you"; "I appreciate your efforts."
- Apologizing to one's spouse when wrong - for example: "I am sorry"; "I didn't mean it."

- Being inclusive in one's conversation - for example: using "we" instead of "I".
- Being willing to be responsive and helpful to one's spouse.
- Giving or sharing credit with one's spouse.
- Encouraging, cheering and comforting one's spouse.
- Holding, touching and kissing one' spouse in public (public displays of affection).

Chapter 6

# Trust and Decisions

*Choice* is the act of selecting from the alternative courses of actions. Choice is a major ingredient of decision making, and it involves alternatives and preferences. The nature of available alternatives and the personal interests at stake will determine the kind of choice a person will make. A person that has his or her interests aligned with God's will, makes decisions that glorify God, and a person that prefers his ego and fame makes decisions that will gratify the world. Life is full of decisions with varying degrees of consequences. Some consequences are easily endured, enjoyed and managed while others are devastating, irreparable and eternal. Everyone is created with the freewill to make a choice. Matthew 6:24 warns that *"No man can serve two masters: for either he will hate the one, and love the other; or else he will hold to the one, and despise the other. Ye cannot serve God and mammon."* Couples should decide to serve and follow God. They should choose marriage and make the sacrifice necessary to save and keep it. Couples should love and cherish the spouses they have; not the spouses they wish they could have.

### 37. What should I do if I discover troubling information about my spouse's past life?

Marriage begins at the wedding. Both church and court weddings require couples to engage in marriage counseling before the joining and the issuance of marriage license at the wedding. One of the main reasons for counseling among others is to ensure that couples work out their differences, address secrets, and understand the concept of marriage. Good marriage counseling will help the couple to become better acquainted with each other, covenant with, and be comfortable with one another's history and prepare them to handle future challenges. The disclosure of a spouse's past life may be deliberately hidden or inadvertently stone walled from the other spouse during courtship and counseling. However, the belief is that if one did not ask for it, it is not important to the other, and it should not matter to one now. If one of the couple asked about it then, and the other person lied, then trust can be lost. Unlike regular contracts, non-disclosure of relevant information does not impair the marriage covenant.

> ***"When morning came, there was Leah! So Jacob said to Laban, "What is this you have done to me? I served you for Rachel, didn't I? Why have you deceived me?" Laban replied, "It is not our custom here to give the younger daughter in marriage before the older one."*** Genesis 29:25-26

Though Jacob was deceived after he failed to ask all relevant questions, he could not dissolve his marriage to Leah due to non-disclosure because the marriage had been consummated.

One of the most important questions posed at a wedding is "*if anyone has any reason why these two people should not be joined together in holy matrimony, that person should speak now or remain silent forever*". Even in court weddings, this question is implied through the signing of a marriage application form by the couple. The signing of these forms imply that the information provided is accurate, complete, that one knows everything necessary prior to marriage; and that no person, issue or the non-disclosure of past information will impair another person's decision. To be true to yourself, are you sure the disclosure of this same information would have changed your feelings, emotions, and ecstasy for your spouse at that time? The truth is, most couples care less about any information at this time except for love, sex, and marriage.

Marriage involves an entire package. One marries everything about their spouse including his or her past, present, and future. If one marries in a hurry, it probably was because that was what the situation demanded at the time he/she met his/her spouse. One cannot turn back the hand of time; perhaps you were young in age then, but now you are older and wiser, and you think you should not have married; well, it is too late. One cannot have buyer's remorse at this moment. Your status might have changed from being unemployed to having stable employment, or from being a renter to owning your own home, or from being single to being a mother or father. Since a person cannot return to their old status, they should not regret their marriage just because of the non-disclosure of a spouse's past information. Genesis 2:25 reads *"And they were both naked, the man and his wife, and were not ashamed."*

All you need to do when you discover troubling or negative information about your spouse's past is to thank God for allowing your spouse to marry you; at least the troubling information did not kill your spouse. One needs to pray for their spouse, and look for ways to help him or her overcome and/or move beyond the information. I cannot pretend to know the proportional consequences or stress of the discovered information on you, your spouse, and your family, but the and information should be viewed from a positive perspective and from faith perspectives since you were brought into marriage to help each other. It is a test of one's maturity, patience, and faith, so this is not the time to be ashamed of your spouse, or to regret the life you share together. Neither should you abandon your marriage. Remember that spouses in a lasting marriage cover each other's nakedness and overlook past errors.

38. **Now that I am married, what are my options within the marriage?**

Life is about choices. Choice makes life complex, exciting, and even pleasurable. Without choices, life becomes simpler but boring. Choice offers us alternatives, options, and preferences. We make a choice to marry. After marriage, there are three options available as a spouse under both spiritual and physical perspectives.

Options under the spiritual perspective are:

- **Follow God** - The first option is to follow God and His will. This requires couples to remain married no matter what. The effect of this option is that there will be harmony and unity of purpose, a blissful marriage experience, a lasting marriage, strong and unconditional love, a peaceful home, joyful and blessed children that glorify God's name. This can be achieved when couples:
    - Accept Christ as Lord and Savior.
    - Obey the word of God and His principles on marriage.
    - Understand that God is a party to the marriage.
    - Demonstrate love and respect for one's spouse.
    - Refuse to abuse or mistreat one's spouse.
    - Resolve marriage crisis and conflict in God's way.
    - Parental or fatherly presence and care for children and family.

- **Follow the World** - The second option available to couples, is to follow the world. The effect of this option is disunity of purpose, chaotic family, unruly children, separation of couples, and termination of marriage. This is achieved when couples:
    - Disregard or abandon Christ, His church and the word of God.
    - Engage the principles and doctrines of the world.
    - Practice infidelity, abuse or mistreatment.
    - Abandon one's responsibilities to the children or their partners.
    - Lack of love for one another and being disrespectful.
    - Engage the courts in marriage crisis and conflict.

- **Follow Your Heart** - The third option is when couples follow their hearts. This option is the hybrid of the two previous options. With this option couples seek their individual happiness, which may sometimes contradict the will of God. It is about whatever makes a spouse feel good or happy. The effect of this option is a dysfunctional or unstable marriage, breakage of marriage and remarriage. This is achieved by:
    - Rejection of sacrifice, compromise, forgiveness, patience and other godly virtues that make for lasting marriage.
    - Acceptance of God's principles only to the extent that they make the couple happy.
    - The condition of the heart which is wicked and selfish.
    - The significant influence of public opinion and culture.

The three similar options under the physical perspectives are:

- **Work at It**: The first option to a couple is to work on the marriage. Couples must put forth an effort and fight to salvage the marriage. Neither spouse can take the other spouse or marriage for granted. Married couples must be proactive, innovative, and creative. There must be a change in attitudes, approach and actions. This type of change requires much work and must include constant prayer and supplication such as spending quality time with one another, communicating better with each other, changing certain behaviors that will be more pleasing to God. When persons in marriage work together insurmountable odds can be overcome and marriages will endure the test of time and situations.

- **Do Nothing About It**: The second option is to do nothing or be reactive. This occurs when couples engage in playing and incorporating the blame game and the result is to raise the white flag or surrender to the problems and issues. Whatever is going on in a marriage is not the in-laws' fault, or the churches fault, or your parent's fault. It is nobody's fault but the couples and the inability to address human differences that come with marriage. Persons are imperfect therefore those imperfections bleed over into marriages. The blame cannot be placed on one spouse alone. Spouses are equally responsible to address any issues that arise in the marriage. If nothing is done to address the issues, then failure and demise of the marriage is imminent. The fact that someone did something last year, month or week is not an excuse for giving up on the marriage.
- **Being Indifferent About it**: The third option is when a couple becomes indifferent about their marriage. This happens when nothing matters any more. The couple has adapted and is no longer doing things to be reactive. In this case, the action or inaction of the couple only promotes lack of passion and fire and ultimately the marriage dies. The couple's relationship has become weak and they are now indecisive about the marriage and have no insight about what can be done to revive the marriage.

At this point the couple doesn't even know what they desire any more. The effect of this option is that the marriage relationship is on life support. It has become boring, lacks spark, and becomes vulnerable to extinction. In other words, "the thrill is gone". What was the attraction has now become a distraction.

39. **As a wife, should I go into ministry even if my husband is not in agreement with it?**

In marriage, the husband and wife are one. The action or inaction of one spouse will directly and significantly affect the other spouse. One of the reasons the world is rejecting marriage is that spouses want to maintain their independence and not be accountable to the other spouse. This is not a godly marriage. A marriage in which dependency and accountability are missing cannot endure. The answer to a question of whether a wife should go into ministry without the approval or support of her husband is NO. This does not only affect the wife, the same applies to the husband as well. A man or woman who wants to go into ministry or answer the call of God on their life should seek spousal support and understanding of the call to ministry.

Due to some unique attributes of ministry, a spouse needs a higher level of support from the other spouse than the level that he or she needs for any other career or vocation. These attributes of ministry are:

- **Ministry involves divine calling** - Career path is a product of individual ambitions but ministry is a product of vision. People should enter into ministry to answer God's call upon their lives and not as a vocation.

  ***"Therefore, O king Agrippa, I was not disobedient unto the heavenly vision."***
  Acts 26:19

> ***"And the LORD answered me, and said, Write the vision, and make it plain upon tables, that he may run that readeth it. For the vision is yet for an appointed time, but at the end it shall speak, and not lie: though it tarry, wait for it; because it will surely come, it will not tarry."***
> Habakkuk 2:2-3

When God gives a man or woman a vision, He makes available the grace that is necessary to fulfill the vision. The man or woman should keep, cherish, nurture, and wait for the appointed time of that vision. In marriage, the timing of the vision falls under two periods:

- **The pre-marriage vision** - This is a vision received before marriage which is or is not yet carried-out. On one hand, if the vision is being carried-out and the man or woman is already in the ministry, the man or woman who intends to marry the visionary must be ready to support the spouse and the ministry. On the other hand, if the vision is not yet carried-out, the scenario dictates that the man or woman would have discussed or failed to discuss the vision with his or her prospective spouse before marriage. Either way, the man or woman with the vision may choose to wait and seek the understanding, support and approval of his or her spouse before entering the ministry.
- **Post-marriage vision** - This is a vision that is received after the marriage. The man or woman cannot force the timing and fulfillment of the vision on the other spouse. The man and/or woman must consult pray and trust God to convince the other partner and seek divine revelation about the vision. The marriage relationship is superior to ministry.

> ***"So they are no longer two, but one flesh. Therefore what God has joined together, let no one separate."*** Matthew 19:6

- **God places the institution of marriage above the ministry such that even ministry should not separate the spouses.** A man or woman cannot claim the vision is divine and is from God so he or she does not need the support or approval of his or her spouse. Some celebrity pastors and ministers of the gospel who have divorced their husbands or wives in the name of ministry may want us to believe that they are working for God but they have erred. They cannot cherry-pick the part word of God they want to believe. If they preach prosperity, faith, and obedience, they should also preach marriage, patience, and endurance. In fact, no one can be zealous in doing God's work more than God Himself.
- **Ministry involves family engagement** - Unlike other career paths that may not require the involvement of the other spouse and family members, ministry requires complete commitment of all members of the household. Membership of ministry is voluntary and not permanent. Members, supporters, and partners come and go when you least expect it. In the case of married couples, you and your family are the only permanent members and partners therefore you cannot ignore spousal support.
- **Ministry involves building one's livelihood on the spirituality and benevolence of other people** - Because ministry is about service without a specific price tag, men and women in ministry live on the voluntary contributions of people being served. Most of the time where their salaries are paid, the pay is not commensurate to the services rendered.

> ***"If we have sown spiritual seed among you, is it too much if we reap a material harvest from you?"*** 1 Corinthians 9:11

Though they are entitled to a livelihood, money should not be the focus of any man or woman in ministry. Unfortunately, many have seen ministry as a means of making money and getting rich quick. Ministry is different from charitable organizations that receive block or matching grants from the government.

- **Ministry attracts opposition and persecution** - Since divine ministry is confronted with the spirituality of mankind and the kingdom of God, and Satan is against the kingdom of God, there is conflict between ministry and Satan.

> ***"For a great door and effectual is opened unto me, and there are many adversaries."***
> 1 Corinthians 16:9

> ***"We are troubled on every side, yet not distressed; we are perplexed, but not in despair. Persecuted, but not forsaken; cast down, but not destroyed."*** And 2 Corinthians 4:8-9

Satan attacks ministry and the people in ministry through opposition, persecution, and enemies.

To enjoy a lasting marriage relationship no one should rush into ministry, and certainly not without the support and blessings of the spouse.

40. **How can I trust someone who has violated or compromised my trust in the past?**

*The American Heritage Dictionary* defines trust as the *"firm belief in the integrity, ability and character of a person or thing."* In order words, trust is the confidence we place on the words and actions of a person. A man who knows the behavior of his wife may not have an unyielding trust in the character of his wife, the same as with the woman. Because one of the basics of marriage is trust, a man and woman expects faithfulness to each other in all matters of their relationship. They expect marriage vows to be kept, the marital bed to be undefiled and to be protected from marriage predators. As a matter of trust, couples expect fidelity, openness, truthfulness, devotion, loyalty and commitment to each other. The opposite of these elements of trust are deception, secrecy, non-disclosure, infidelity and abuse. A man must understand that he cannot physically or verbally abuse his wife and expect to retain her trust as a protector. He cannot engage in extra-marital affairs and expect her to trust him as a soul-mate. Likewise, a woman cannot constantly lie to her husband and expect him to be her defender.

Trust cannot be demanded or acquired but rather is earned. Husbands cannot demand a wife's trust except you have proven yourself to her and earned her trust through your actions and character. Trust is not what you pray for but what you develop over time through relationship. The way and manner one relates to a spouse, family and others can be used as evidence of trustworthiness. Trust is not a one-time thing but a series of actions and events over an extended period of time. A spouse will appreciate a one-time kind gesture demonstrated and forgive a one-time mistake made, but a spouse will find it hard to trust that the partner will change from what he/she does over and over again. Trust lost is difficult to regain. Couples should not be manipulative with their marital trust. A marriage relationship becomes sick when trust is compromised.

When trust is violated and compromised, the couple can heal and trust again through these actions:

- **Trust God** - Marriage partners are God, man and woman. God is the manufacturer, inventor and source of marriage, and it makes sense to refer back to Him when there are challenges in marriage. He is faithful and trustworthy. As a child of God, one should believe and trust Him first. If you trust God, it will not be too hard to trust your spouse again, especially if God still trusts your spouse. Pray that God will heal the damaged spouse with regard to the distrust and forgiveness can happen that will cause you and your spouse to love and trust again.

- **Remember Your Marital Vows** - One of the significances of the marriage vow is to dissolve plots of marital challenge. Consider your vows when there is doubt about the trust of a spouse. Think about the good memories that have been created and shared with your spouse prior to the distrust. When a spouse truly thinks about their marital vows, trust will return again. Always use love to find ways to resolve problems and differences. Find ways to engage your spouse to amend the distrust.

- **Seek Counseling with Your Spouse** - Life is about knowledge, and counseling provides knowledge. Don't jump into conclusion about anything without adequate evidence; even with raw evidence, both of you need counseling. Circumstances and situations are not always the way they appear. Counseling may reveal the causes of distrust, where one has erred and where one's spouse missed it. Counseling may offer solutions on how to relate better and to regain one's trust.

- **Forgive and Get Healed** - Forgiveness is a must in any lasting marital relationship. Offenses come in different sizes and shapes with minor and major pain and consequences. Forgiveness is for both spouses. One needs to forgive a spouse when he or she violates the others trust. Even if the offense is infidelity, one should have the heart and desire to forgive. This may not be easy but with God, the third party in marriage, all things are possible, and you can do all things through Christ. After forgiveness, give yourself time to fully heal while assisting your spouse to seek additional help for whatever the issues may be.

41. **What is a tattoo, and do I need spousal permission before having one?**

A tattoo is the printing of word, symbol, or inscription on the body or the artistic modification of the body with indelible ink. It is like other body modifications such as piercing, bleaching and tribal marks. Each has been used to be identified with some traditional cultures but has now become a multi-million-dollar business. It does not only produce income and employment for those who are tattoo artists but also some satisfaction for those who receive the printing on their bodies.

From the physical perspective, people wear tattoos to engage in fashion, to adhere to culture, to show they are different, to make a statement or an expression, to identify with or initiate into a fraternity, to remember someone, things or events. While many support it as cool, fun and tasteful, others oppose it for health reasons; for the fact that it creates an indelible mark that may be costly to remove, and for the belief that it is often used to express moral defiance and rebellion.

From the spiritual perspective, tattooing is condemned as an abomination against God, as an adherence to the value of the world, and as a defilement of the body, the temple of the Holy Spirit. It allows the letting of the blood, the invocation of demonic spirits and inscription of marks different from the mark of Christ. The implication of Christians engaging in tattooing is that they have comingled themselves with the world and have made the world darker instead of being a light to it.

> ***"Do not cut your bodies for the dead or put tattoo marks on yourselves. I am the LORD."*** Leviticus 19:28 (NIV)

> ***"Do you not know that your bodies are temples of the Holy Spirit, who is in you, whom you have received from God? You are not your own."*** 1 Corinthians 6:19 (NIV)

The question of whether a married person should obtain permission from his or her spouse before having a tattoo is a question of relationship. If the couple is in marriage relationship, he or she needs the permission of the other spouse before tattooing or piercing his or her body. There is no way around it because when you get married, you give up "I, me, mine, and myself" for "we, us, ours and ourselves".

> ***"The wife does not have authority over her own body but yields it to her husband. In the same way, the husband does not have authority over his own body but yields it to his wife."*** 1 Corinthians 7:4 (NIV)

On the other hand, a person can do anything he or she likes to his or her body without seeking the permission of a spouse if he or she is not married. At any rate, there is no spousal relationship without marriage. Civil or domestic union is not a marriage ordained by God.

Christians should cease and desist from trying to be like or outshine the world in the things of the world. Tattooing may sound cool and fun to a reprobate mind, but it does not give glory to God. It is the Holy Spirit that convicts souls; you cannot win or save anybody, so don't give excuses that you want to be like them, so as to win them. It is okay to live with a tattoo if you had it before you gave your life to Christ as God erased our sins at conversion.

***"The times of ignorance God overlooked, but now he commands all people everywhere to repent."*** Acts 17:30 (EST)

42. **What should I do if my spouse is sick?**

Couples are humans and human beings become sick. Sickness is illness, bad health, uneasy or defective body conditions. Sickness inflicts pain and shuts down a person's ability to function normally. Sickness may last for days, weeks, months or years with varying degrees of impact, from minor to major or mild to serious. Some of these sicknesses come in the form of diseases that are curable or incurable, acute or chronic, and contagious or non-contagious. They may be personal or epidemic in nature.

Sicknesses may be physical, psychological and spiritual. Physical sickness is easily diagnosed with visible symptoms. Examples are: suffering from headache, pain, arthritis, diabetes, heart or liver or lung or kidney disease or cancer. A psychological sickness includes any illness of the mind, psyche, or mental breakdown. Mind relates to intellect, emotions and memory. Some examples of psychological sickness are depression, stress and anxiety, bipolar disorder, Autism, and Alzheimer. Spiritual sickness involves oppression and bondage from evil spirits and demons. Spiritual sickness may use the symptoms of physical or psychological sickness to hide its operations. Examples of spiritual sickness are unexplained illness in form of pain, depression, addiction, or barrenness.

The causes of sickness can be human, environmental, natural and spiritual. Some examples are food poisoning, injury caused by accident, bacterial infections, viral infections, air pollution, imbalance of body hormones and substances, breaking down of body organs, sin committed against God, and attack from demonic powers.

Sin is a cause of sickness.

> ***"Jesus saith unto him, Rise, take up thy bed, and walk. Afterward Jesus findeth him in the temple, and said unto him, Behold, thou art made whole: sin no more, lest a worse thing come unto thee."*** John 5:8;14

Also, attack from Satan or demonic agents can cause sickness.

> ***"Jesus had been saying to him, "Come out of the man, you unclean spirit!" And they came to Jesus, and see him that was possessed with the devil, and had the legion, sitting, and clothed, and in his right mind: and they were afraid."*** Mark 5:8,15

Some illness can be prevented through good diet, immunization, exercise, clean environment, avoidance of sin, and deliverance.

The following are the suggestions of what you should do if your spouse falls sick:

- **Pray for your spouse** -This is not the time to question God, run away from God or leave the church but it is the time to seek God. Even many unbelievers, backsliders, and unserious believers seek God for prayers during the time of illness, but it is also important to seek and serve God when we have good health.

  ***"Is any sick among you? let him call for the elders of the church; and let them pray over him, anointing him with oil in the name of the Lord: And the prayer of faith shall save the sick, and the Lord shall raise him up; and if he have committed sins, they shall be forgiven him."*** James 5:14-15

- **Care for your spouse** - A sick person is weak and needs help and care from the strong. It is the responsibility of the healthy spouse to care for the sick spouse. This is not the time to dump or abandon the sick spouse, file for divorce or bring up old disputes to justify your irresponsibility. Caring for a sick spouse may be a daunting task but it is what must be done.

> ***"We then that are strong ought to bear the infirmities of the weak, and not to please ourselves."*** Romans 15:1

- **Consult doctors** - Doctors and other medical experts have knowledge, experience and wisdom through their training, research and their ability to diagnose and provide treatment for our body. The healthy spouse should take the sick spouse to the doctor for there is nothing wrong in seeking and receiving treatments and medications from doctors. There are things God will do for us and there are things God wants us to do for ourselves.

> ***"Jesus answered them, "It is not the healthy who need a doctor, but the sick."*** Luke 5:31

Jesus was not against a doctor's consultation. Doctors provide treatment but God gives the healing.

- **Engage the family** - Dependent upon the nature of the sickness, it may be a difficult time for ailing family. The healthy spouse should engage both their extended families including willing in-laws. This allows them the opportunity to be part of the recovery process and to provide necessary assistance as they deem fit. The spiritual family, the pastor and members of the couple's church, should be engaged as well. They should understand that there is nothing wrong in seeking help. We are not created to be self-dependent and self-sufficient. We need one another.

- **Make post-mortem plan** - In a situation where the sickness is terminal, the healthy spouse needs to summon courage and make a postmortem plan with the input and contribution of the sick spouse. This is a very difficult task which many may not want to do not only because of cultural and religious beliefs, but also the denial and pain of losing a loving spouse. Postmortem plans are not a legal will, but a plan that details the desires and wishes of the sick person while they are still alive and how things should be handled after death. In the absence of a will, this plan reduces family conflicts that sometimes may take place over the burial, estate and the children of the deceased spouse.

### 43. How long should a spouse wait before remarrying after the death of a spouse?

Death and dying are a part of life and has been since the fall of man. It utilizes different means to end the lives of people and causes range from natural death, accidental, disasters such as tornados, fires, and unexpected diseases.

> ***"Then shall the dust return to the earth as it was: and the spirit shall return unto God who gave it."*** Ecclesiastes 12:7.

The pain of death is that it mostly happens unexpectedly with no adequate preparation from the family and the deceased. Death kills with no recognition of the victim's status. For example, believers, non-believers, young, old, rich, poor, white, black, and brown have died at various times and places. According to the United States Center of Diseases Control and Prevention (CDC) as reported in its National Vital Statistics Report (NVSR), about 2.6 million and 2.5 million people died in US in 2013 and 2012 respectively. Of those reported totals both men and women had equal deaths of 1.3 million in 2013, and 1.3

million for men and 1.2 million for women in 2012. For 2013 data, the CDC report highlights the 5 major causes of death as: heart disease 0.6 million; cancer 0.6 million; chronic lower respiratory disease 0.1 million; accidents 0.1 million; and stroke 0.1 million. If the daily death rate is about 7,000 people in United States with all of its technology, healthcare systems and economic development, how much more is the death rate per day for many third world countries with their unsophisticated healthcare systems and ravaging wars? A spouse may die untimely leaving behind a husband or wife and children. The question of how long a living spouse should wait before remarrying after the death of a spouse depends on the following:

- **The spouse's choice** - The covenant of marriage ends at the death of one of the spouses.

  > ***"The wife is bound by the law as long as her husband liveth; but if her husband be dead, she is at liberty to be married to whom she wills; only in the Lord.*** 1 Corinthians 7:39

  The living spouse is free to marry at any time he or she wishes. It is the living spouse's prerogative and choice. On one hand, he or she can marry the next day, week, month, year or many years later. On the other hand, he or she can choose not to marry again. It is a personal choice.

- **How the living spouse mourns** - The process of grieving may be the same but individuals mourn differently. The general process of grieving involves shock, denial, pain, guilt, anger, bargaining, depression and acceptance. Some people grieve internally by absorbing the emotions and pains while others externalize it in a conspicuous manner. Likewise, some spouses reach a level of acceptance very fast, while it takes others years to accept the reality of the death of their spouse. The living spouse who overcomes mourning faster will not take a long time before remarrying.

- **The nature of a living spouse's job** - The nature of job of a living spouse is a determinant factor in how long it will take a living spouse to remarry. Many pastors and other ministers of the gospel marry within a short period after the death of a spouse to keep themselves from temptations and sins. Pastoral responsibilities include counseling, encouraging and visitation, which can expose the vulnerability of human nature with the opposite sex.

- **The age of the living spouse** - Many living spouses who are advanced in age see no need to remarry, and even if they want to, do not see the rush. They have lived their life to fullness already and only consider marriage for companionship. On the other hand, many living spouses who are young remarry within a year or two after the death of their spouse because they are too young to be widows or widowers. They find new love and remarry because they still need all the benefits of marriage including procreation, recreation, friendship and companionship.

  ***"So I advise these younger widows to marry again, have children, and take care of their own homes. Then the enemy will not be able to say anything against them."*** 1Timothy 5:14

- **The sex of the living spouse** - It is a general belief that women take a longer time to remarry. Could it be because women are more emotional and it takes them a longer time to grieve or detach themselves from the deceased spouse, or that they are not sexually demanding? or that they need someone who will fill the shoes of the dead spouses? Whatever the reasoning, women tend to wait longer than men.

- **Other factors** - There are many reasons while a living spouse may or may not wait long before remarrying after the demise of a spouse. For instance, the consideration of the children of the deceased spouse, the traumatic effect on the living spouse or the nature of the death of the spouse, and the cultures, traditions and beliefs of the living spouse.

44. **How can I handle marriage if my spouse is not as intelligent as I had thought?**

Marriage is an institution established by God to fulfill His will for mankind. God instituted marriage for companionship, complementarity, completeness, procreation and recreation. The assignment God gave mankind would not be complete without the union and partnership of man and woman.

Marriage reveals the nakedness of the couple to each other. This nakedness includes their secrets, weaknesses, pretenses, personalities, and inadequacies. In a God-fearing marriage, the couple will not be ashamed of this nakedness; but in a selfish secular marriage, couples look for ways to leave their spouses, one of which is the detection of weaknesses.

Marriage unites two people who are different in sex, level of education, reasoning, perspective, and opinions. Based on natural instincts and worldly standards, spouses are enthused when their spouse is highly intelligent, smart, attractive and rich and dislikes when the case is the opposite. This couple possibly married because they discovered positive, irresistible attributes, characteristics, benefits, and advantages about their spouse that they could not let go. Unfortunately, it is after marriage that negative discoveries about their spouse's nakedness are made. Thereafter, buyer's remorse sets in after they get what they wanted and their needs are already met. Marriage is a covenant not a contract, so slogans and catchy phrases like "Buyers Beware" or "as is" cannot be displayed at a wedding.

Complaining about the intelligence of one's partner after marriage is fundamentally wrong. What did you discover or discuss with your spouse during courtship? Having a short period of courtship is not an excuse. Marrying in absentia or engaging in a long distant relationship is not an excuse either. Except one is blind and deaf, this issue of education or academic intelligence should have been discussed. The issues that were not raised then were not relevant then and shouldn't be relevant now that you have enjoyed the best of your spouse. Now is not the time to complain or throw your spouse off the bus because of the flimsy excuses of lack of skills, intellect, or educational achievements, these had no bearing before marriage and should have none now.

If the level of your spouse's intelligence or education is an issue, what is expected of you is to nurture, help and cultivate your spouse to blossom like roses, shine like stars and glitter like gold. It's your responsibility to cover his or her nakedness and weakness instead of shaming or embarrassing him or her. Couples should see themselves as one and work together to achieve great accomplishments as a single-family unit. Couples should address issues that come their way to strengthen their relationship instead of weakening their marriage. They should love each other because love covers all sins and weaknesses. Love allows one to esteem and value one's spouse despite his or her weaknesses and errors. Love is the giving that makes a sacrifice for the development of one's spouse.

### 45. Do my marriage vows really matter, especially when I am tired of the marriage?

Marriage begins with the wedding, during which couples exchange marital vows to establish the contractual aspect and the right of consummation of the marriage covenant. In discharging this vow, the officiating minister may read out the vow to the couple separately or jointly, or the couple may read out the vow to each other jointly or in unison. In some other cases, it may be a combination of an officiating minister and the individual spouses reading out different parts. Whichever method is adopted, the content and context of the vows or pledges are similar to the following samples:

> *"Do you take this man/woman to be your husband/wife, so that both of you will live together according to the God's order on marriage? Will you love him/her, obey him/her, honor him/her, and cherish him/her throughout your life? Will you reject other men/woman and cleave to him/her alone as long as you both shall live?"*

> *"I, ABC accept you XYZ, as my wedded wife/husband today to have and to hold, for better, for worse, for richer, for poorer, in sickness, in health and in all circumstances. I will love you and cherish you according to the will of God, for the rest of my life ('till death do us part), in the name of the Father, the Son and the Holy Spirit."*

From these samples vows or pledges, there are a few phrases that are of obvious significance, such as: *"both of you will live together", "love, honor, cherish him or her", "for better, for worse, for richer, for poorer, in health and in all circumstances", "as long as both shall live or 'till death do us part."*. The implication of these phrases is that the marriage covenant is a permanent commitment that implies that couples are to live together irrespective of circumstances and be in the union until the death of either or both of them.

Couples should know that their marriage vows matter. Couples have to be faithful to their vows and the marriage covenant. There are many bad circumstances that could arise to force persons to break the vows, including tiredness, boredom, finances, arguments, crisis, or public opinions, but couples or spouses cannot give in. When a marriage vow is broken, spouses fail, through committing sin and celebrating evil.

Couples should recognize that tiredness is part of nature. The lack of strength, energy and motivation to continue a task is not the end of life. When we are tired or bored, we rest, take a break and create exciting moments to regain energy but we don't terminate appointments or commit suicide. Likewise, when couples grow tired of marriage:

- It is not the time to break marriage vows or covenants, but rather it is time to seek help in order to rejuvenate and spice up the marriage.
- It is not the time to put away a partner in separation or divorce, but rather it is the time to address whatever issues are causing tiredness.
- It is not the time to reveal the dirty linen in the marriage, but rather it is the time to celebrate the good memories that have been enjoyed with a spouse in marriage.
- It is not the time to be unfaithful or abusive, but rather it is the time to pray and seek God to give the spouses new wine.

Chapter 7

# Love and Sex

*Selfishness* is a synonym for individualism and egotism. It is the lack of care for another's interests, preferences and welfare. Selfishness makes no sacrifice for others and it has no place in marriage. A selfish spouse does not consider the feelings of the other spouse. Selfishness embodies the "I", "Me" and "My" syndrome. But marriage changes "I" to "We", "Me" to "Us" and "My" to "Our". Marriage changes individualism to collectivism, and independence to interdependence. Marriage allows one to share food, resources, time, energy, body, and interests with one's spouse. It allows the couple to walk together as one in unity as a team. Amos 3:3 reads that *"Can two walk together, except they be agreed?"* Couples should not only prefer their spouse to any other person but they should also esteem them above themselves. Couples should remove selfishness and pride from their character. They should be humble and willing to share life, goods, and themselves with their spouse.

46. **What is Sex?**

Sex means different things to different people but in marriage it is intercourse through the genitals or sexual organs. Sex is an important issue in marriage because through it the marriage covenant is consummated. Men and women are sexual beings as their sexuality involves their body, soul and spirit. In marriage, sex is described as:

- **A lubricant of marriage** - Sex is God's idea and it is permitted in marriage. It soothes wounds and binds the friendship of the couple. It brings excitement, intimacy and connection between the couple. It brings warmness, fun and happiness.
- **The climax of romance** -Sex allows for the stimulation and arousal of genitals and sexual organs that produces orgasm. It brings pleasure and ecstasy that leads to closeness of friendship.
- **A means of procreation** - Sex allows man to release sperm into a woman's fallopian tube through the vagina. These sperm cells join the woman's egg cell, which is later fertilized to become pregnancy. That's the magic of God's creation of sex; thus accomplishing procreation.
- **A means of recreation** - Sex is for both procreation and recreation. Sex is a natural instinct created by God for man's pleasure. It is to be enjoyed in the context of marriage. This allows sex to meet the emotional and physical needs of couples without resulting in pregnancy.
- **Spiritual** - Loneliness in man is not only caused by physical and emotional reasons but also by spiritual ones. The last work of creation is the discovery of man's and woman's nakedness without shame. Couples worship and draw closer to God through their sexuality.

***"The husband should fulfill his marital duty to his wife, and likewise the wife to her husband. The wife does not have authority over her own body but***

***yields it to her husband. In the same way, the husband does not have authority over his own body but yields it to his wife. Do not deprive each other except perhaps by mutual consent and for a time, so that you may devote yourselves to prayer. Then come together again so that Satan will not tempt you because of your lack of self-control."*** I Corinthians 7:3-5

Satan recognizes the spirituality of sex as he uses it as a weapon of lust and makes mankind sin against God. No wonder sex is commercialized and popularized as the coolest thing to do even outside the boundary of marriage.

47. **What are the types of sex available for couples?**

Sex involves the body, soul and spirit. It is one of the exciting aspects of marriage. It is a good exercise. It reduces stress and improves immune systems. There are basically four types of sex and they are:

- **Vaginal Sex** - This is the traditional sex involving the vagina and the penis. It involves a man and a woman, with the penetration through the vagina. This kind of sex is God ordained and allows for procreation and recreation.

- **Anal Sex** - This is anal penetration with the penis. It involves man and woman or man and man with the penetration through the anus. This kind of sex is for recreation only and it is not God ordained. The anus is not made for penetration and pregnancy cannot take place through the anus. Unlike the vagina, the anus is not self-lubricated and lacks protective tissues against viruses and bacteria. A large penis may cause tearing to unprotected anal tissues. Anal sex is mostly practiced by homosexuals, of whom God disapproves. Homosexuals are one of the main at-risk groups of AIDs as many incidences of HIV are reported among them.

***"That is why God abandoned them to their shameful desires. Even the women turned against the natural way to have sex and instead indulged in sex with each other. And the men, instead of having normal sexual relations with women, burned with lust for each other. Men did shameful things with other men, and as a result of this sin, they suffered within themselves the penalty they deserved."*** Romans 1:26-27

The October 2016 Fast facts of the United States Centers for Disease Control and Prevention (CDC) states that, *"Anal sex is the riskiest sexual behavior for getting and transmitting HIV for men and women."*

- **Oral Sex** - This is the use of the mouth to stimulate and arouse a man or woman to obtain orgasm. Since foreplay and romance is part of good sex, there is nothing wrong with oral sex. The scripture is silent on this except that it encourages couples to enjoy and not deprive each other of sex. Oral sex is not for procreation but for recreation. Hands, legs, and body, including mouth or tongue, can be used to stimulate and arouse our spouses for them to have an orgasm. The only issue is that it should be a mutual agreement between the couple and both spouses should enjoy it. If your spouse does not like it then it would be selfish if you demand it.

- **Masturbation** – This is another type of sex where a person engages in self-stimulation and arousal of his or her body to obtain orgasm. It is interesting to know that the scripture is silent on masturbation. Masturbation may be good or bad depending on who it is directed to. Godly sex practice directs sex to be pleasurable to the spouse. Sex becomes lust when the pleasure is directed towards someone other than the spouse. Masturbation is not for procreation but for recreation.

The question many believers may face is which sex type should they practice? Honestly, apart from anal sex, which is completely ungodly, I do not have an answer, except to encourage couples to practice the type of sex that is by mutual agreement, hygienic and is consistent with their level of spirituality.

48. **Does anything go when it comes to sex in marriage?**

One of the challenges Christian couples face in marriage is the question of sex. The questions, to mention a few are: What can married couples do in sex? How can they satisfy each other in bed? What type of sex should a couple practice? Unfortunately, the church has avoided this important topic and allowed the World, Hollywood, Bollywood, Nollywood, and Ghallywood to lead and teach us concerning this topic. The following factors should be considered when it comes to the practice of sex in the context of God:

- **Legitimacy** - God created sex within certain boundaries.

  **Firstly, sex is permitted only in marriage.** It becomes sin when practiced outside marriage. Men or women who have sex before marriage even during their courtship commit fornication while a married man or woman who has sex with anyone apart from his or her spouse commits adultery. Sex is therefore with spouses.

  ***"Give honor to marriage, and remain faithful to one another in marriage. God will surely judge people who are immoral and those who commit adultery."*** Hebrews 13:4 (NLT)

  **Secondly, sex is for married couples who are of opposite genders.** The idea of homosexual coupling or same-sex marriage is not God's idea. God created them male and female. No matter how convincing the argument of man, it is not tenable with God. Importantly, God does not argue with man, He allows man to win the argument through freedom of choice. *"Do not practice homosexuality, having sex with another man as with a woman. It is a detestable sin."* Leviticus 18:22 (NLT)

**Thirdly, sex with animals is taboo**. Bestiality is ungodly though it is a common practice in our world today. How gross it is for a man or woman to have intercourse with a dog or goat? Sex with an animal is nothing but perdition.

***"A man must not defile himself by having sex with an animal. And a woman must not offer herself to a male animal to have intercourse with it. This is a perverse act."*** Leviticus 18:23 (NLT)

- **Secrecy** - Sex is not for public consumption. Couples are permitted to have sex in confidentiality and in secret. For children of God, public sex is wrong. Even in the home, doors should be locked especially when children are grown. Many couples violate this principle in thinking that sex should be spontaneous therefore should be done in the park, road side, in the car, public bathrooms, and even hospitals, where it can be viewed by others. It is ungodly for couple to videotape or record sexual acts to be distributed for sale, blackmail or for whatever reason. Pornography violates this principle.

  ***"Then each of you will control his own body and live in holiness and honor - not in lustful passion like the pagans who do not know God and his ways."***
  1 Thessalonians 4:4-5 (NLT)

- **Consent** - Couples should agree and be comfortable with their sexual practices. Amos 3:3 (KJV) reads *"Can two walk together, except they be agreed?"* For a married couple to make sex enjoyable to each other, they should agree on:

Firstly, what types of sex they will have. The types are vagina sex, anal sex, oral sex and masturbation. Couples should desist from whatever type of sex their spouse is not comfortable with.

Secondly, what types of sexual positions should a couple assume? There are different sexual positions. Some positions give men more enjoyment than women, and vice versa. Communication, consideration and agreement are necessary for both to derive pleasure.

Thirdly, the time they will have sex. Scriptures encourage couple not to deprive each other of sex but there are times when a spouse may not be in the mood. Spouses should make sacrifices to satisfy each other but there should be no rape or forceful sex among couples.

- **Hygiene and Health Concern** - The couple should educate themselves to ensure that their sexual practice is not detrimental to their health or create health issues for either or both spouses. For instance, sex may need to be on hold during a wife's menstrual period. Condoms may need to be used if one spouse has a sexually transmitted disease. Anal sex may be eliminated due to tissue tearing, pills or medication may be used for a heart condition, and certain sex position may be adopted due to a spouse's body condition.

- **Satisfaction** - One major complaint in marriage is lack of satisfaction of one spouse.

Firstly, a couple should not deprive each other of sex. Husband and wife should be lovers, and give their bodies to each other especially in sexual intimacy. It is an act of selfishness to refuse your wife or husband sex.

***"The wife hath not power of her own body, but the husband: and likewise also the husband hath not power of his own body, but the wife."*** 1 Corinthians 7:4 (KJV)

Secondly, every sexual activity should be directed towards the satisfaction and fulfillment of each other's sexual desires. Neither spouse should physically or mentally have sex with anyone other than each other. Even in masturbation, it should be directed towards one's spouse.

***"But I say unto you, That whosoever looketh on a woman to lust after her hath committed adultery with her already in his heart."*** Matthew 5:28 (KJV)

Thirdly, couples should derive pleasure in sex with their spouses. Although not in all situations, husband and wife should experience orgasm when having sex with each other. Husbands and wives must discover what arouses and stimulates their spouse, and make necessary sacrifices. Sex is an act of giving.

***"Be devoted to one another in love. Honor one another above yourselves."*** Romans 12:10 (NIV)

- **Spirituality** - Couples should consider their spirituality when it comes to sex. Our sexual activities should bring us closer to each other and give glory to God. We should not involve ourselves in any sexual act that is against the will of God. Anal sex is ungodly and should not be practiced by the children of God. Fasting should make us put sex on hold outside of marriage.

49. **What would you do if your spouse always refuses to have sex with you?**

This question is more prominent in the hearts of husbands than wives. Without sex, there is no marriage. The scripture recognizes the unavoidability of sex as it encourages men and women to marry. The importance of sex cannot be over-emphasized in marriage as it affects everything. The life of a married couple intensifies through sexual involvement. A spouse that is unhappy in bed may not be productive in his or her office. A couple who have problems with sex may have problems with communication, trust, and finances. In addressing this question, we will focus on the reasons why a spouse may refuse sex, the dangers of refusing sex, and the recommendation to address the issue.

These are some reasons why a spouse may refuse to have sex with his or her partner.

- **Unresolved issues** - Sex affects everything and everything affects sex in marriage. A wife may refuse sex because of her concerns over an issue or matter that is being ignored or is not addressed by her husband.
- **Tiredness** - A spouse may have a hectic day at home, work, school or business, which makes him or her lack the energy necessary for sex. This fatigue may be physical, psychological or spiritual.
- **Non-anticipation** - A spouse may claim he or she is not in the mood for sex just because he or she is not anticipating or expecting it under the prevailing circumstances.
- **Sickness** - A spouse may refuse sexual activity because of illness or recovery from illness. The urge or demand for sex during this time comes because the demanding spouse believes his or her spouse is well, fully recovered and not under serious illness.

- **Punishment** - A wife may refuse sex in order to get even and punish her husband. This is using sex as a punishment or reward mechanism. A man may reject this idea by refraining from have sex with his wife.

- **Extra-marital Affairs** - An unfaithful spouse who is having extra-marital affairs may refuse sex with his or her spouse. Infidelity and adultery come with guilt of sin and hatred of one's spouse.

- **Unhealthy Practice** - A wife may refuse sex during her menstrual period for health reasons. Also, a wife may refuse oral and anal sex for health reasons.

- **Not Enjoyable** - A spouse may refuse sex when he or she does not enjoy it with the partner. Sexual satisfaction means different things to different people. To some foreplay, romance, duration of the act, orgasm, and communication after the act are all important to their enjoyment of sex.

The decision for not having sex may be reasonable and rational but sometimes it may just be an excuse. Couples should understand that there are dangers in refusing sex in marriage. These dangers may include:

- **Complicating the existing issues** - A spouse who refuses sex because of unresolved issues may be complicating the same issue. Sex is to be separated from ongoing issues for the enjoyment of the couple. Satisfying your spouse with sex may be the key to resolving the issue.

- **Bruising the spouse** - Constant refusal of sex may bruise and kill the mental ability and creativity of the spouse. Sex means different things to men and woman. While most women can stay long without sex most men cannot. Men use sex to release tension and anxiety as they release various brain chemicals during sex such as adrenaline and prolactin which make them relax and sleepy after sex. Sex brings happiness, excitement and motivations, and lack of it brings grudges, discouragements, and resentment.

- **Spouse looking elsewhere** - Refusal of sex has consequences. Don't say "he will be alright", "he can handle it", or "I don't care". A wife who refuses sex with her husband is pushing him to look elsewhere. Many husbands deprived of sex by their wives have resorted to sinful masturbation, pornography and infidelity.

- **Counter-Reactions** - The refusal of sex may lead to a counter reaction especially when it is perceived as a reward or punishment. Sex is not a means of reward but rather it is the glue of marriage. Sex is not for punishment but rather it is the power source of marriage. Sex is linked to everything in the couple's life. If sex is good, everything will work towards good. And if sex is refused, good things may be messed up.

Sex is the lifeline of marriage and it should not be interfered with. A couple who has good sexual relations has hope of improving communication, restoring trust and resolving crisis. Following are some recommendations to redress the refusal of sex:

- **Co-ownership of Couples' bodies** - A husband should recognize that his body belongs to his wife, and a wife should understand that her body belongs to her husband. They should be willing to share their bodies with each other and not give excuses.

  *"The husband should fulfill his marital duty to his wife, and likewise the wife to her husband. The wife does not have authority over her own body but must yield it to her husband. In the same way, the husband does not*

*have authority over his own body but must yield it to his wife."* I Corinthians 7:3-4

- **Make Schedule for Sex** - For the start and to avoid excuses, couples should make a schedule for sex. This allows couples to determine how many times they want to have sex in a week and the time of the day they want to have it. It may sound monotonous or unromantic, but this will help to create expectation, anticipation and responsiveness until the couple matures. Scheduled sex should not rule out spontaneous sex.

- **Make-up Sex** - Sometimes a spouse will have a genuine reason to refuse sex. In such situations, the spouse who refuses should see it as his or her responsibility to ask for it the next time. For instance, a wife may be too tired to have sex on Tuesday night at her husband's request, but she should see it as her responsibility to request for it on Wednesday or Thursday or the next time. Couples should have their coded language or signals they use to request sex.

- **Non-Bargain Device** - Couples should refrain from using sex as a bargain device either as a means of reward or punishment. Doing this is a lack of respect to your spouse and the marriage. The conspirator who uses sex to extract concessions or rewards from their spouse is no better than a prostitute.

50. **Should Christian couples subscribe to sex education?**

We live in the age of information where the rate of dissemination is close to the speed of light. Everywhere one looks there is information. Information being a part of knowledge is vital to existence and the fulfillment of mankind. Knowledge shapes thoughts and ideas, gives insight and wisdom, and influences actions and behaviors. There is no doubt, knowledge is power but there is good and bad knowledge. Good knowledge empowers us with thoughts and ideas to do the will of God while bad knowledge stimulates us with insight and wisdom to do contrary to God's will. Education invents and uses information to produce knowledge.

In the past, the world was not overcharged with sexual images and advertisements, so couples married as virgins. This allowed the couple to grow in sexual intimacy as they engaged more and more with each other. Then younger couples received sex education by asking questions from the older couples. The situation is different today. Sex is now widely expressed through sexually explicit images, advertisements, music, and films. If one of the spouses has been sexually active before marriage, it could create unnecessary pressure on the novice, (the inexperienced or virgin spouse.) There is nothing wrong with Christian couples engaging in sex education as long as such education helps them to fulfill the purpose of God and does not contradict the will of God. Such sex education may provide benefits such as:

- Preventing pregnancy through birth control and contraceptive use.
- Ensuring healthy sex practices using lubricants, condoms and other sexual enhancements.
- Resolving marital crisis and conflicts through sexual seminars and counseling.
- Ensuring sexual satisfaction through the understanding of techniques and positions.
- Ensuring sexual stimulation through sex toys, books and videos.

Sex education becomes worthwhile when both spouses are involved and learn together and the knowledge does not lead to self-gratification or satisfaction of sexual lust through masturbation and pornography.

51. **Why do spouses cheat in marriage?**

It is unimaginable to think about this but it does happen even among Christians. One of the rationales for the demise of marriage is infidelity. Many will argue that the Bible permits divorce on the grounds of sexual immorality such as fornication and adultery.

> ***"But I say unto you, That whosoever shall put away his wife, saving for the cause of fornication, causeth her to commit adultery: and whosoever shall marry her that is divorced committeth adultery."*** Matthew 5:32

The Scriptures encourage man and woman to perform their marital obligation of sex to their spouse, and discourages the defilement of the marital bed through cheating or infidelity.

> ***"Nevertheless, to avoid fornication, let every man have his own wife, and let every woman have her own husband."*** 1 Corinthians 7:2

> ***"Give honor to marriage, and remain faithful to one another in marriage. God will surely judge people who are immoral and those who commit adultery."*** Hebrews 13:4

The question is why do Christian couples cheat on their spouses? The reasons are many but here are a few:

- **Un-regenerated Hearts** - There are many church goers, Christ-professed and carnal minded Christians today whose hearts have not been touched and transformed. They talk the talk but they fail to walk the walk. Remember, Christ said Moses allowed the people of old to divorce and do all sorts of things in marriage because their hearts were hardened. Unless your heart and that of your spouse is changed, renewed, born-again, and transformed there is a possibility of cheating.

- **Unintended Artificial Incentives** - Couples sometimes create incentive for their spouses to cheat without knowing. For instance, a couple who lives separately due to distance from work, school or business may be creating an unintended incentive of cheating; a spouse who frequently travels for business or work may be creating negative incentives; a couple who has separate bank accounts or live their lives independent of each other may be creating unintended incentive of infidelity. Couples that create the ungodly arrangement of a so-called open marriage may also welcome cheating.

- **Spousal Abuse** - A spouse who has been abused by his or her spouse may lose the sense of confidence, security and closeness with such an abuser. Abuse may be physical, emotional, financial and spiritual therefore the abuser can have control and power over the victim. Abuse removes the interest, tenderness and anticipation for sexual intimacy, and could make a spouse look for sex outside of the marriage.

- **Revenge** - This is when either spouse turns sex into a punishment or reward mechanism whereby he or she only offers his or her body when the spouse does well, and withholds it when he or she fails the test. A spouse who keeps refusing sex is indirectly asking the other spouse to look elsewhere. Many Christians that lack self-discipline turn to pornography, masturbation, isolation and hatred because of their spouse's refusal of sex. Most proponents of polygamy cited their spouse's refusal of sex as one of the reasons for turning to polygamy. And those that cannot engage in polygamy end up cheating.

- **Unhappy Marriage** - Many engage in cheating to express their unhappiness with their spouse. For instance, a spouse may claim that the other spouse is no longer attractive or appealing to him or her; that the spouse does not give sexual satisfaction; that the spouse is not romantic; that the spouse is a workaholic and has no time for them; that there are frequent arguments and conflicts; and that they are no longer compatible, among many other reasons.

- **Natural causes** - There are cases of cheating and infidelity among believers especially because of illness, loss of job, and loss of financial or material possessions on the part of a spouse. This is usually the case when the object of love that brought the couple into marriage is no longer available. A man who marries a woman because of her physical beauty and educational accomplishment is likely to cheat if her beauty is marred because of accident or if her academic license is revoked. A woman who marries because of the man's good job will not only be disappointed but may disappear when the job is lost.

- **Personal Background and History** - there are people who engage in infidelity because of their personal beliefs and background. The first time one cheats may be considered a mistake but how can we account for the second, third and fourth times? Sometimes, it is a personal problem linked to their background, beliefs and association. Some people don't believe they can stick to one woman or man for their entire life. Some learned the experience from their parent, believing that it works for their parent and it will work for them as well.

Irrespective of one's situation, a believer is not expected to cheat on his or her spouse. If one engages in cheating, it is because they are not born again. And if one deprives their spouse of his or her marriage right, they are also not born again.

> ***"Therefore to him that knoweth to do good, and doeth it not, to him it is sin."*** James 4:7 (KJV)

52. **What are the techniques of good love-making?**

Sex is an important issue in marriage. Sex outside of marriage is illegitimate and attracts the wrath of God. This type of sexual act affects every aspect of marriage. A couple that has an excellent sex life will enjoy an excellent relationship, friendship and understanding. They will have a high energy level, an active mental ability and a low stress level. An excellent sex life will aid positive developments in other areas of a couple's life, including their career, job, business, finances, health, and productivity. Nicky and Sila Lee, in *The Marriage Book,* highlight six qualities for great lovers to include communication, tenderness, responsiveness, romance, anticipation and variety. For sex to be enjoyable and create great love making, these attributes will be evident:

- **Communication and Compromise** - In a marriage relationship, communication is everything including sex. Communication should reveal to one's spouse your sexual needs, desires, interests and enjoyment. Let your spouse know your fears, philosophy, beliefs and experiences about sex. To have good sex with your spouse, he or she should know how you want to or can be aroused, and what stimulates an orgasm and pleasure within you. Communication should foster compromise. Couples should reason together, bear with each other, and engage to satisfy each other. This is achievable through communication and compromise.

- **Care and Connection** - Couples need to be sensitive, affectionate and tender to their spouses. Most women complain of tiredness as a reason to refuse sex to highlight their husband's insensitivity and uncaring attitude. The mission to have sex at night should not start that night; it should at least start from the morning by finding out how she is doing, assisting or joining her in house chores, holding and playing with her to lessen her stress, speaking with and appreciating her to boost her emotions. Caring and connecting should not be a one-time occurrence nor a strategy used for sex day but it should be an ongoing and regular ingredient of marital interaction. It will be difficult to have or enjoy good sex with someone whom you have just abused physically or verbally. Good sex requires continuous joy, trust, love, care, tenderness, positive interactions and much affection but abuse, strife, repression and tyranny are killers of these responses.

- **Romance** - Another quality of good sex and lovemaking is romance. Most women hate men that are not romantic. Romance is the creation of excitement, enthusiasm and adoration for someone you love. Romance is the summation of what you say, do and give. It is also about the environment you create, the places you go, and the surprises you make for the person you love. It is the responsibility of the husband to be romantic to his wife. Without romance, sex is a boring and monotonous experience. Romance adds the flavor to relationship and makes arousal easier and most enjoyable.

- **Expectation** - It is important for couples to create, learn and understand the language, code and signal for sex. I have heard different codes like "Fellowship Night", "Tiger Night", "Dinner Night", "Debate Night", "Dance Time", "Off Day", "Game Time", "Rush Hour" and the like utilized to signal sex time for couples. Using these codes and languages creates expectation and anticipation for the couple. Spontaneous sex can sometime turn out to be good sex but expectation allows couples to prepare their body, mind and spirit for the sexual adventure.

- **Spicy Changes** - Good love-making cannot be monotonous sex. There is a need to spice it up with some extraordinary changes and surprises. Spouses don't need to look for sex outside of marriage. All that is needed is a little change from the way they normally have sex. For instance, the couple could change or vary the time and place that they have sex, and change or vary their style and sexual position. Instead of always having sex at night, have some at night, but also engage each other during the day and early in the morning. Instead of always having sex on the bed, try having some acts on the bed but also other places in the house such as the sitting room, on the couch, on the floor, on the stairs, in the shower, in the kitchen, in the garage, in the laundry room and even in the closet. Occasionally the couple can go spend time together in a hotel. Instead of having sex always by lying down in the bedroom, try having sex by sitting, bending or standing depending on the body size, shape and health of the couple. Couples must be creative and intentional when it comes to their sex life, styles and interactions and keeping marriage fulfilling, exciting and lasting.

- **Requisition and Acceptance** - Couples should make requests and accept invitations from their spouse for sex. Acceptance of such requests should not be with reluctance or half-hearted, but with excitement, enthusiasm, cheerfulness and whole-heartedness. In the Christian marriage, each spouse should know that many attributes of marriage are united through sex and that your body belongs to each other. A spouse should not refuse sex to engage in spiritual activities such as prayer and fasting. When a wife or husband has a non-responsive attitude towards sex despite good communication, care and romance, the non-response is, with all probability, due to underlying and unresolved issues that have been ignored by the couple. Acceptance of a sex invitation is an easy task by men and women in a healthy marriage relationship and environment.

- **Foreplay** - Foreplay is another attribute of a good lovemaking. It involves both physical and psychological activities that prepare a couple for sex. It helps the couple to create sexual arousal. While it helps men to have erection, it helps women to have a lubricated vagina. Examples of foreplay are kissing, cuddling, tickling, touching, role-playing, talking, and massage.

- **Satisfaction** - Good love making brings sexual arousal and satisfaction to the couple. Sexual satisfaction differs for different people. For one, it may be the caring, connecting, romance and tenderness that take place before the actual sex act. For another it may be reaching an orgasm. For another, it may be the warmth, trust and communication that sex brings. Couples should strive to determine and understand what provokes sexual arousal, fulfillment and satisfaction to their spouses and be provided without inhibition or hesitation.

53. **What does it mean to be romantic with your spouse?**

Romance is the creation of the feeling of excitement, enthusiasm, joy, and emotional attractiveness to the one you love. Romance creates a strong desire of warmth, closeness and intimacy with that special someone. It excites the mind, stirs up the imagination, soothes the body as well as stimulates the senses. It is the flavor of a relationship and arouses men and women to intimacy. Good romance may involve the expression of the following:

- Special Act - Such a special act may be a small, medium or giant thing, word, activity, event, or episode.
- Creative Act - This act involves thoughtfulness, energy, time, money, and skills to woo or dazzle the intended person.
- Sincere personality - The act comes from a sincere and loving heart and personality that appreciates, cares, esteems and values the person.
- Unexpected Act - This is a surprise to the person. The act is not demanded. It is about creatively making anything or event romantic. Creating additions or improving on something already known or demanded can still be romantic.

Most women want romantic husbands. Romance makes the wife the goddess, the sweetheart, the sunshine, the dearest of the husband. Romance is the summation of what is said; what is done; what is given; the environment that is created; the places gone; and the surprises made. These depend on the interests, preferences and likeness of one's spouse. Do not try what she does not like. The components of romance are:

- **What We Say** - A romantic journey starts with words. What we say to her? How do we describe her body, eyes, breasts, feet, buttocks, thighs, hands, neck, or lips? To be romantic, we cannot see any flaw in her. We need to recognize her dress, her hair, her shoes, and accessories.
    - Talk to her and whisper into her ears.
    - Appreciate her beauty, work and achievement.

- **What We Write** – Like words, writing is the expression of our thoughts, feelings and opinions. It is romantic to write nice things to or for her.
    - Compose and read her a poem.
    - Compose and sing her a song.
    - Write her a letter, a note or email.
    - Send her a text.
- **What We Do** – We are romantic by our actions. Not just about doing the house chores, but about doing something she wants to get done. Showing care and admiration through one's actions involves knowing and reading her mind.
    - Making her breakfast or dinner.
    - Doing her laundry.
    - Carrying her in your arms or on your back or playing with her.
    - Kissing, touching, rubbing or cuddling her.
    - Getting the car door for her.
- **What We Give** – There is a saying that "you can give without loving but you cannot love without giving." It is romantic to buy or give her special things.
    - Buy and mail her flowers and roses.
    - Buy her a gift or gift card.
    - Give her your time, presence and attention.
    - Give her a nice massage.
- **Create a Warm Environment** – It is romantic to create an inviting environment that is devoid of conflict, arguments and stress for her.
    - Light up candles.
    - Play nice music.
    - Create cool lighting.
- **The Places We Go** – It is romantic to take her to memorable and special places.

- Take her to a short and unexpected vacation.
- Take her for chocolate or cake or ice-cream ride.
- Take her to the park, movie, theaters, concerts, games, shows.
- Take her for a boat ride.
- Go on a date.

- **The Surprises We Make** - It is romantic to give or make her burst into laughter, surprise, and "Wow!!!" and "Yeah!!!" moments.
  - Make her laugh for joy through hilarious jokes, and treatments.
  - Touch her heart in a special way.

54. **What do the Scriptures say about romance?**

The Song of Solomon is considered to be a poem of love. It is important for couples to learn some great lessons from this book of the Bible. Here are some highlights:

- **Touch Her**
  Song of Solomon 2:6 reads, *"His left hand is under my head, and his right hand doth embrace me."*
- **Feed Her**
  Song of Solomon 2:3 reads, *"As the apple tree among the trees of the wood, so is my beloved among the sons. I sat down under his shadow with great delight, and his fruit was sweet to my taste."*
- **Speak to Her**
  Song of Solomon 2:10 reads, *"My beloved spake, and said unto me, Rise up, my love, my fair one, and come away."*
- **Listen to Her**
  Song of Solomon 2:8 reads, *"The voice of my beloved! behold, he cometh leaping upon the mountains, skipping upon the hills."*

- **Admire Her** - Admire her eyes, hair, teeth, lips, body, neck, breasts, tongues, feet, waist, nose, head, and arms. Solomon 4:1-5 read, *"Behold, thou art fair, my love; behold, thou art fair; thou hast doves' eyes within thy locks: thy hair is as a flock of goats, that appear from Mount Gilead. Thy teeth are like a flock of sheep that are even shorn, which came up from the washing; whereof everyone bear twins, and none is barren among them. Thy lips are like a thread of scarlet, and thy speech is comely: thy temples are like a piece of a pomegranate within thy locks. Thy neck is like the tower of David builded for an armoury, whereon there hang a thousand bucklers, all shields of mighty men. Thy two breasts are like two young roes that are twins, which feed among the lilies."*
- **See no flaws**
  Song of Solomon 4:7 reads, "*Thou art all fair, my love; there is no spot in thee.*"
- **Buy her gifts**
  Song of Solomon 5:1 reads, "*I am come into my garden, my sister, my spouse: I have gathered my myrrh with my spice; I have eaten my honeycomb with my honey; I have drunk my wine with my milk: eat, O friends; drink, yea, drink abundantly, O beloved.*"
- **Take her on travels and vacation**
  Song of Solomon 7:11 reads, "*Come, my beloved, let us go forth into the field; let us lodge in the villages.*"
- **Make her the only one**
  Song of Solomon 6:8-9 read, "*There are threescore queens, and fourscore concubines, and virgins without number. My dove, my undefiled is but one; she is the only one of her mother, she is the choice one of her that bare her. The daughters saw her, and blessed her, yea, the queens and the concubines, and they praised her.*"

Chapter 8

# Unity and Success

*The word of God* is the secret of success. The word of God comes in the form of *logos*, written or spoken words, to give information and enlightenment. It also comes in the form of *rhema* or revealed words to give spiritual understanding, freedom and life. The word of God has the integrity of God; it is settled forever, and it cannot be broken. The word of God produces peace; it gives profits; it voids fear; and it leads to a path of righteousness. The word of God has many representations such as water for cleansing, hammer to break hardened situations or heart, balm to heal, seed to sow, fire to burn or refine, mirror to reflect, rain to refresh, lamp or light to guide, weapon to defend and war, food to nourish, and power to create faith. The word of God consists of instructions that must be obeyed, promises that must be enjoyed, and truths that change facts. Joshua 1:8 reads that *"This book of the law shall not depart out of thy mouth; but thou shalt meditate therein day and night, that thou mayest observe to do according to all that is written therein: for then thou shalt make thy way prosperous, and then thou shalt have good success."* Couples should engage in the word of God to enjoy success in their marriages. They should not allow satanic influence, worldliness, and lack of faith to hinder them from studying, meditating and obeying the word of God.

55. **What is the meaning of a successful marriage?**

A successful marriage is said to mean different things to different people. It is argued that success is relative and every couple should decide what makes their marriage successful. It is also argued that a successful marriage today can be a failed marriage tomorrow, depending on the circumstances facing the couples. However, a successful marriage can be described as a growing and blissful marriage, or a high-quality marriage. God's intention of marriage is to make it good, successful and lasting. Marriage is successful when it is enjoyed rather than endured, when the couple becomes each other's best friend, and finds comfort, security and stability in each other. The benchmark of marital success is not based on money, status or material things but on the following:

- **A successful marriage glorifies God**: God is the third party in marriage and a successful marriage should center on God. When God is removed from a marriage relationship, such a marriage is a failure and a time bomb waiting to explode.

  ***"Except the LORD build the house, they labor in vain that build it: except the LORD keep the city, the watchman waketh but in vain.*** Psalm 127:1 (KJV)

  A successful marriage is run on the life manual of God's word. The barometer of success cannot be on public opinions, celebrity gossip magazines or the secular laws of governments.

- **A successful marriage is filled with love and respect:** Love is a powerful ingredient in any relationship, including a marriage relationship. It allows the couple to engage in good communication and cherish, respect and believe in each other.

***"Three things will last forever - faith, hope, and love--and the greatest of these is love.*** 1 Corinthians 13:13 (NLT)

There is nothing wrong in marrying for love but the relationship should involve the three categories of love. These are *Eros* or erotic love, *Phileo* or brotherly love, and *Agape* or unconditional love. These three types of love should exist in a successful marriage. Sexual and brotherly love will fade but Agape love will last. Agape love is not arrogant or envious but it is patient and forgiving.

- **A successful marriage experiences little or no conflict:** Conflict is normal in life or relationship and a successful marriage has its own share of conflict. Conflict arises as a result of disagreement or violation of personal interests or values but a successful marriage manages it as a learning experience that fosters growth and maturity.

  ***"Do all that you can to live in peace with everyone."*** Romans 12:18 (NLT)

  Couples in a successful marriage value peace, unity and harmony. They identify and address the sources of conflict before it surfaces, proactively create boundaries and engage in self-discipline and self-respect in order to mitigate conflict. They put work into their marriage, refuse to take each other for granted and resolve conflict as soon as it arrives.

- **A successful marriage is devoid of abuse or victimization of spouse**: There are plenty of manipulations, maltreatments and oppressions in today's marriages, which lead to separation and the breakup of many marriages. Physical abuse, domestic violence and imprisonment of spouse are common in today's failed marriages. These vices and miseries are not congruent with a successful marriage.

***"In the same way, you husbands must give honor to your wives. Treat your wife with understanding as you live together. She may be weaker than you are, but she is your equal partner in God's gift of new life. Treat her as you should so your prayers will not be hindered.*** 1 Peter 3:7 (NLT)

There should be mutual respect and restraint among couples. Couples should desist from playing the cards of emotional, sexual and financial abuse. Husbands, your muscles are there to protect your wives.

- **A successful marriage is characterized by godly, well-behaved children**: One of the responsibilities of couples in marriage is to raise godly children. A woman is a wife to her husband and a mother to her children. Likewise, a man is a husband to his wife and a father to his children. The marriage is successful if these responsibilities are not outsourced to others that have no interest and stake in the children.

  ***"Train up a child in the way he should go: and when he is old, he will not depart from it.*** Proverbs 22:6 (KJV)

  Parents have responsibilities over their children when the children are young but they lose these responsibilities when the children have come of age and become adults. A marriage is successful when the children are well behaved and have good manners.

- **A successful marriage blesses others** - A marriage is not successful except it becomes exemplary for other young marriages to follow. A man's marriage is his reflection. A man's eloquence, intelligence and other personal qualities are not as effective as his marriage in influencing people.

  ***"Ye are the light of the world. A city that is set on a hill cannot be hid. Neither do men light a candle,***

***and put it under a bushel, but on a candlestick; and it giveth light unto all that are in the house. Let your light so shine before men, that they may see your good works, and glorify your Father which is in heaven."*** Matthew 5:14-16 (KJV)

Marriage is so important to God that the scriptures compared the relationship between Christ and the church to the marriage relationship between husband and wife. Marriage is successful when it becomes a source of inspiration for others and when others see it as a model.

- **A successful marriage ensures unity of purpose** - Marriage allows two to become one. A marriage is successful when husbands and wives are united. This unity is not only in parenting children but in finance, interests, vacations and more.

  ***"And said, 'For this reason a man will leave his father and mother and be united to his wife, and the two will become one flesh'? So, they are no longer two, but one flesh. Therefore, what God has joined together, let no one separate.*** Matthew 19:5-6 (NIV)

  God's command on marriage is the unity of husbands and wives, without allowing anyone or anything to separate them. The unity of a couple is a great mark of a successful marriage.

56. **What is marital blissful?**

Most men and women in a marriage relationship enter with the goal of a joyful and successful marriage. To achieve this goal, many of them waited for years in preparation, spent a lot of money, and started their marriage with a beautiful well-organized wedding. In all sincerity, they overcame all odds, covered all details and married their childhood friend, soulmate or heartthrob to ensure a blissful marriage. But the moment they got into it, they realized that marriage was a different institution than what they imagined, and that it required different skills as well as wisdom. However, marriage can be successful, blessed and blissful with the understanding and implementation of the following:

- **The Parties in Marriage** - For a marriage to be successful, a couple needs to recognize the three parties in marriage and the responsibilities of each party. These parties are God, Man and Woman.
    - God is the creator of the marriage institution and the ultimate joiner of the couple. As a creator, He establishes the principles and sets the boundaries that guide marriage. A couple that desires a successful marriage should follow God's principles and live their lives within His boundaries. As a joiner, God yearns for both individual and collective relationship with husbands and wives. This means that husband and wife should have a relationship with God first before they can have a successful relationship with each other.
    - The Man is the husband and head of his wife in marriage. He is a father to the children of the marriage. He is a family man, a leader and a provider to his wife and family. A man who recognizes and fulfills these responsibilities is not far from a successful marriage.
    - The Woman is the wife and help mate of her husband in marriage. She is the mother of the children of the marriage. She is a home maker and a family woman. She is called to submit to her husband. She is also

called to complement rather than compete with her husband.

- **The Parties outside the Marriage** - Marriage creates responsibilities for parties inside and outside the marriage. As stated above the parties in a marriage are God, husband, and wife. The parties outside of the marriage are called internal and external stakeholders. The internal stakeholders are children and step children, while the external stakeholders are in-laws such as the parents, brothers, sisters, nieces, nephews, aunts, uncles and cousins of both the husband and wife. Other external stakeholders are friends, colleagues and community.
    - The internal stakeholders together with the couple form the nuclear, blended or immediate family. Children are a blessing to the marriage and they should not be used as a wedge in the marriage.
    - The external stakeholders together with the couple form the extended family. These people are available to the couple for association, socialization and fellowship. They should not determine the existence or extinction of the marriage. They can give information and counsel to the couple but their recommendations are merely advisory.
- **The Environment of Marriage** - Environment is important and could be a determining factor in the success or failure of a marriage. The environment is the practice and circumstance under which one lives and operates. Environment is dynamic as it changes from time to time and place to place. The environment of marriage could be internal or external. The internal environments are the norms, cultures, customs, traditions and practices of the families of the two individuals in the marriage, while the

external environment is the community, country, culture, norms, opinions, governments, and laws of the city and country where the couple resides. It is no surprise that the family history and practices of the husband or wife affects how the couple relates to each other. Also, many husbands cry foul about the draconian treatment from their wives, due to the culture and laws of the developed countries in which they live. Couples should understand their environment and ensure that they ignore any negative environmental influence. The fact that others are doing a particular thing is not enough reason or an excuse to do it. Yielding to public opinion is not the same as yielding to the word of God.

- **Resolution of Marital Crisis** - There is an inherent crisis in every relationship, including marriage. These crises range from minor to major and manifest in the forms of financial, communication, childbearing, parenting, sex, in-laws, and other domains. Couples should identify and formulate how to resolve crises before they happen. There are many resources available for marital conflict resolutions. Couples should engage in relationship development through marriage training, seminars, books, counselors, and mentorship. Couples should engage the church and its leadership as a major resource of a successful marriage.

- **The Gift of Marriage** - The institution of marriage is a gift from God. It is what makes a man or woman complete; it is the antidote of natural loneliness. Marriage is not only for procreation; it is also for recreation. As a result, marriage requires work and effort. There is no marriage that is heaven made. A man and woman enter marriage by their own choice and volition, and they should therefore be ready to work for their marital success. Each spouse should give his/her total self for the good of other spouse. Each should make sacrifices for the other.

57. **What attributes do husbands admire in their wives?**

It is commonly said that "Happy wife, happy life". It also goes that "Happy husband, happy marriage". It is selfish to concentrate on the wives while we neglect the husbands. The purpose of a godly marriage is that each spouse should first please God and secondly please their partner. The idea of the worldly marriage is for a spouse to please himself or herself. Christians should know that the responsibility of a blissful marriage is the duty of both husband and wife.

> ***"Do nothing from selfishness or empty conceit, but with humility of mind regard one another as more important than yourselves; do not merely look out for your own personal interests, but also for the interests of others."*** Philippians 2:3-4 (NIV)

Marriage or no marriage, a Christian is expected to be happy and holy. He or she should help his or her spouse to achieve the same. When you do what your spouse likes, you make them happy, and you too will be happy. There are things wives do or behaviors wives have, that their husbands like. We will examine a few out of a long list. This list is not ranked in order of importance.

- **Beauty and Physical Outlook**: Husbands like to brag about their wives' beauty, especially when they maintain their exquisite look after childbirth. Married women should not ignore their bodies based on the excuses that they are married, they have birthed children, or they have no time. Exercise, diet, dressing, and hair styles can contribute to the physical outlook and beauty of a woman. Beauty is natural and it has nothing to do with excessive make-up which makes a person look like a model; nor is it about excessive jewelry that leads to debt; or provocative dressing that exposes one's nudity.

- **Abilities, Talents & Interests:** Husbands like wives that are endowed with natural and mental abilities and talents, especially when they complement those of the husbands. Some wives know their abilities, talents and interests before marriage while others discover them after marriage. Regardless of when they are acquired, abilities, talents, skills and interests like music, sports, communication, and humor makes husbands proud and excited about their wives. Most husbands are happy when their wives can sit down and watch football, basketball or soccer with them instead of complaining.

- **Cheer-leading the Husbands** - Husbands like wives that encourage and motivate them to succeed. They are happy when their wives become their main fan and supporter. They glow when they know their wives have their backs and are there to cheer them in whatever situation. Proverb 16:25 (NIV) reads *"Gracious words are a honeycomb, sweet to the soul and healing to the bones."*

- **Job, Career and Profession** - Husbands rejoice when their wives are successful in their jobs, careers and professions, especially when they know that such successes are not wedged against the marriage. Most husbands go to a great extent and make enormous sacrifices to ensure that their wives succeed in her endeavors because it makes them happy.

- **Maturity** - Husbands like wives that are spiritually and emotionally matured. They like wives that love and follow God. They are happy when their wives are forgiving, prayerful and exhibit virtues of God. Husbands also like wives that are mentally and intellectually sound, and can engage in arguments, debates and rigorous reasoning.

- **Home Making**: Husbands like wives that prioritize the care of the home and children. They like wives that take the home-maker and family woman roles seriously by making sure that homes are peaceful and have necessary provisions. Many husbands like to cook, do laundry, buy groceries and help in many household chores but they like it more when their wives take charge of these responsibilities while they assist and complement her. Husbands pursue big and energy-sapping tasks such as repairs, mowing and carrying or lifting heavy objects as their main chores.

- **Love Making**: Husbands like for their wives to enjoy sex with them. Most husbands make demands for sex more than their wives, and they are happy when their wives show interest, and availability, and willingly participate in the lovemaking.

- **Friendly**: Husbands like wives who are friendly both in nature and attitude. They are happy when their wives are approachable, kind and hospitable. They enjoy it when their wives keep good friends and relate peacefully with their siblings, parents and others.

- **Loyalty and respect**: Husbands like wives that are loyal and faithful to them. Husbands are happy when their wives agree with and project them well in the public. Husbands like it when there is a unity of purpose and vision with their wives.

- **Marriage-oriented**: Husbands like wives who believe in the marriage. Husbands believe that wives who want their marriage to work will accept the leadership of the husbands and play their part to maintain peace and harmony in the home.

58. **What attributes do husbands hate about their wives?**

Husbands may want to simply reverse the things that they like most about their wives to get to the things they hate about their wives. This may be easy and convenient but in reality, what the husbands like and hate may be different in type and variability. The dislikes listed below reflect some of the actions, behaviors and attitudes that wives display and demonstrate toward their husbands.

- **Nagging** - Nagging is the over-flogging of issues or matters. Such lead to complaining, scolding, nitpicking, and anxiety. Naggers raise the issues that should not be raised, repeat over and over again, issues that should be mentioned only once, indirectly view themselves as better and the spouse who is being nagged as stupid. Most husbands hate wives who nag at them.

- **Disrespectful** - One thing husbands cherish most from their wives is respect. They want respect regardless of the situation or circumstance. For instance, when they are weak, fail in their responsibilities, and the wives earn more money than them, they still want to be respected. Most husbands hate wives who lack respect for them both in private and public.

- **Unintelligent** - Since marriage occurs under numerous and varied circumstances and love overshadows reality before marriage, a married couple may realize that some things are not the way they thought about their partner. Some of the new discoveries after marriage may be that the wife is not sensible, logical, and intelligent enough to communicate or behave at the level the husband wants or desires. Sometimes, married women receive no motivation to develop and they stop improving themselves in learning. Husbands hate wives who cannot communicate intelligently in private or publicly except and unless the husbands lack such abilities.

- **Maltreatment of Parents** - Husbands hate wives that are unfriendly and hostile to their parents and siblings. Most husbands love their wives and children but they also love their extended family. Husbands understand and accept their obligations and responsibilities, and they know that their nuclear family is priority. Despite this knowledge, some wives view the extended family of her husband as intruders and enemies, and they mistreat and disrespect them. Most husbands hate attitudes such as this from their wives.

- **Complaint and Criticism** - Complaint is the expression of displeasure over a particular incident or behavior, while criticism is the expression of displeasure over one's personality. Complaint specifies but criticism generalizes behavior or attitudes. While complaint may be good sometimes criticism is bad most of the time. Even what we call constructive criticism damages relationships especially when it is wrongly or mischievously expressed. Most husbands dislike complaint and criticism from their wives.

- **Finance and Career** - Husbands are the providers, while wives are the homemakers. However, due to the complexity of the modern world that has turned women into strong contenders in the market place, many women engage in very attractive careers and professions, own profitable businesses, and earn good money. Men and women are now putting money together to run and provide for the home. Most husbands hate wives who are not ambitious and career-minded. They also hate wives who refuse to release her money for the benefit of the home and marriage.

- **Lack of Submission** - Because there cannot be two captains to steer the ship, husbands become distasteful towards wives who contest the leadership of the home being entrusted to them. Most husbands agree that there will be deliberations in making decisions and are willing to compromise in achieving unity, but they hate insubordinate and stubborn wives that always want to have their way.

- **Dependent** - Husbands hate wives who are still attached to their parent's apron string. Marriage is for men and women who are matured physically, emotionally, financially and spiritually. Husbands view themselves as married to two women when their mothers-in-law have something to say about every issue of their home and marriage.

- **Denial of Sex** - Sex is one of the reasons why the scriptures commanded man and woman to marry, and they should not deprive each other of love making. Unfortunately, sex that ought to lubricate marriage and unite the husbands and wives emotionally has become a bargaining medium for couples. Husbands hate wives that constantly express dissatisfaction with and are disinterested in sex or love-making.

- **Spiritualism and occultism** - In the process of seeking answers to questions and solution to problems, many people engage in occultism, spiritualism, demonic acts and witchcraft. Though they claim to be Christians they consult and conjure evil spirits, herbalists, palmists, psychics, and tarot card readers. While many husbands have no problem with their wives being Christians like them, they hate their spouse's involvement in this kind of occult practice.

59. **What attributes do wives admire in their husbands?**

Human beings are different in their likes and dislikes. Either from the gender or cultural standpoint, what appeals to men may be different from what interest women. Because of this heterogeneity, it will be difficult to assume that every woman will like the same attributes about her husband. While some women like pragmatic and romantic husbands, others may prefer passive but supportive husbands. Generally, the list below, not in the order of importance, details some of the traits, characteristics and attributes women like about their husbands.

- **Strength** - Most women like men who are energetic and physically strong. Such women brag about the physique of their men, and enjoy a sense of protection in their husband's muscular build. With such enormous strength and energy, doing household chores, running errands, and fixing and repairing things around the house are not a burden but rather a pleasure to such men. Many wives also attest to this strength when their men can last for a long time during lovemaking.
- **Romance** - Women like men who have perfected the art of romance. Romance is not just one thing we do, but a combination of things that create bonds of affection and love. It includes the words we speak, the works we perform, the places we go, the resources we spend (i.e. time, skills, money), the smiles and laughter we create, the songs we sing, the timing we use, the food we cook, the affection we give, the togetherness we share and the environment we create.
- **Sacrifice** - Wives cherish husbands who make sacrifices for them, their children and their step-children. They esteem husbands who prefer them to husbands' parents, brothers, sisters and friends. They value husbands who are ready to give up jobs, careers, businesses and hobbies for them and their children. Wives appreciate husbands who

do not only provide resources to them but also spend time with them. They treasure husbands who are ready to spend on them and their children.

- **Trust** - In this world of deception, infidelity, lies and betrayal, many wives cherish husbands who are truthful, honest, faithful and trustworthy. They like it when there are no rumors or appearance of distrust with their husbands. Wives relish the feeling that there is no other woman out there to compete with, and that the future of their children will not be compromised by any secret wife or children. They like the feeling that their husbands have their back.

- **Maturity** - Wives like matured husbands. They cherish husbands that will treat them like queens, pamper them with love, overlook their errors, listen to their concerns, and allow them to shine. Wives, because of the emotional nature of women, appreciate husbands that honor them, even when there is crisis or disagreement. A husband's maturity is not in his physical age or material wealth but in his actions and character.

- **Compatibility** - Many wives like husbands who are compatible with them. Wives like it when the gaps and differences between them and their husbands are not wide. They like it when their husbands think and reason like them. Wives crave for similarity with their husbands in respect of interests, beliefs, finance, family, traveling, and sports.

- **Love** - Wives like husbands that love them. Love is one of the most important needs of women in marriage, and wives appreciate their husbands for it. They want their husbands to understand and exercise their love language. They want to sleep and wake up in the unconditional love of their husbands. They want the love of their husbands both in the open and in secret.

- **The Look** - Like men that cherish beautiful women, women appreciate handsome men. The scripture is correct when it says that "men look at the outward appearance". Some ungodly married women have engaged in "one-night stands" infidelity not because they want to marry the man but because they got carried away with the physical appearance of such an adulterous man. Wives cherish the look and physical appearance of their husbands.

- **Leadership** - Wives like husbands that demonstrate good leadership. Many wives have no issue with submission and they appreciate husbands who exercise skillful judgment while and when leading them. They like it when their husbands show responsibility, honesty and humility through their leadership. They revere husbands who genuinely consider, consult and seek out their interest and welfare.

- **Support** - Wives like husbands who support and encourage them, not just to flourish as wives, homemakers and mothers but also to be fulfilled in any career path they choose. Wives as female children before marriage had jobs, talents, education, professions, careers, businesses and contributed to the finances of the family. They like husbands who cheerlead for them to achieve greater heights and accomplishments in life.

60. **What attributes do wives hate about their husbands?**

Husbands and wives have their likes and hates. Wives are repulsed by some things about their husbands. These are actions, characters and behaviors a husband exhibits that are repugnant to his wife. These are issues that if not well managed can lead to crisis in marriage. These dislikes are not listed in the order of importance.

- **Non-playful and non-romantic**: Wives hate husbands that are not romantic and are too stiff to play with. Many wives dislike it when their husbands are not creative, pragmatic, spontaneous and hilarious in creating an atmosphere of love.
- **Too rigid in traditional Role**: Wives detest husbands who are too rigid in their understanding of the traditional definitions of roles of husbands and wives. They hate husbands who believe wives should stay in the kitchen to be seen but not heard. Wives hate when their husbands cannot join in the kitchen or in household chores.
- **Non-appreciative or too demanding**: Wives abhor husbands who complain or take them for granted, and husbands who are too demanding and not appreciative. Married women see their roles as wives, mothers, homemakers and lovers as challenging tasks that need constant appreciation from their husbands.
- **Non-Sexual**: Wives dislike husbands who are sexually weak and not able to satisfy them in bed. Many wives have problems with husbands who cannot sexually last long but ejaculate before they reach an orgasm.
- **Non-hygienic**: Wives hate husbands who mess up the house, and do not assist or clean up after themselves. Many wives complain about their husbands littering the home with socks, shoes, books and other personal belongings.
- **Extended Family**: Wives dislike husbands who care and spend on their extended family more than their immediate

or nuclear family. A wife's primary focus is on her children, herself and her husband; any attention to others should come only after the immediate and blended families are adequately provided for.

- **Bad Habits**: Many wives dislike husbands who engage in bad habits such as snoring, overeating, oversleeping, sleepwalking, and discourteous behavior.
- **Domineering**: Wives dislike husbands that are too domineering and cannot seek or take advice from anyone. Such husbands are always right, always perfect, and do not need the input of their wives. Such husbands cannot bring out the best of their wives.
- **Abusive:** Most wives detest abusive husbands. They cannot stand the physical, psychological or financial abuse or violence from their husbands.
- **Non-Spiritual**: Wives dislike the ungodly attitude of their husbands. Many wives want their husbands to be the spiritual leader of their home, leading them in prayer and worship of God both at home and church.

61. **How do you create a good relationship with your spouse?**

Good relationships between spouses are consequential if the marriage is going to thrive. A good relationship brings happiness and joy. It allows couples to fulfill their goals and desires. Good relationships are not the absence of disagreement or crisis between spouses but the reduction of crisis to the barest minimum and resolution of crisis in a godly and peaceable manner. Good relationships create understanding and a friendly bond. Couples with good relationships enjoy peaceful homes and have less friction. They give good accounts of themselves, other people give good accounts of them, and they serve as mentors and good examples to other couples. To create good relationships, the following are pertinent.

- **Communication** - A couple who will have a good relationship will learn to communicate well. Communication is the starting point. Simply put, communication involves talking and listening. Couples cannot have a good relationship with one whom is talked to carelessly. Words should not come across to your spouse as disrespectful, insulting and humiliating. One spouse cannot attack, criticize, nag or condemn the other and expect him or her to smile at you. A good relationship allows spouses to discuss all matters. You must talk to your spouse, and not at your spouse. How a spouse listens to the other spouse shows good or bad relationship. No spouse can create a good relationship by listening selectively or defensively.

- **Intimacy** - Couples can use intimacy to create a good relationship. Intimacy involves sex and romance, and is very important in a marriage relationship. A couple should not deprive each other of intimacy. Romance is the creation of feelings of excitement while sex is the climax of love. Sex is the caressing, foreplay, kissing, and fondling that climax with intercourse. Some couples can have intimacy without a good relationship, but they cannot have a good relationship without intimacy.

- **Dating and Courting** - To ensure good relationship before marriage, the couple begins their journey with dating and courtship. To create a good relationship after marriage the couple should not discard dating and courting. Dating allows couples to go outside the home and to do things that promote interaction and togetherness; for instance, going out to eat, watching a movie together, and watching or playing games together. Courting allows couples to create an avenue to know each other more and better; dating will, for instance, enable the couple to have a learning experience that includes discussion or crisis resolution time, create memories by vacationing or visiting historical and interesting places. Couples must use every occasion and event to create and have fun. They must play and laugh at and with each other often.

- **Celebration** - To create a good relationship, a couple should learn to celebrate each other. Couples that have good relationships minimize criticisms, reduce condemnation and increase celebration. Words and phrases like "Thank You", "You look fabulous", "I love you", "You are smart" and "How can I help" will not be in short supply. Celebrations of birthdays, wedding anniversaries, graduations, promotions and other achievements will be a big deal and event. There will be appreciation of a spouse's work, roles, and many acts of kindness. There will be acknowledgments of appearance, dressing and outlooks. There will be honoring of in-laws for their roles and contributions to the couple's life.

- **Unity and Sharing** - Couples can create a good relationship as they strive to share and do things together as a family unit. Marriage turns two people in to one. The two are expected to act and live as one family. By uniting, a couple will ensure good relationship. Couples are encouraged to unite by:

    - Living together - Couple cannot have good relationship when they live apart. A couple should live together in the same house, in the same room and sleep on the same bed. A temporary separation even due to work can cause a big problem for the couple. However, if such separation is unavoidable, the couple should ensure that there are other means of cultivating the continuous flow of a good relationship. While living in the same house, spouses should discourage sleeping in different rooms or on different beds even during times of disagreement.

- Combining Resources - A couple should combine their resources as a family unit. This can be achieved through the use of joint bank accounts and hybrid account methods. Different account methods and the issue of money are well explained in chapter 3. It will be hard to ensure a good relationship with your spouse if there are constant disagreements about money. Couples who are living in the United States should file their tax returns together. The filing of separate returns by a couple is a sign of problems such as financial irresponsibility, deception and bad relationship.
- Do things together - Couples should learn to enjoy each other's presence, company and friendship through doing things together; for instance, bathe together, travel together, visit families and friends together, cook together, clean or do household chores together, exercise together and even relax together.

- **Spiritually knit** - One important way for couples to ensure a good relationship is to unite spiritually. It is said that a family that prays together stays together. Couples should endeavor to have the same faith, attend the same church, pray together, study the bible together, fast together and encourage each other in the Lord. Your spouse should not only be your friend but also your prayer partner.

62. **How should a child be raised in a household where parents belong to different religions?**

The marriage institution is not a boxing ring or wrestling match or a fighting arena for spouses to decide whose interests, faith, and perceptions are better or superior. It is a place where a couple should seek the interest of one another, and work together in harmony to keep the peace and to please each other. There are different reasons why a spouse may find himself or herself in this kind of marriage where the spouses are not both Christians or of the same faith. These reasons include:

- **Ignorance** - A Christian may out of ignorance marry an unbeliever despite the warning of the scriptures. Hosea 4:6 reads *"My people are destroyed for lack of knowledge: because thou hast rejected knowledge, I will also reject thee ..."* For a couple seeking to overcome this kind of ignorance, it is highly recommended that they regularly attend Bible study, fellowship and worship with the saints, and study and meditate on the Word of God...

- **Choice** - Some Christians deliberately married unbelievers in the name of love, desperation, rationality, and world influence. 2 Corinthians 6:14-15 reads, *"Be ye not unequally yoked together with unbelievers: for what fellowship hath righteousness with unrighteousness? And what communion hath light with darkness? And what concord hath Christ with Belial? Or what part hath he that believeth with an infidel?* The initial plan and attitude was that they could handle the situation, change or convert the spouse to a believer in Christ, and that the difference in faith does not matter.

- **New Birth Experience** - Some spouses who were not Christians before marriage may get converted and believe in Christ after marriage, but their spouses are not converted.

- **Backsliders** - These are Christians who backslide and convert to another religion. Some are in this situation because their spouses who were Christians before marriage became deceived by Satan and subsequently denounced their faith in Christ.

In any of these situations where the couples are of different faiths, there may be a compromise between the couple to allow each spouse to practice his or her own religious preference. There may be constant disagreements between the couple as they fight for superiority of their religion of preference. This disagreement and conflict will affect many things including the rearing of children and whether the children will be taken to church. The degree of disagreement will depend on two factors - the gender of the spouse, and the level of acceptance of religious faith. A male spouse, the husband, may exercise more control over the female, the wife. An aggressive, strong or fanatical spouse may be more combative than a passive non-combative spouse.

For a Christian in this situation of disagreement about training and taking children to church, the following are recommended:

- **Do not fight** - There is no need to fight a spouse over taking children to church. We do not wrestle against flesh and blood.

- **Pray and trust God** - Pray and believe for God to touch the heart of your spouse. The hearts of the king, including your spouse, are in His hands.

- **Negotiate with your spouse** - Marriage requires compromise and the harnessing of visions and goals.

Since you are not prevented from practicing your own faith, you can negotiate to have the children in church sometimes if not all of the time. Negotiation requires making decisions with others by meeting the interests of the parties involved.

- **Bear the fruit of Righteousness** - Christian spouses need to live out their faith with good attitude, character and behavior. Believing spouses should shine their light and let people see their good works and glorify God. The unbelieving spouses should see Christ and the Bible effectively at work and being lived out in the lives of believing spouses.

Chapter 9

# Spiritualism and the World

*The word of man* is logical, reasonable and philosophical. Man differs from any other creature in creation because he received the breath, nature and likeness of God, and because he has the authority to control and rule other creatures. Man has enormous power, creativity and wisdom to conjure words and ideas that are powerful and motivating. He is blessed with uncommon oratory, literary, scientific, social skills and knowledge to create his own environment. Men and women like Mahatma Gandhi, Nelson Mandela, Abraham Lincoln, Socrates, Aristotle, Mother Teresa and Margaret Thatcher have given the world great words, values and ideologies that many continue to follow. There is nothing wrong with the word of man, we all produce thousands of words daily and yet we go to school to learn how to create more words. But the word of man should not be preferred over the word of God. The word of man is limited and can change. The words of man may be facts but cannot be truth all the time like the word of God. The truth of God's word is not only superior to facts, but it can change facts. 1 Corinthians 1:25

reads, *"For the foolishness of God is wiser than human wisdom, and the weakness of God is stronger than human strength.* Couples should prefer the word of God over the words of their friends, co-workers, celebrities and the world. Couples should build their marriages on the scriptures, the Bible and not on worldly magazines, newspapers and novels.

63. **Should Christians practice family planning?**

Family planning is a medical process that people use to prevent or postpone pregnancy. Family planning is synonymous to birth control and is achieved through the use of contraception. The planning allows couples to control the spacing and number of children they want to have. Some examples of items and procedures used as birth control are condoms, pills, spermicidal foams, gels and lubes, hysterectomy, vasectomy, and tubal ligation. This list does not include abortion. However, there are two schools of thought on this question.

The first school of thought believes that a Christian should not engage in birth control. Here, the argument is based on God's command.

> ***"And God blessed them, and God said unto them, Be fruitful, and multiply, and replenish the earth, and subdue it: and have dominion over the fish of the sea, and over the fowl of the air, and over every living thing that moveth upon the earth.*** Genesis 1:28

This school of thought emphasizes that:

- **Christians should have many children** - They say Christian couples should not limit the number of children they have, arguing that the number should be determined by the natural fertility of the couple as well as menopause.

- **Christians should obey the word of God** - It is claimed that Christians who practice birth control are carrying out their own will instead of God's will, and that family planning is disobedience to God's word.

- **Christians should trust in God** - Many Christians fail to have multiple children due to economic, political, social and financial reasons. The argument is that factors such as economic development, population control, social peer-pressure, and women's liberation make many believers reject God and accept the world.
- **Children are a blessing from God** - It has been argued that children are a blessing from God, and that God has a purpose and plan for them. Some say that God may punish those who engage in birth control with respect to delay in childbirth and barrenness.

The second school of thought believes that there is nothing wrong when Christians engage in birth control. The argument is based on choices.

> ***"Today I have given you the choice between life and death, between blessings and curses. Now I call on heaven and earth to witness the choice you make. Oh, that you would choose life, so that you and your descendants might live!*** Deuteronomy 30:19

The emphasis for this school of thought is:

- **Man is created with choice** - We are created with freewill, conscience and freedom. God does not impose Himself on us. Though there is consequence for our choice, He gives us the ability to choose. For instance, we choose to be saved or to remain sinners, to give sparingly or bountifully, or to love or hate. It is our choice to determine the number of children we have. God will not hold you guilty for having one child or two children or ten children if that is your choice. Birth control may be necessary to ensure that you plan the number of children you can rear in God's way.

- **Man cannot help God -** Sometimes God uses angels and man as servants to carry out His errands and to fulfill His purpose. Psalms 104:4 reads, *"Who maketh his angels' spirits; his ministers a flaming fire.* As Jesus said in the matter of worship, God can raise stones to worship Him, God does not need man to populate the earth. If He did, He would not allow anything to reduce the population of the people on the earth. He would not allow war, epidemics, famine, pestilence, earthquakes, tornados, hurricanes, or death to terminate man, and yet expect man to populate the same earth.
- **The meaning of "be fruitful and multiply"** - The fruitfulness and multiplication commanded in the scriptures are not just about womb fruitfulness and population growth. This also means the make-up of man so that man has everything in him to grow, expand, be fruitful and increase in every area of his endeavor.
- **Sex is more than procreation** - Normally and in the absence of any impediment, every act of sexual intercourse of a man and woman should lead to pregnancy. But sex in the proper context is not just for child bearing; it is also for recreation, pleasure, healing, and the spiritual bonding of husband and wife.

Based on the above rationales, there is nothing wrong for a Christian to practice family planning, use contraceptives and engage in birth control if the purpose is to prevent, delay or space pregnancies. But a Christian should not engage in birth control if the sole purpose is to terminate or eliminate existing pregnancies as with abortion.

64. **Should Christians engage in renewal of marriage vows?**

Marriage is the joining together of two people to become one. It prohibits the joining of three, four or more. Man has to leave his father and mother to become part of the marriage of two people. God detests sex before marriage to ensure children are not conceived or born outside the marriage of two people. Marriage is not a contract that is easily amended and revoked, not a vow or promise that is easily fulfilled or refused, but a covenant that should last till death separates the couple.

Renewal is an act of extending the original period of time when something is effective or valid, or the state of being made new, fresh, or strong again. This implies that, if there is no renewal, the thing in question may become invalid, stale, weak and ineffective. Since the marriage covenant is both spiritual and physical, this means that:

- The renewal of the marriage vows connotes the cancellation or invalidation of the original vow and the establishment of a new vow which supersedes the old one. The act of renewal can be perceived as creating multiple marriage covenants.
- Renewal of marriage vows becomes an ordinary ceremony that has no significant spiritual benefits but spiritual disadvantages. The court will not issue a new marriage license or certificate. The wedding date does not change. The new marriage vows and other marriage rites demean the marriage covenant. The marriage covenant is violated where there are more than two people, specifically when children are included. Many years of living together with plenty of sexual activity is also a violation of the marriage covenant.
- The renewal of marriage vows is like giving marriage a terminal duration other than until death. To alleviate the pain of divorce, the world is proposing a marriage contract

that should expire and be renewable every 7 or 10 years. This gives couples the option to cancel or extend the marriage contract at agreed time periods.

There are many things we do today innocently and with good intentions opening the door for the devil to attack our faith and belief. What we accept as Christians should be based on our relationship with and knowledge of God and His word. But today, what we accept is based on how many people have accepted it, how long it has been accepted, and the caliber of people who have accepted it. Because many so-called great and influential people, including Christians, are spending huge amounts of money on the renewal of marriage vows, and because of unprecedented public attacks on those who are against it, many matured Christians don't ask questions anymore about why we do what we do?

Among the many excuses, two main excuses are often given by the supporters of renewal of marriage vows:

- It is a celebration of our love as couples.
- We did not have the time and the resources to plan or have an elaborate church wedding when we were married.

Among many attacks, the following are the two leading attacks against the opponents of the renewal of marriage vows:

- They are too spiritual.
- They have no money to organize it.

The marriage covenant is more than a contract and a vow. Because marriage has spiritual implications, I believe that Christians should not engage in the renewal of marriage vows or multiple marriages. While there is good intention with the idea, it trivializes the institution of marriage, violates the marriage covenant, and opens the door for the world to change the definition of marriage. The good intention of enhancing the joy of marriage can be achieved through the celebration of marriage anniversaries, vacations or retreats for couples, marriage memories and other creative ways to spice up marriages.

65. **What is "open marriage," and should Christian couples practice it?**

Open marriage relationship is a worldly idea to combat the institution of marriage. Open marriage relationship is an agreement between spouses to engage in sexual activities with other people apart from each other. This idea is based on spouses giving each other physical, emotional and sexual freedom to become intimately involved with other people. It is also an idea to bring another man or woman into the marital bed as a sexual partner. An open marriage relationship is described as:

- **Freedom of a spouse to have sex outside of marriage without committing adultery**. The secularists claim that this is not adultery as the spouse has the permission and consent of his or her partner.
- **Freedom of a spouse to have sexual intercourse with others without cheating**. The practice will prevent spouses from lying or hiding their relationship with others. There is no accusation of secrecy and infidelity among spouses.
- **Freedom to love your spouse without owning him or her**. Secularists claim that marriage should not be a wedge for spouses to own and control each other. A spouse should have the freedom to do what he/she wants without restriction, embargo and jealousy.
- **Freedom to engage in sexual acts with multiple partners to defeat the illegality of polygamy**. This practice allows a man to have sex with his wife and other

women at the same time. Likewise, it gives a woman the opportunity to have sex with men other than her husband, or allows a couple to invite other couples to their bedroom and exchange spouses.

The supporters of open marriage relationships argue that it addresses:

- **The menace of divorce** - They suggest that many divorces today are due to cheating and infidelity. The open marriage relationship will cure this.
- **Outdated Traditional Marriage:** They claim that monogamy, that is, marriage of one man and one woman, is not working for this new generation. The millennium generation is different from the traditional folks who stay on one job, live in one city and stay married to one man or woman for their whole life. Open marriage relationships, they argue, will allow people to try new things in their monogamous marriage relationships and other quasi-polygamous relationships without violating the laws, statutes, and constitutions of their state and countries of residence.
- **Sex scandal** - They claim that many careers have been abruptly crushed because of an influential person engaging in extra marital affairs. They argue that open marriage relationships will stop this.
- **Sex Freedom** - They claim that open marriage allows couples to have sexual freedom without any boundary or restriction. It allows the choice of polygamy, exchange of spouses, and multiple sex partners without the guilt of adultery or infidelity.

For Christians who have the fear of God in them, this should not even be a consideration. This is the sign of the last days. Satan is working hard to turn the heart of men and women towards himself and against God.

> ***"But mark this: There will be terrible times in the last days. People will be lovers of themselves, lovers of money, boastful, proud, abusive, disobedient to their parents, ungrateful, unholy, without love, unforgiving, slanderous, without self-control, brutal, not lovers of the good, treacherous, rash, conceited, lovers of pleasure rather than lovers of God— having a form of godliness but denying its power. Have nothing to do with such people.*** 2 Timothy 3:1-5

Christians should not engage in this practice for the following reasons:

- **Marriage is an institution of God** - The marriage institution consists of God, man (husband) and woman (wife). The open marriage relationship releases God from the marriage. Marriage is compared to the relationship between Christ and the church. Open marriage relationships pollute the body of Christ.
- **Adultery is a sin** - the secularists may count sex outside marriage as a sporting or extra-curriculum event but God calls it adultery. Adultery is a sin punishable by God. Christians are to live above sin and the world.
- **Polygamy is not God's will** - Polygamy is against the will of God. It was allowed during the time of the law because of the hardness of men's hearts but it is not permitted under this time of grace.

  > ***"I will give you a new heart and put a new spirit in you; I will remove from you your heart of stone and give you a heart of flesh."*** Ezekiel 36:26

- **Marriage is a covenant** - The world may redefine marriage as a contract or a mere relationship, but for God marriage is a covenant. Contrary to the open marriage relationship, marriage vows must be kept.

66. **What is the "don't ask, don't tell" policy in marriage?**

There was a "don't ask, don't tell" policy in the United States Armed Forces, which was recently repealed. The "don't ask, don't tell" policy in marriage entails keeping a secret about whatever it is not asked. The US military policy addresses the sexual orientation of service men and women. The marriage policy addresses all marital matters. In marriage, there are questions of whether to tell a spouse about your feelings, financial transactions, travel plans, goals and visions whether they are good or bad. The existence of this policy in a marriage relationship is evidence of:

- **Breakdown in communication** - Where there is lack of communication in the marriage relationship, there will be secrecy and hoarding of relevant information between the couple. A situation where a spouse cannot freely epress his or her feelings to the other spouse without argument and strife will make such a spouse to find it difficult to volunteer marital information except when asked. Such a spouse gives the excuse of letting sleeping dogs lie by not sharing the information with the other spouse.
- **Lack of Trust** - "Don't ask, don't tell" is in operation when there is no trust between the couple. And where there is no trust, a couple will lie to each other, hide information and keep secrets from each other. One of the spouses may engage in business transactions or financial projects without the knowledge and consent of the other. The issue with this policy is that the spouse does not provide relevant information until the other spouse asks. And if the other spouse does not ask, the information is concealed until the secrecy is revealed. This may be toxic to the marriage.
- **Individualism** - This practice is a common one in a marriage relationship where an individual spouse can do

his or her own thing. A situation where each spouse works and keeps his or her own money exclusively, and discloses little or no information about finances, will encourage this policy. In this kind of situation, there is no transparency and the spouses can keep relevant information from each other.

When a couple practices the "don't ask, don't tell" policy in marriage, they open doors to problems that, left unresolved, could break up or bring an end to their marriage. With this policy, infidelity, distrust and deception can creep in, thus, demeaning and destroying the marriage. It is better to be open with a spouse in every situation. Sometimes, spouses fail to reveal a matter to their spouse not because of this philosophy but because of error and omission due to forgetfulness. In such a case, whenever a spouse recalls a matter, he or she should share it with their partner. An important principle in marriage is full disclosure of information as and when it is due.

### 67. What is abortion, and should a married Christian woman have an abortion?

Abortion is the termination of a pregnancy to prevent the birth of a child. The difference in contraception and abortion is that contraception prevents the pregnancy while abortion terminates or destroys it. Pregnancy can be terminated through medical abortion or surgical abortion. Medical abortion uses pills to create miscarriage and removal of pregnancy, while surgical abortion entails either vacuum aspiration or dilatation and evacuation. Abortion is legal in most of the States in United States with little or no restrictions. According to an Orlando women's center in Florida; 22% of all pregnancies in United States end in abortion, 50% of these women are younger than 25 years with 33% between age 20 and 24. 17% are teenagers, and these women come from every religious affiliation; 43% are Protestant, 27% are Catholic, and 13% are Born-again or Evangelical Christians.

In God's perspective as codified in the Bible, the word of God, abortion is a sin of murder, the shedding of innocent blood. Most often, abortion is not an accidental or self-defense killing but a premeditated killing. God is against it. The argument that pregnancy is just a fetus and not human is against God's will because life begins at conception. Here are some Scriptures:

> ***"Thou shalt not kill."*** Exodus 20:13
>
> ***"By thee have I been holden up from the womb: thou art he that took me out of my mother's bowels: my praise shall be continually of thee."*** Psalm 71:6
>
> ***"For he that said, Do not commit adultery, said also, Do not kill. Now if thou commit no adultery, yet if thou kill, thou art become a transgressor of the law.*** James 2:11
>
> ***"Before I formed you in the womb I knew you, and before you were born I consecrated you; I have appointed you a prophet to the nations."*** Jeremiah 1:5

When a man and a woman engage in sex, conception or pregnancy is bound to occur except there are hindrances. Sex is exclusively reserved for married couples. A teenager engaging in sex is committing fornication, and bringing curses to his or her life. Christian parents should return to their responsibilities of training their children in the way of God. Teenagers engaging in abortions are committing murder, shedding the blood of innocent babies and thereby bringing curses and judgments on them-selves. The unfortunate part is that many Christian parents encourage their teenage daughters to carry out abortion in order to avoid personal embarrassment and the stigma of their children having babies out of wedlock. They seek to protect their names, social status, image and reputation with no regard for their faith in God.

For married couples, sex serves two main purposes: procreation and recreation. Couples engage in sex to enjoy themselves as husband and wife, to unite physically, emotionally and spiritually, and to conceive and birth children. The reasons why married couples may engage in abortions are:

- **Unplanned pregnancy** - About 33% of all pregnancies are unplanned because the couple thinks they are not ready, done with bearing children, and they lack financial resources to care for the needs of the child after birth. This makes ungodly souls to seek for termination of pregnancy. However, these unexpected and unplanned excuses have no place in the will of God.
- **Misunderstanding family planning and abortion** - Every couple can choose the number of children they want or don't want to have through birth control or family planning. Family planning helps to prevent conception, while abortion helps to destroy the conceived child. As a married Christian, the fact that you don't want more children is not a reason to abort a pregnancy; it is murder.
- **The complication of pregnancy** - Sometimes pregnancies are not healthy and the babies in the wombs are not developing properly, there is always the challenge of whether to abort such pregnancies or not. In such situations, it requires much faith for a Christian woman to believe God and keep the pregnancy. While I do not pray for such situations for anyone, my encouragement for any woman or couple who finds themselves in such a situation is to trust and believe God. It is for your good. However, they will not be under the judgment of God if they choose to abort such pregnancies. Like people die of illness, the pregnancy can be terminated because of the baby's illness.

- **The health of the mother** - Another challenging scenario is when the health of the woman is at stake. Pregnancy may endanger the health of the mother, and it may require an abortion to save her life. In this case, it should be done as a last resort. Whenever there is complication, it is not wrong to save life even if it is the life of the mother.

Every choice and decision we make in life has consequences. The fact that we are not instantly judged by God does not mean He will not judge Christians and non-Christians for murder committed through the abortion of pregnancies. Ecclesiastes 10:8 reads *"He that diggeth a pit shall fall into it; and whoso breaketh an hedge, a serpent shall bite him.* Sometimes people go through situations in life that defy prayer; these may be the rewards of the breaking of marriage covenants and shedding of innocent blood. However, there are healthy and sick pregnancies, the sick pregnancies could be aborted to save the life of the mother, but we cannot abort healthy pregnancies irrespective of our logic and reasonableness without attracting the wrath of God.

68. **What did I lose when I got married?**

For many people marriage is an albatross hung around their necks. They detest marriage because of their beliefs, bad experiences and general misunderstanding of marriage. They see marriage as the main cause of woes or problems and unnecessary evil. They regret their marriages and provide many arguments to discourage others from engaging in it. These are some of the things they claim to have lost in marriage.

- **Identity** - They claim to have lost their identity, personality and uniqueness. They assert that their beautiful appearance and handsome physique are lost in marriage especially after child birth. They hate marriage for losing their voices, personal space, interests, hobbies, and self-confidence. These feelings are most obvious when their spouses do not share their interests. For example, a spouse who loves traveling may blame marriage as a reason for not traveling enough.

- **Independence** - Marriage demands dependence or interdependence; therefore, they blame marriage for losing their freedom to do whatever they like, go out to wherever and whenever they like, associate with whomever they like, and spend their money on whatever they desire. This is evident when their spouses are controlling and domineering.
- **Career** - Since couples must agree and make sacrifices for each other, many, especially women, regard marriage as the termination of career, business and professional pursuits. Marriage may require couples to move to new locations, cities, states and countries, thereby warranting one or both spouses to leave their well-paid jobs or careers and take up new opportunities in their new location or residence. They claim that the birth and the challenge of raising children diminished or ended their career progress.
- **Life** - Apart from the list of interests, many believe that marriage snatches away their life from them. For instance, they complain of the loss of friends, names, respect, and honor. They hate the restriction marriage places on them. They dislike the loss of personal privacy. They detest sticking or giving their love and body to just one person. They despise the reproach of infidelity, adultery and unfaithfulness when they sexually share their bodies with someone other than their spouse.

The perception that marriage is a loss has brought tremendous implications to the institution of marriage such as: high rate of divorce, redefinition of marriage and diminished faith.

- **High Rate of Divorce** - Divorce is a common phenomenon in our world. There are many things that distinguish Christians and non-Christians; unfortunately, divorce is not one of them anymore. The rate of divorce is skyrocketing and there is not much difference between the divorce rate of first and second marriages. The idea that divorce is a great loss to people is no longer valid. Some unexpectedly walk out of their marriages for no reason.

- **Redefinition of marriage** - It is a shame that God is no longer relevant to man. The number of atheists, non-believers and backsliders is increasing at such a fast rate that everything of God including marriage is being redefined or destroyed. The God-established biblical marriage is being replaced with open marriage relationships, homosexual and polygamous marriage. The belief that marriage is a loss is another reason for the diminished importance of marriage.

- **Diminished Faith** - Marriage is a product of faith, and it can only be appreciated and successful in our walk with Christ. Faith teaches virtues such as love, forgiveness, patience, forbearance, kindness, and peace. These virtues are tested in marriage. Believers who are called to promote faith and win others to faith will only diminish faith when marriage means nothing but a loss to them. Jesus said in Luke 18:8 that *"... Nevertheless when the Son of man cometh, shall he find faith on the earth?*

Marriage, like any other relationship, has its ups and downs. It is not a light endeavor for two people of the opposite sex, different backgrounds, interests and abilities to live together as husband and wife. There may be feelings of loss but in the real sense marriage is gain. For those who cannot handle marriage hiccups, they should not marry in the first place. It is better not to marry than to destroy the institution of marriage through divorce. Interestingly, God created and excused some people from marriage. Matthew 19:12 exhorts that *"For there are some eunuchs, which were so born from their mother's womb: and there are some eunuchs, which were made eunuchs of men: and there be eunuchs, which have made themselves eunuchs for the kingdom of heaven's sake. He that is able to receive it, let him receive it.* But since you choose marriage, may you receive the grace and strength to overcome stress and negative feeling of loss in your marriage.

69. **What did I gain when I got married?**

Marriage is a blessing endowed to men and women from God. It is a mystery that unites man and woman for procreation, recreation and dominion. Marriage is God's idea to cure the inadequacy, loneliness and incompleteness of man. It allows for dependence of husband and wife on each other. It demands the separation of spouses from other men and women and exclusive coupling with his or her spouse only. What we gained when we got married can be explained under the categories of spiritual, psychological and social-economic benefits.

- **Psychological Benefits** - Two are better than one because if one is cool, the other will warm him or her.
    - Love - Apart from salvation, marriage provides the best love story man has ever known. We have read and seen people who for love got married against all odds and sentiments. Marriage provides opportunity to share life with someone special.

- Companionship - Marriage creates friendship, confidentiality and companionship. It does not only cure loneliness, but it also cures the guilt and embarrassment of having sex.
- Family - Marriage births family and allows couples to create and pass a legacy to their progenitors. It is unfortunate that the degeneration of marriage is the reason many children are born out of wedlock and raised by single parents.

- **Social-Economic Benefits** - In the United States of America, there is a continuous fight by the Lesbian Gay Bisexual & Transgender (LGBT) community for the recognition of same-sex union as marriage. At the time of writing this book, 21 countries have legalized same-sex marriage including the USA and Ireland. The fight is not only about discrimination but also the social, economic, political and legal benefits of marriage, which include:
  - **Medical Benefits** - The spouse is the next of kin and has the responsibility to make medical decisions upon the incapacitation of the other spouse. A spouse can also include the other spouse in his or her health insurance benefit plan.
  - **Legal Benefits** - In most cases, a spouse is excused from testifying against the other spouse in court. Also, adoption of children is a right reserved to a couple.
  - **Financial Benefits** - Couples can file a joint tax return. A wealthy person can accrue greater deductions and exceptions in their estate and trust return. A deceased spouse can also pass inheritance to the living spouse. In community property States, the property acquired during marriage is jointly owned by

both spouses and shared equally between spouses upon divorce and death.

- **Immigration Benefits** - A spouse with a lesser immigration status can enjoy the greater immigration benefits of his or her spouse.

- **Spiritual Benefits** - Marriage is not about man alone. It is about God's plans and purposes. One of the principles of creation is seed. This principle allows a creature to be made one time and to subsequently reproduce and multiply itself or kind through the seed within it. This is not just about procreation but also about:
  - Fulfillment of God's purpose.
  - Enjoyment of God's favor and blessing.
  - Worshipping of God.
  - Building of God's kingdom.
  - Rearing of God-fearing children.

Marriage is not about what we gain or lose, but it is about our faith, family and future. Faith, because it promotes God's purpose and gives pleasure to God; family, because it leads to joy and peace and promotes the welfare of family and community; future, because it affects our lives, legacies and the next generations.

70. **Would you consent to a spouse sleeping with another person in return for material or monetary gains?**

The world is full of amazing principles, some of which are godly, and others are devilish. Principles and beliefs such as "you scratch my back, I'll scratch yours", "tit for tat", and "political pay back" are now common. The idea that everyone has a price encourages fraud, bribery and nepotism. To obtain favor from a politician or seek political appointment, huge donations are made to their campaigns. To obtain business opportunity or promotion at jobs, many do all sorts of things for their bosses, wealthy employers and friends such as offering their children, spouse, or themselves to work for less, cleaning their houses and mowing their lawns for free, giving discounted vacation packages or gifts, just to mention a few. To discourage this kind of influence-peddling, many government institutions and professional organizations restrict their employees and members from receiving gifts above certain amounts. For instance, the former Governor of Virginia State, Bob McDonnell and his wife Maureen, were convicted of fraud charges, including receiving the gifts of a Rolex watch, and a $15,000 check for their daughter's wedding, though later discharged of charges by the Supreme Court. Former Illinois Governor Rod Blagojevich was also convicted of an attempt to sell or trade the former senate seat of President Barrack Obama for campaign cash and donations. Influence-peddling is illegal in the world of politics. Unfortunately, in relationships, the idea is sometimes taken to another level. The idea of a person sleeping with someone in positions of power with the intent of winning favors, a job or business is ludicrous. It is bad enough for a single or unmarried person to engage in sex before marriage, thereby committing fornication. It is even worse for a married man or woman to engage in affairs outside marriage, thereby committing adultery. But how should we explain the idea of a couple consenting to the idea of the other spouse having sex with another person outside of marriage just because they need something from the person or the person promised the spouse or couple a huge sum of money, favor, business opportunity, promotion, or something of value? This is consensual trade sex, not an open marriage or rape. An act like this is:

- **Adultery** - A married person who sleeps with another person other than his or her spouse engages in adultery.

Adultery is a grievous sin against God and one's body, the temple of the Holy Spirit. Proverb 6:32 (KJV) reads, *"But whoso committeth adultery with a woman lacketh understanding: he that doeth it destroyeth his own soul.*

- **Prostitution** - Sex for money or favors is nothing but prostitution. Prostitution is immoral. God is not only against prostitution, it is against the laws and constitutions of many States and Countries. Proverb 23:27-28(NLT) reads that *"A prostitute is a dangerous trap; a promiscuous woman is as dangerous as falling into a narrow well. She hides and waits like a robber, eager to make more men unfaithful."*

- **Abomination** - Acts like this, are not only sin (adultery and prostitution), they are also an abomination against God. It is a rejection of God's principles, wills and purposes for marriage. It is the defilement of the temple of Holy Spirit. 1 Corinthians 6:13 (NLT) reads that, *"You say, "Food was made for the stomach, and the stomach for food." (This is true, though someday God will do away with both of them.) But you can't say that our bodies were made for sexual immorality. They were made for the Lord, and the Lord cares about our bodies.*

- **Divorce** - No matter the motivation or needs that lead to this idea, the end result is divorce. When the dust has settled and eyes are opened, the other spouse will recognize that he or she is not naturally wired to share his or her spouse's intimacy with other people. This subsequently bruises emotions and deflates the egos of the couple. Sometimes, people hide behind polygamy and open marriage concepts, while those are ungodly; the idea of consenting to sexual relations of your spouse outside of marriage is nothing but a demise of marriage. Matthew

19:9 (NIV) reads *"I tell you that anyone who divorces his wife, except for sexual immorality, and marries another woman commits adultery."* For instance, Sarah consented with Abraham and offered her maid, Haggai, to sleep with Abraham. The end result was strife and the sending away of Haggai and Abraham's son, Ishmael. The world is still spinning out of control from the aftermath of such an arrangement. There was also a man who, because of his impotence following after the birth of their first child, allowed his wife to have affairs with other men. This was done with the intention of having more children. The wife consented and had two more children out of wedlock before the marriage collapsed. Unfortunately, the wife has returned the two kids to her concubine, the rightful father.

71. **How can I cope with my spouse's involvement in spiritism, witchcraft or occultism?**

Man is a spirit who lives in a body and possesses a soul. Because of man's spirit nature, he loves to relate in the realm of the spirit. Scriptures and science are not congruent as they sometimes agree and disagree. Scriptures are not only superior to science but existed before it. Interestingly, science is leaning more towards confirming the scriptures. The scriptures identify three places of inhabitance as heaven, earth and beneath the earth. Each place of inhabitance has its own unique body and spirit. Spirit dominates the heavens and underneath the earth but body dominates the earth. God and angels also dominate heaven while Satan and demons dominate beneath the earth. Men and women involve themselves in Spiritism to interact, interfere or participate in the affairs of heaven and beneath the earth. Through the Holy Spirit, Christians engage in prophesy, word of knowledge, word of wisdom, and speaking in unknown tongues to partner with heaven. Likewise, witches, wizards, occultists, herbalists, and necromancers use evil spirits to influence, deceive, manipulate and cause serious destruction and havoc by partnering with Satan and demons from beneath the earth.

There are people who believe in Spiritism and those who do not. There are three categories of believers of Spiritism, and one category of non-believers. Here are the four categories:

- **Holy Spirit Believers** - These are Christians who believe in the Holy Spirit only. They involve, participate in or stay under the operation of foundational gifts, spiritual gifts and ministerial gifts of the Holy Spirit.

    - Foundational Gifts - Romans 12:6-8 reads, *"Having then gifts differing according to the grace that is given to us, whether prophecy, let us prophesy according to the proportion of faith; Or ministry, let us wait on our ministering: or he that teacheth, on teaching; Or he that exhorteth, on exhortation: he that giveth, let him do it with simplicity; he that ruleth, with diligence; he that sheweth mercy, with cheerfulness.*

    - Spiritual Gifts - 1 Corinthians 12:7-10 reads, *"But the manifestation of the Spirit is given to every man to profit withal. For to one is given by the Spirit the word of wisdom; to another the word of knowledge by the same Spirit; To another faith by the same Spirit; to another the gifts of healing by the same Spirit; To another the working of miracles; to another prophecy; to another discerning of spirits; to another divers kinds of tongues; to another the interpretation of tongues".*

- Ministerial Gifts - Ephesians 4:11-12 reads, *"And he gave some, apostles; and some, prophets; and some, evangelists; and some, pastors and teachers. For the perfecting of the saints, for the work of the ministry, for the edifying of the body of Christ".*

- **Evil Spirits Believers** - Those who believe in spirits other than the Holy Spirit. Examples include Ogun (the god of iron), Ifa (the god of divination), Sango (the god of thunder), and many other spirits that work with star readers, and rock or animal worshipers. Evil spirit believers include herbalists, white garment or Pentecostal prophets or pastors who invoke spirits other than the Holy Spirit. Matthew 7:15 reads, *"Beware of false prophets, which come to you in sheep's clothing, but inwardly they are ravening wolves.*
- **Commingled** (Holy Spirit and Evil Spirits) Believers - Those who believe in the Holy Spirit and other spirits. This is determined by what works or is most expedient at a particular time. They are in church today and in the herbalist's shrine tomorrow. 1 Samuel 29:7-8 reads, *"Then said Saul unto his servants, Seek me a woman that hath a familiar spirit that I may go to her, and inquire of her. And his servants said to him, Behold, there is a woman that hath a familiar spirit at Endor. And Saul disguised himself, and put on other raiment, and he went, and two men with him, and they came to the woman by night: and he said, I pray thee, divine unto me by the familiar spirit, and bring me him up, whom I shall name unto thee.*
- **Non-Believer** - Those who do not believe in Spiritism. These people are logic- and science-minded. The fact that one does not believe doesn't change or remove the existence of it. Many deniers who later experienced or

became victims of operations of evil spirits testify to their existence.

The question here deals with a Christian spouse who does not want his or her spouse to engage in category 2 and 3 above. To address this question, it is important that we identify why anyone would be involved in witchcraft and the occult either as a practitioner or a seeker. Some of the reasons are:

- **Family History and Background** - It may be hard for some people to leave what they have known since childbirth and inherited from their parents. Just as some are born into Christian families, others may be born into idol worshipping families.
- **Religious Practice** - People may accept this as their religious practice and except God saves them, it may be hard to get them out.
- **Personal Problem** - Some people found themselves in this practice in their quest to seek solutions to certain problems. Issues such as sickness, barrenness, poverty, bad dreams, failure, and death have led people to herbalists, star-readers and witches.
- **Social Status** - Some engage in Spiritism to seek power, relevance and acceptance among their peers. Some people are in fraternities and cults today because of power, fame, affluence, women or friends.

These are suggestions of how to handle marriage if a spouse is involved in evil spirits, witchcraft and cults:

- **Do not join or participate in it -** Every Christian should engage heaven through the Holy Spirit but should not engage "beneath the earth" through evil spirits. If your spouse is engaging false prophets or herbalists, do not be a part of it.

- **Pray and Believe God** - Pray for your spouse. Trust God that He will open your spouse' eyes to see that God hates this.

- **Support Your Spouse to Overcome the Issue** - There may be reasons why your spouse is involved in this. You can support him/her to overcome this influence by: engaging the spouse in discussion, encouraging them to attend counseling, providing them support to solve the underlying problems in a godly way, and engaging them in a deliverance service.

- **Do not divorce** - This is not a reason to seek divorce. Marriage issues are meant to be addressed and resolved. They are not the path nor should they be a reason to dissolve the marriage covenant.

72. **How can someone be freed from a spiritual husband or wife?**

There are two realms, namely the physical and spiritual realms. The physical realm is the metabolic and cosmic world; the one we live in. It is the world of logic, senses, nature, government, economy and science. The spiritual realm is the world of faith, power and the invisible. It is occupied by God and Satan with different operations.

- **God is good and associates with righteousness but Satan is evil and associates with wickedness.** John 10:10 explains that, *"The thief cometh not, but for to steal, and to kill, and to destroy: I am come that they might have life, and that they might have it more abundantly.* God is a giver of life while Satan is a thief and destroyer of life.

- **God uses angels and heavenly host as servants to carry out His work**. Psalm 104:4 reveals that, *"Who makes his* *angels spirits; his ministers a flaming fire"*. Satan uses demons and evil spirits to implement his own assignments. Ephesians 6:12 confirms that, *"For we wrestle not against flesh and blood, but against principalities, against powers, against the rulers of the darkness of this world, against spiritual wickedness in high places.*

- **God is omniscient and resides in heaven.** Satan is only in one place at a time, and resides under the earth. Isaiah 66:1 (KJV) reads, *"Thus saith the LORD, The heaven is my throne, and the earth is my footstool..." Philippians 2:10 (NIV) reads "that at the name of Jesus every knee should bow, in heaven and on earth and under the earth.*

There is a relationship between the spiritual and physical realms. However, the former is superior to the latter. Nothing happens in the physical realm without its root and initial occurrence in the spiritual realm. Because man is made up of spirit, soul and body, he relates with both realms. Though the spirit realm does not waste time on the details, most of the things man does in the physical realm can be done in the spiritual realm. Here are three examples to mention a few:

- **Man or woman can be served food in the spirit either by angels or demons**. Elijah was served food by an angel in 1 Kings 19:5-6 (KJV) *"And as he lay and slept under a juniper tree, behold, then an angel touched him, and said unto him, Arise and eat. And he looked, and, behold, there was a cake baken on the coals, and a cruse of water at his head. And he did eat and drink, and laid him down again.*
- **Man or woman can be made to travel in the spirit.** The Spirit of God took Philip away in Acts 8:39 (NIV) *"When they came up out of the water, the Spirit of the Lord suddenly took Philip away, and the eunuch did not see him again, but went on his way rejoicing.*
- **Man or woman can be talked to in the spirit**. King Saul consulted a witch to invoke the spirit of Prophet Samuel

who was already dead and buried. 1 Samuel 28:11-15 reads, *"Then the woman asked, whom shall I bring up for you? Bring up Samuel, he said. When the woman saw Samuel, she cried out at the top of her voice and said to Saul, Why have you deceived me? You are Saul! The king said to her, don't be afraid. What do you see? The woman said, I see a ghostly figure coming up out of the earth. What does he look like? He asked. An old man wearing a robe is coming up, she said. Then Saul knew it was Samuel, and he bowed down and prostrated himself with his face to the ground. Samuel said to Saul, why have you disturbed me by bringing me up? I am in great distress, Saul said. The Philistines are fighting against me, and God has departed from me. He no longer answers me, either by prophets or by dreams. So I have called on you to tell me what to do.*

A man or woman can have both spiritual and physical spouses. Depending on the covenant, the effect of the spiritual marriage may or may not allow someone to marry in the physical realm. A married man or woman who has a spiritual spouse will face unexplained conflict, fight, misunderstandings, crisis or issues in his or her physical marriage.

The reasons people have spiritual spouses may include:

- **Covenant** - To escape the problems of life, people enter into or inherit covenants whose full consequences they don't understand. Someone who has a delay in child birth may consult herbalists, witches and other agents of Satan, and make sacrifices that initiate him/her into a covenant. Blood covenant is powerful, dangerous, transcends life and is difficult to cancel.

- **Curse** - People who have legitimate authority and right through conquest, birth, and purchase can bless and curse another. A spiritual spousal relationship is a bondage that may result from curse. Isaiah 49:24 reveals, *"Shall the* *prey be taken from the mighty, or the lawful captive delivered?*

- **Sexual Sin** - One dangerous way people engage in spiritual entanglement is ignorance through sex. Marriage involves contract (agreement) and consummation (sex). It is not only Sexually Transmitted Diseases (STD) that one should worry about when having sex with someone you are not married to, but the spiritual implication as well.

A man or woman with a spiritual spouse can be freed through the following:

- **Salvation** - Accept Christ as Lord and Savior. Salvation through the blood of Jesus Christ washes away our sins and errors. It gives freedom from sins, deliverance from curses, and justification from guilt. 1 Corinthians 6:11 reveals that, *"And such were some of you: but ye are washed, but ye are sanctified, but ye are justified in the name of the Lord Jesus, and by the Spirit of our God.*

- **Deliverance** - Deliverance is a spiritual warfare through the Holy Spirit to unlock the settled work of Satan in the life of believers. Some difficult situations that involve a covenant may require deliverance.

- **Abstinence** - The scriptures encourage us to flee from fornication and adultery for a reason. Jesus told the woman caught in the act of adultery to go and sin no more so that serious danger will not happen to her. 1 Corinthians 6:18 (NLT) reveals that, *"Run from sexual sin! No other sin so clearly affects the body as this one does. For sexual immorality is a sin against your own body.*

73. **Should a Christian engage in polygamy?**

Polygamy is the practice of having more than one spouse at a particular time. This differs from a monogamous marriage, which is the practice of one man and one woman. Polygamy is practiced as either polygyny or polyandry. Polygyny is a marriage practice that allows a husband to have two or more wives. Polyandry is a marriage practice that allows a wife to have more than one husband. Most times, polygamy is mentioned in respect of polygyny, a practice that allows a man, the husband to marry many wives but everyone presumably condemns the practice of polyandry. In order words, what is good for the goose is not good for the gander. Men can have many wives, but women cannot have many husbands. These are the myths of a polygamous marriage:

- **Polygamy is a natural thing** - The argument is that one woman cannot satisfy the sexual desires of man. The sexual desires of men are stronger than those of women, and since women have a menstruation period during which they cannot engage in sex, it makes sense for men to have more than one wife. The problem with this argument is that marriage is not only for sex but rather it is for the unity of two people with mutual interests who are in love and want to raise a family together.

- **Polygamy discourages and cures infidelity, adultery and divorce** - The argument is that polygamy allows competition among the wives to offer their best to the husband, thereby discouraging the husband from going outside the many wives he has. And even when he has other women outside, the wives at home will not bother since each of them shares her husband with other wives anyway. There is also no guilt of and no conflict about infidelity, and there is no divorce. The problem with this argument is that God is a party in marriage and the issue of infidelity or adultery is not only about the woman, it also involves God. It is a sin.

- **Polygamy reduces the problem of women's population** - The argument is that women are more than men, and there are many women who have reached marriageable age without husbands. Polygamy, as this argument goes, allows women who are without husbands and are willing to be the second, third or fourth wife to marry. The argument here is either God does not exist or God is not fair to women. Well, this assumption is wrong because the population of male and female is fairly the same. The Department of Economics and Social Affairs of United Nations in January 2015 estimated that the world population ratio of male to be 50.4% and that of female to be 49.6%. The point is that man will use any excuse to justify its ungodly acts and activities.
- **Polygamy cures barrenness in the marriage** - This rationale is that there is no need to wait on or believe God for children. If your present wife is having a delay in childbirth, you can easily marry another wife that will birth children for you. The argument is that the wife cannot blame the husband for engaging in polygamy for the sake of having children. On the other hand, will men allow women to marry a second husband for the sake of having children if the infertility is caused by the husband? Faith in God encompasses our entire life, and anyone that cannot believe God even for the birth of children cannot claim to be a Christian.
- **Polygamy was practiced in the Bible** - Many argue that polygamy is good because it was practiced in the Bible. Yes, it was practiced in the Old Testament of the Bible, but Jesus came and corrected the error of the Old Testament. Jesus despised it in the New Testament. He said in the

beginning it was not so, and only people with hardened and unconverted hearts will engaged in it. John the Baptist died because of his sermon against polygamy or polyandry.

> ***"For Herod himself had sent forth and laid hold upon John, and bound him in prison for Herodias' sake, his brother Philip's wife: for he had married her. For John had said unto Herod, It is not lawful for thee to have thy brother's wife.*** Mark 6:17-18

The scriptures encourage Christians and church leaders to be husband of one wife.

> ***"A bishop then must be blameless, the husband of one wife, vigilant, sober, of good behavior, given to hospitality, apt to teach."*** 1 Timothy 3:2

• **Polygamy is a policy tool** - Many people argue that polygamy was a common practice in the last century and was acceptable in certain cultures. They contend that it was practiced in both western and African countries and served people well until governments kicked against it. The governments used it as social and economic policy like any fiscal and monetary policies. Polygamy was lawful until governments made laws against it, its proponents argue. The problem here is that marriage is bigger than culture and government. Marriage is an institution of God.

But these are the reasons why Christians should not engage in polygamy.

- **The Significance of Creation** - Man and woman were created in the image and likeness of God as male and female. God did not create two women or three women and a man but rather He created a man and a woman as a symbol of perfection. Like the trinity, a symbol of marriage is God, man and woman, anything outside of this is against the template of creation. In the beginning, it was not so.

- **The Equality of the Sexes** - Christians are to protect the dignity of God's creation including women. God created man and woman equal and one was not less than the other. Christians should not wait for the Feminist movement before they treat women well. Any man that will not permit his wife to practice polyandry should not practice polygyny.
- **The Condition of Men's Heart** - Jesus said abuse of marriage is a function of the man's heart condition. It is a difficult task to discourage an unbeliever with a hardened heart from practicing polygamy but this practice should not be heard of among believers whose hearts God must have touched.
- **Marriage is the symbol of the Church** - The relationship between Christ and the church is like the relationship between the husband and wife. As Christ is only married to the church, a husband should only be married to his wife. As Christ loves the church, likewise a husband should love his wife.

74. **What is the impact of generational history on the institution of marriage?**

Generation is used to describe the set of people who were born and lived through the same experience, events and time. At the time of writing this book, the United States of America classified generations into Traditional, Baby Boomers, Generation X and Millennials. Management uses generation concepts to predict the behaviors of people in the workplace. Generation concepts can also be used to explain the transformation in homes, schools and churches. This question focuses on these four generations and how each one treats marriage.

- **Traditional** - These are those born between the years 1922-1945. Among others things, they witnessed the stock market crash, the Great Depression and Pearl Harbor. They are stable, sacrificial and respectful in character. They are also uncomfortable with conflict, but dedicated and loyal to their commitments. In this generation, the husband worked and the wife took care of the home and children. This generation respected marriage and did everything to make the marriage work.
- **Baby Boomers** - These are people born between the years of 1946 and 1964. They experienced civil rights, women's rights, Vietnam, and the assassinations of President John Fitzgerald Kennedy (JFK) and Martin Luther King Jr. (MLK). This generation heard about their parents' suffering due to their loss of savings and investments as a result of the Great Depression, and they vowed not to be or ended up like their parents. They were optimistic and willing to go the extra mile by breaking things apart. They became repressive and repugnant to established structures including faith, family and the social system. Their women went to work and personal gratification became common. They hated or avoided conflict but accepted separation and divorce. This marked the beginning of the collapse of the institution of marriage.
- **Generation X (Gen X)** - These are people born between the years of 1965 and 1981. They witnessed the Watergate scandal, the marketing of the personal computer, the fall of the Soviet Union and Desert storm. They are pragmatic, global thinking, techno-literate and self-reliant. This generation had both parents at work but became adapted

to television and video games. Many of their women are financially stronger than the men. This generation questions authority and distrusts leadership. This generation yearns for fun and informality. They are impatient and uncertain. Within this generation, the marriage institution is questioned and non-marriage relationships are common.

- **Millennial or Generation Y (Gen Y)** - These are people born between the years 1982 and 1995. They witnessed violence such as the Oklahoma City bombing, the Columbine massacre, school shootings; the 9/11 Terrorist Attack; War in Iraq, and Technological Development. They are multitasking, diverse, sociable and confident. They lack structure and have communication problems. They were raised by pre-and after school programs and single parents. They have a happy syndrome and want rewards for showing up. Due to the structure of marriage and their trophy mentality, this generation has no problem in getting married today and getting divorced tomorrow.

These four generations engage the institution of marriage in different ways. The Traditional generation is stable in marriage. Baby boomers hate conflicts and accept divorce and separation as a solution. The Gen X group hates authority, and are quick to end their marriages, and engage in other kinds of relationships such as open marriage, and live-in couples. The Gen Y wants happiness without structure or boundary, and sees no value in marriage. However, the saints of God are people of a chosen generation. The believer's generation is different irrespective of the period of birth and experience in the worldly generations of traditional, baby boomers, Gen X or Gen Y. The believer's generation is Generation Jesus or Gen J. In this generation, our purpose is to glorify, praise and worship God. Our genetic predisposition is to do the will of God, like what

Jesus likes and hate what He hates. And our goal is to represent God on earth and be the light of the world and the salt of the earth. Those from Gen J will keep, cherish and use their marriage to serve and glorify God.

> ***"But ye are a chosen generation, a royal priesthood, a holy nation, a peculiar people; that ye should shew forth the praises of him who hath called you out of darkness into his marvelous light.*** 1 Peter 2:9 (KJV)

75. **How has modern society affected the responsibilities of women in marriage?**

Before the Great Depression of 1930s, most households had a single breadwinner, the man. During the depression, there was a devastating global, financial and economic meltdown such that about 30 million Americans lost their jobs or their sources of income. The local, state and national banks were closed for almost two weeks, and governments rationed food to the people. This experience led to new strategies of social and economic survival for households. One of these strategies was the creation of dual sources of income by couples with the implication that children would have to raise themselves. Other events such as the Second World War, the Vietnam War, the dot.com boom, the Civil rights movement, the Women Rights movement, and many others solidified these management or preventive strategies of households. The effect of these was that the roles and activities of husbands and wives have changed in marriage. Husbands, as the heads of the homes still maintain the salient role of keeping the marriage and family together. However, husbands should treat their wives with honor and with the understanding that:

- **Women are in the workplace** - Women are not only homemakers but also joint wage earners/breadwinners.

They do the same, or better, quality jobs than men. They have better qualifications and/or experience and make more money than men.

- **Women have a voice** - Women are educated, travel and are smart. They can think critically on their own. They have their own ideas and opinions on any given subject.
- **Women are leaders** - Like men, women are founders, Chairpersons or Chief Executive Officers (CEO) and managers of multi-million-dollar companies and organizations. They are pastors, prophetesses, teachers, evangelists, teachers and bishops of churches and ministries. They are mayors, governors, prime-ministers and presidents of governments in municipalities, states and nations.
- **Women have identity** - Many women have achieved great things and made a name for themselves. Like men, they have changed the course of history and won the highest prizes including the Nobel Prize.
- **Women are respected** - Like men, women have rights and privileges; rights, such as the right to vote and be voted for, the right to own property, the right to sue and be represented, and the right to live without abuse. Women, through the Feminist movement have engaged in activism and won major legislations.
- **Women are in Sports** - Like men, women engage in all manner of sport activities as players, coaches, referees, administrators and owners.
- **Women are in the Military** - Military forces are no longer a privilege exclusively reserved for men. Women are not just in the military but they also engage in all facets of the armed services, including taking on combat roles. They

are both in regular and elite groups. They are in the Army, Navy, Air Force, Marines and National Guard.

Generations affect every aspect of man's life including marriage. But God does not change and His words remain unchanged. His principle on marriage does not change. Though man and woman were created equally in the image and likeness of God, God made man to lead the family in the institution of marriage. Like any organizations that must have leadership, marriage has its own leadership in the man. While there is nothing wrong with the involvement of man and woman in different roles and responsibilities as determined by the complexity and development of the world, the believers in Christ should recognize their responsibility to serve as the light of the world, through the sanctity of their marriages.

Chapter 10

# Abuse and the Law

*L**ove* is the heart of marriage. It is the music that refreshes the soul of marriage. Love glues two people with different backgrounds, customs, cultures, stories, statuses and sometimes languages together in marriage. Love is said to be blind because people in love overlook errors, weaknesses, shortcomings and wrongdoing in their spouses. Love is the fulfillment of the law and it covers all sin. Love does not contradict or violate the peace of others. It breaks boundaries and limitations and can make stories too good to be true. Love embraces, cares and cherishes. It is not envious, proud and abusive. Love is not only sexual and brotherly but it is sacrificial and unconditional. Love is not lust but it dies for what it holds, keeps what it has and nurtures what it gets. Romans 12:9 reads that, *"Love must be sincere. Hate what is evil; cling to what is good.* A couple should learn to love each other. They should recognize that love and hate cannot be together. Couples should lean on God because love is God.

76. **What is marital or spousal abuse?**

*The American Heritage Dictionary* defines abuse as "to use wrongly or improperly or excessively, misuse, hurt, or injure by maltreatment." Myles Munroe of blessed memory said that "where purpose is not known, abuse is inevitable." Abuse is not one of the purposes of marriage but it is one of the leading causes of the dissolution of marriage. Marital abuse or abuse of one's spouse is tantamount to irresponsibility and a lack of respect for the institution of marriage. Abuse in marriage comes in form of domestic abuse, violence or disturbance.

In United States of America, the Tennessee State law coded in TCA 39-13-101(a) states that, "*a person commits assault who: intentionally, knowingly or recklessly causes bodily injury to another; intentionally or knowingly causes another to reasonably fear imminent bodily injury; or intentionally or knowingly causes physical contact with another and a reasonable person would regard the contact as extremely offensive or provocative* And the same Tennessee law in TCA 39-13-111(a) states that, "*domestic abuse victim means any person who falls within the following categories: adults or minors who are current or former spouses; adults or minors who live together or who have lived together; adults or minors who are dating or who have dated or who have or had a sexual relationship, but does not include fraternization between two individuals in a business or social context; adults or minors related by blood or adoption; adults or minors who are related or were formerly related by marriage; or adult or minor children of a person in a relationship that is described above.* This means domestic abuse can be perpetrated by both males and females irrespective of social, culture, economic or religious status. It also implies that domestic violence can be committed against a spouse, children, fiancée, fiancé, mothers, fathers-in-law, grandparents, boyfriend, girlfriend, and exes. There are different types of domestic abuse, including physical, emotional, sexual and financial.

- Physical abuse is to exert and/or inflict pain and injury on someone using physical contact and force; for instance, throwing an object, pushing, pressing, choking, kicking, hitting, punching, cutting, battering or to endanger someone. Physical abuse may leave a scar on the body of the victims.

- Emotional abuse is an injury to someone's feeling and sense of self-worth, relevance and independence. This is to demean and trash someone's personality, attributes, and opinions to the point that the person begins to feel useless and worthless. Examples of this include yelling, criticisms, blaming, name-calling, threatening, isolating, humiliating, intimidating, bullying, and other acts that psychologically impair someone. Emotional abuse may not leave a scar like physical abuse but its effect is nonetheless negative and damaging and can leave mental scars.

- Sexual abuse is physical and emotional pain and injury caused to someone by forcing them to participate in unwanted, non-consensual and unsafe sexual activity. This includes but is not limited to rape, incest, sex with children or minors, forced sex with spouse, and degrading or uncomfortable sex with a spouse.

- Financial abuse is emotional pain and injury caused to someone through the use of money or economic activities; for instance, deprivation of access to money or the bank account; withholding of money, check, debit or credit card; sabotaging a spouse's employment by causing absenteeism, tardiness and job loss; and destroying property.

Christians should desist from domestic abuse and violence. Apart from the fact that domestic abuse is a crime punishable under the law with a jail term, God's command to His children is to love one another as He loves us. In a relationship, there is bound to be disagreement and arguments but these should not result in domestic violence that is physical, emotional, sexual and financial abuse.

> "***Husbands, love your wives and do not be harsh with them.*** Colossians 3:19
>
> ***"In your anger do not sin, do not let sun go down while you are still angry."*** Ephesians 4:26

77. **What is the rationale for increased incidences of domestic violence and spousal abuse?**

Domestic abuse is the exertion of pain and injury on the body and feelings of one's spouse or family member. It does not only create physical scars such as bruises and cuts but it leaves the victims with mental and psychological scars such as depression, stress and panic disorder. Domestic abuse is not only common in the secular world; it is growing in churches and in Christian marriages and homes. Domestic violence has no regard for age, gender, race, ethnicity, nor income levels, and men, women, children, and the elderly can be victims of domestic violence. For example, in the United States, the National Coalition Against Domestic Violence estimates that 1 in 3 women and 1 in 4 men will experience domestic violence at some point in their lives. They also report that 1 in 15 children are exposed to domestic violence each year. The reasons for domestic violence vary and may include:

- **Power and Control** - People engage in domestic abuse and violence because they want to exercise power and control over their victims. Domestic violence is described as an abusive behavior in a relationship, directed by one partner (abuser) to another partner (victim) to maintain power and control over the latter. This power and control are obtained through coercion, manipulation, threats, hitting, kicking, intimidation, isolation, and blame.

- **Revenge and Injustice** - People engage in domestic abuse and violence to repay or revenge the wrong doings of other people. While this should not be an excuse, children who are exposed to domestic violence while growing up may accept violence as a normal way of life and become abusers themselves. Someone who felt maltreated in other areas of their life may also resort to redress the injustice against their spouse and family members.

  "***Do not repay anyone evil for evil. Be careful to do what is right in the eyes of everyone. If it is possible, as far as it depends on you, live at peace with everyone. Do not take revenge, my dear friends, but leave room for God's wrath, for it is written: It is mine to avenge; I will repay, says the Lord.*** Proverbs 12:17-19

- **Personality Problem** - A tree is known by its fruit; likewise, a person is known by his or her character. People engage in domestic abuse and violence to display their personality and character traits. There are people with abusive personalities and no matter how you try to tame them, they will reveal themselves. Examples of abusive personalities include extreme jealousy, sudden mood swings, unrealistic expectations, isolation, blaming others, hypersensitivity, forcefulness and aggression. This is the reason Christ gave us a relationship and not a religion with God. The true believers in Christ will not only talk the talk but they will walk the walk. The true believers have become new creatures and old things have passed away.

- **Drug and Substance** - Drug abuse and controlled substances are a contributing factor to abusive behavior. Drugs or narcotics are substances whose possession and usage are illegal while controlled substances are those whose possession and usage may or may not be legal depending on circumstances such as prescription. Senses and judgments are impaired by the uncontrolled usage of drugs and controlled substances like cocaine, and heroin.

- **Cultural Norms** - There are cultures and beliefs that encourage the gender dominance that leads to domestic abuse. A culture that allows husbands or wives to physically or verbally abuses each other is contradictory to the will of God. One of the reasons many African husbands are having problems with their wives is the inability to reconcile the African culture of restriction with that of women in the Western culture of liberation and freedom. Marriage is not a cultural institution but it is God's institution.

78. **What are the signs that someone is in an abusive marital relationship?**

Domestic abuse among Christians is not a rare situation in this age. Anywhere you look there is domestic abuse. Men and women abuse one another. Husbands abuse their wives physically. Wives abuse their husbands verbally. Children are assaulted, raped and sexually violated. Elders, parents and in-laws are deprived of healthcare, clothing, food and money. Families are to exist and to love and care for their members, but are now traumatized by abuse. Abuse is not only about physical injury but it may be emotional and economic. The following are the signs to be aware of when a spouse is being abused in marriage.

- **Feeling of fear** - An abusers' purpose is to have control and exercise power over their victims. This is achieved through fear, intimidation, harassment, blaming, exploitation, coercion, isolation, humiliation, threats, and manipulation. The first sign to know if you are being abused is to check your feelings and thoughts. If you are fearful and afraid of your spouse that is a problem. A spouse is in an abusive marriage relationship when there is unhealthy fear of the other spouse; a feeling of being hurt or harmed; being unable to express oneself, is becoming a pattern and a way of life. Another sign of an abusive marriage relationship is when a spouse cannot discuss certain issues; constant yelling from your spouse; constant restriction of movement or association with other people.

- **Abusive Behaviors** - One-time incidents may be overlooked and forgiven since mistakes do happen. But if the incidents become regular, then it is abusive behaviors or way of life. Examples of abusive behaviors are: insult or ridicule, throwing objects, hitting or slapping extreme jealousy, blame or criticism, excessive anger, forcefulness and bullying.

  ***"But the things that proceed out of the mouth come from the heart, and those defile the man. "For out of the heart come evil thoughts, murders, adulteries, fornications, thefts, false witness, slanders*** Matthew 15:18-19

- **Past Experience** - It is important to examine your spouse's past experiences in terms of childhood and previous relationships. It is a fact that children who live in homes and witness spousal abuse or who are themselves abused, grow up to become abusers or victims. A person who has a record of domestic abuse, child molestation, or sexual abuse may also become a repeat offender in the new relationship. Unless spouses with past experiences of domestic violence get healed, domestic violence may become a normal way of life for them and there is a possibility for them to abuse others or to become victims of abuse.

- **Environment and Community**- Evil communication corrupts good manners. Families, friends and the people you spend time with may contribute to domestic violence behaviors. If your best friends are abusers and they don't see anything wrong with domestic abuse, you too may soon join in the practice, unless disassociation occurs. You need to choose who you relate with as there is a possibility of them influencing you.

It may be difficult to know with certainty that someone is being abused; however, there is a possibility that someone in an abusive relationship may exhibit these signs: frequent bodily injuries; numerous phone call threats and harassment; unexplained absences from work, church and other meetings; restriction from associating with family and friends; full of anxiety and stress; and limited access to a couple's property and money.

79. **How does domestic abuse affect marriage?**

Domestic abuse is evil and is not from God. God is for tolerance, perseverance and forgiveness, and His nature is peace and harmony.

***"Make every effort to live in peace with everyone and to be holy; without holiness no one will see the Lord.*** Hebrew 12:14 (NIV)

For believers, domestic abuse is not only sin to God but it can also create the following effects:

- **Divorce** - One of the leading causes of divorce is domestic abuse. Education and development have helped to identify abusive and non-abusive behaviors. Many abusive behaviors that people practiced in the past but have been hidden under the cloak of gender superiority, culture and religious sentiment are no longer acceptable. Since marriage cuts across cultures, the most difficult issue to resolve in marriage is domestic abuse. Many may even consider infidelity and financial issues as part of domestic abuse.
- **Children's Behaviors** - Domestic abuse has a tremendous mental effect on the children of both the abuser and victim. Children who witness the abusive behavior of their parents against each other or other people will not only suffer abuse themselves as children but they may also become abusers as adults. Children that receive abusive training from their parents may abuse others. Proverb 22:6 (KJV) reads, *"Train up a child in the way he should go: and when he is old, he will not depart from it.*
- **Health Challenge** - Domestic abuse leads to physical and psychological injuries. Examples of physical injuries may include broken bones, red eyes, bleeding nose or mouth, twisted arms, open wounds, and headaches. Examples of psychological injuries are stress, depression, forget-fulness, sleep deprivation, flashbacks, and anxiety. These injuries may affect both the primary victim - the spouse,

and secondary victims - the children, families, friends and community.

- **Economic and Social Costs** - Domestic abuse creates financial burdens to the abuse victim and society. This can be measured by: loss or reduction in household income; cost of law enforcement, legal and medical cost, and loss of productivity. The U.S Department of Housing and Urban Development reported that domestic violence is the third leading cause of homelessness among families.
- **Faith** - The faith of a domestic abuser will be called to question. Children of God are called to be lights of the world. They are not called to abuse their spouse, family and friends but rather to love and be kind to them. They are called to exemplify the nature and character of God toward their spouse. Christians should not tarnish the nature of God nor their faith in God.

Domestic abuse is a crime not only against the victim(s), but also against society. It is both a civil and criminal offense punishable with punitive and compensatory measures ranging from the award of money to probation to prison time. Police officers, lawyers and courts are involved in domestic abuse cases. In the United States, there are about 21 States that have mandatory arrest while some others have preferred response arrest for domestic violence assaults. For instance, New Jersey uses mandatory arrest as stated in her Statutory Annotation 2C:25-21 that *"When a person claims to be the victim of domestic violence, and when a law enforcement officer has responding to the incident finds probable cause to believe that domestic violence has occurred, the law enforcement officer shall arrest the person who is alleged to have subjected the victim to domestic violence and shall sign a criminal complaint..."*Tennessee on the other hand, uses preferred response policy as stated in Tennessee Codes Acts - TCA 36-3-619 that (a) *"If a law* *enforcement officer has probable cause to believe that a person has committed a crime involving domestic abuse, whether the crime is a misdemeanor or felony, or was committed within or without the presence of the officer, the preferred response of the officer is arrest."* And (b) *"If a law enforcement officer has probable cause to believe that two (2) or more persons committed a misdemeanor or felony, or if two (2) or more persons make complaints to the officer, the officer shall try to determine who was the primary aggressor. Arrest is the preferred response only with respect to the primary aggressor. The officer shall presume that arrest is not the appropriate response for the person or persons who were not the primary aggressor. If the officer believes that all parties are equally responsible, the officer shall exercise such officer's best judgment in determining whether to arrest all, any or none of the parties.* In most States, domestic violence offenders or defendants arrested remain in jail without posting of bond for a specific period of time ranging from a few hours to the time of the appearance hearing in court. In the State of Tennessee, it is 13 hours. This implies that physically hitting, kicking or slapping of your spouse that warrant a 911 phone call to the police can land you in jail for a minimum of 13 hours. It can also lead to one-year probation and a period of anger management classes and counseling.

As believers, our first point of seeking redress is not calling the police but rather calling on God and the men and women of God He has put in place as our pastors and spiritual leaders. Since every child of God must have a pastor and belong to a church, this will not be a difficult task. They are there to counsel, correct and guide you. The unfortunate thing is that some men of God are abusers themselves. God will lead you to stay under the leadership of servants of God who you respect and can call on in time of trouble.

80. **What is Feminism?**

The Feminist movement is a social movement whose goal is to fight against male dominance, female subordination and the oppression of women. The Feminist movement is called by names such as Women's Rights Movement, Women's Liberation, and Women's Freedom. This movement believes that men and women are equal by nature but are not treated equally. Feminist activists believe that society makes men superior and women inferior. They believe that the unalienable rights of women should not be violated, withdrawn or different from those of men. The aim of this movement is to fight against gender injustice and inequality that affects women in all aspects of life. For the purpose of this book, the following are few examples of the injustices and oppressions that the Feminism movement fights against:

- **Women were refused the right to quality education.** Many parents assumed it is a waste of time and money to educate their daughters.
- **Women were refused the right to share in the property or inheritance of their husbands or parents.**
- **Women were prevented from speaking in public.** Society believed that women were only to be seen and not heard, and that the kitchen was a woman's rightful place.
- **Women were refused the right to vote and be voted for.** They were disenfranchised and not included in political activities.
- **Women were refused the right to control their own bodies.** They could not decide when to have and keep a pregnancy using contraception and abortion.
- **Women were refused the right to work, conduct business and earn equal wages for equal work.** Many in

society believed that they were to depend on their husbands rather than make a living for themselves.

- **Women were refused the right to participate in religious activities**. They could not speak or occupy leadership positions in the church.
- **Women were refused the right to decency**. They were compelled or forced to marry early or to marry those they did not love and were raped. Their husbands could divorce them but they could not divorce their husbands.
- **Women were refused the right to legal redress**. They could be victimized, abused and violated without legal recourse and rights.
- **Women were refused the right to sexual liberation.** They could not have multiple sexual partners, many husbands, and have sexual pleasures, while men were adored for having multiple sexual partners and wives.
- **Women were refused the right to marriage equality.** They saw no reason why lesbians should not be allowed to have a legal marriage instead of a civil union.

In other words, the women's liberation movement was and is a fight against injustice and oppression that cuts across the political, economic, religious, legal, and social lives of women. In my opinion, since the world system operates on advocacy and lobbying of interest groups as one of the methods of social engineering, the women's movement has partially done a good job and at the same time created enormous problems. Some of the landmark achievements of the movement in the United States are the Voting Rights Act of 1920 that gave equal rights to men and women to vote and be voted for, and the Civil Rights Act of 1964 (Title VII) that makes it illegal to discriminate against a person on the basis of race, color, religion, national origin, or sex. On a negative note, the movement has contributed to numerous divorces, same-sex marriages, single parenthood, social vices, and abortions. The Supreme Court decision on Roe v. Wade (1973) made abortion legal in all 50 States. During the summer of 2015, as I was writing this book, the country of Ireland in Europe, made same-sex marriage legal through a referendum, and the U. S. Supreme court through a close decision of 5 to 4 has legalized same sex marriage in all 50 States.

81. **What is the biblical view about Feminism?**

Oppression and unequal rights that victimize and undermine the interests of women date back to the beginning of time when Adam and Eve were sent out of the Garden of Eden. And the history of the Feminism movement or Women's Right movement dates back to the time of Moses. The Old Testament's emphasis on the male child is a permissive will of God. For instance, Adam and Eve probably had other female children but the emphasis was only on Cain and Abel. Only the first born male child died in Egypt when the Angel of destruction passed through the land. Male children were commanded to join the Israelite army. King Saul gave his daughter in marriage as a gift or reward to David for killing Goliath without finding out his daughter's interest. The list of events in the Old Testament that prioritize men is long. God permitted it only because men wanted it to be so.

The perfect will of God, however, is that men and women are equal as they were both created in His image and likeness. For instance, during the distribution of the Canaan land, only the male children were given land, inheritances and properties until the five daughters of Zelophehad started the first Feminist or Women's Right movement. They protested with Moses and through God they changed the law and customs of the land.

***"The daughters of Zelophehad son of Hepher, the son of Gilead, the son of Makir, the son of Manasseh, belonged to the clans of Manasseh son of Joseph. The names of the daughters were Mahlah, Noah, Hoglah, Milkah and Tirzah. They came forward and stood before Moses, Eleazar the priest, the leaders and the whole assembly at the entrance to the tent of meeting and said, "Our father died in the wilderness. He was not among Korah's followers, who banded together against the LORD, but he died for his own sin and left no sons. Why should our father's name disappear from his clan because he had no son? Give us property among our father's relatives." So Moses brought their case before the LORD, and the LORD said to him," What Zelophehad's daughters are saying is right. You must certainly give them property as an inheritance among their father's relatives and give their father's inheritance to them. "Say to the Israelites, 'If a man dies and leaves no son, give his inheritance to his daughter. If he has no daughter, give his inheritance to his brothers. If he has no brothers, give his inheritance to his father's brothers. If his father had no brothers, give his inheritance to the nearest relative in his clan, that he may possess it. This is to have the force of law for the Israelites, as the LORD commanded Moses."***
*Numbers* 27:1-11

God granted Zelophehad's daughters their demand because, in the beginning, man and woman were made equal. It was the hardness of heart and customs of man that made man superior and woman inferior.

Jesus, for the sake of gender equality defended the woman that was brought to be stoned to death because of adultery. The accusers in their discriminatory way saw no wrong doing with the man who was the woman's partner in crime. Jesus in John 8:7 (KJV) systematically told the men that "*...He that is without sin among you, let him first cast a stone at her.* Interestingly, every one of them left the scene. At another time, the Pharisees also confronted Jesus to find out whether it was lawful for a man to put away his wife for any cause. The Pharisees, like Sir William Blackstone, did not agree with Jesus' answer. Blackstone said "Husband and wife are one; and that one is the husband". They further asked "why did Moses then command to give a writing of divorcement and to put her away? This question was asked to emphasize their belief that men are superior to women.

> ***"Jesus replied, "Moses permitted you to divorce your wives because your hearts were hard. But it was not this way from the beginning. I tell you that anyone who divorces his wife, except for sexual immorality, and marries another woman commits adultery.*** Matthew 19:8-9 (NIV)

His answer was harsh to them. He taught that though women are to be submissive to their husbands in marriage yet they cannot be maltreated without consequence.

The advocates of the Women's Rights Movement always point to the writing of Apostle Paul to the Church in Corinth to discount the Bible and Christianity. They characterize Christianity as chauvinistic, homophobic and a promoter of oppression and injustice to women. Their favorite scripture is:

> ***"For God is not a God of disorder but of peace—as in all the congregations of the Lord's people. Women should remain silent in the churches. They are not allowed to speak, but must be in submission, as the law says. If they want to inquire about something, they should ask their own husbands at home; for it is disgraceful for a woman to speak in the church.*** 1 Corinthians 14:33-35 (NIV)

The Women's Rights advocates' emphasis is always on verses 34-35 but they ignore verse 33 and the context of this scripture. Every student of the Bible knows that the Church at Corinth was a problematic church. Every chapter of the book of 1

Corinthians was written to address different problems in the church. For instance, there was division, fighting about baptism, incestual behavior of a son sleeping with his father's wife or step mother, a communion meal turned to dinner, prophesy and speaking in tongues, and disorderliness. How could Paul who did not condemn women from speaking in tongue or prophesying in Chapter 11, tell women to keep silent in Chapter 14? The point is that there were serious disagreements, disorderliness and uncontrolled display of spiritual gifts in the church by women to the point that women were no longer subjected to the leadership of the church. As part of the steps in handling this problem, Apostle Paul wrote that women should be silent in the church and be submissive to their husbands, his point being that a woman who is not submissive to her husband may not submit to the leadership of the church. This emphasizes the same biblical principle that it is only in marriage that women are expected to be subject to the leadership of their husbands. The translation of woman should have been wives.

82. **How does Feminism affect the Christian Marriage?**

The Feminist Movement fights against systems that deprive women of their rights of equality with men. There is absolute justification for the movement to curb maltreatment of women by men, customs, organizations and government. While they have recorded astonishing achievements in many areas, they have also pushed the limit to create devastating consequences in other areas. Different legislations were enacted and social and cultural changes were made to give equal opportunities and rights to men and women. The effects of these are both positive and negative. A few examples are:

- Equal voting rights - Men and women can vote and be voted for.

- No Sex Discrimination - Men and women can seek employment for the same positions or opportunities. Men can be a company's CEO and women, likewise.
- No Compensation Discrimination - Men and women can receive equal pay for equal work.
- No Violence against Women - Women can seek both criminal and civil prosecution of violent crimes against them. This crime includes sexual assault, domestic violence, dating violence, and stalking.
- Equal Reproductive Right - Women can have safe and legal abortions, use birth control freely, and obtain quality sex education without legislative barriers.
- No Discrimination based on sexual orientation - Women are free to be physically and emotionally attractive to the same or opposite gender. In other words, women can be straight, lesbian or bisexual without discrimination.

Christian women should understand that some of these rights and opportunities are against the law of God. For instance, abortion and homosexuality are against the will of God. While there is nothing wrong with other rights that empower women, care must be taken to use these rights appropriately and in a godly manner. The world's freedom is not equivalent to God's freedom.

> ***"As free, and not using your liberty for a cloak of maliciousness, but as the servants of God.*** 1 Peter 2:16 (KJV)
>
> ***"For, brethren, ye have been called unto liberty; only use not liberty for an occasion to the flesh, but by love serve one another."*** Galatians 5:13 (KJV)

God brings husband and wife together as one in marriage. He told the wife in Genesis 3:16 (NLT) that *"Then he said to the woman, "I will sharpen the pain of your pregnancy, and in pain you will give birth. And you will desire to control your husband, but he will rule over you.* While this is not a license for husbands to maltreat and abuse their wives, it is an order in marriage for husbands to lead their wives. Here are the few effects of Feminism on Christian marriage.

- **High Rate of Divorce** - Christian wives should not allow Feminism or the Women's Right movement to redefine marriage for them. There is no question about the equality of husbands and wives in creation, value and virtues but wives are expected to submit to their husbands to make marriage work. The Feminist idea that wives should be independent of their husbands is a violation of the marriage tenets and is the reason for the skyrocketing rate of divorce in Christian marriage.
- **High Rate of Abuse and Domestic Violence** - Feminism has turned minor issues into major issues of conflict, and ensured that laws are in favor of women. For instance, a normal marital argument is now sometimes considered emotional abuse that may land a husband in jail. Issues that used to be easily resolved are now turned into major court cases. Ungodly actions and the retaliation of unsanctified Christian men against their wives are now reasons for high rates of domestic violence in Christian marriages.
- **High Rate of Single Parenthood and Unmarried Single Women** - Feminism has taught that women are empowered to do without men. They have sexual freedom to have multiple sex partners, abort unwanted pregnancies, divorce unwanted husbands, and raise children as single parents. The bad news is that Christian women have bought into this movement and there are now more single mothers in the church than among unbelievers. The implication of this is that many Christian

men are now scared to go into marriage. Consequently, there are many unmarried single women.

- **High Rate of Social Vices** - The Feminist movement failed to realize that the lack of father and mother in the life of children has led to high rates of crime, violence, school dropout, teen suicides and an increase in the population of young people in jails and prisons. The family is the foundation of the society, and when the family is destroyed, the society becomes corrupted. Christian women and men should keep their family from the corruption of the Feminist movement.

Chapter 11

# Crisis and Resolution

*The battle* may be destructive. It is a fight between two or more people or parties. A battle may be a result of disagreement and the misunderstanding of issues such as ideology, interests, rights, and properties. It may also ensue because of anger, revenge, or jealousy. Battles produce winners and losers. While winners walk away with joy and happiness, losers are angry, bitter and sad. Battles create casualties and spoils. Examples of casualties are the dead and displaced, damaged and destroyed properties, and incapacitated and dethroned governments. An example of the spoils of battle is the taking over or seizure of lands, cities, properties, and other tangibles goods. Battles occur between friends and enemies but it creates fewer friends than enemies with long lasting and devastating effects. Christians should carefully pick their battles. There are battles we don't need to fight or be involved in. We may know how the battle starts but we may not know how it will end. The casualty of the battle may outweigh the spoils. Psalm 37:8 (NLT) reads, *"Stop being angry! Turn from your rage! Do not lose your temper - it only leads to harm.* In marriage, Christians should not engage in battles with their spouse. They should not turn their spouse, children and family into casualties of war. In marriage, the battle is the Lord's.

83. **What are the sources of crisis in marriages?**

Crisis or conflict is inevitable in a marriage relationship. A marital crisis ranges from minor disagreements to major fights. Conflicts may arise with any issue in a couple's life. Examples of marriage conflicts are disagreements about traveling, food, clothing, children, finances, entertainment of guests, and shopping. A marital crisis is the inability of the couple to harness their separate opinions and ideas. The good news about a crisis is that it can be managed; the bad news is that the effect of an unresolved crisis can be damaging and costly. In order to identify the sources of marriage crises, let's examine the first marriage crisis in the scriptures.

> ***"The woman said to the serpent, "We may eat fruit from the trees in the garden, but God did say, 'You must not eat fruit from the tree that is in the middle of the garden, and you must not touch it, or you will die.'" "You will not certainly die," the serpent said to the woman. "For God knows that when you eat from it your eyes will be opened, and you will be like God, knowing good and evil. When the woman saw that the fruit of the tree was good for food and pleasing to the eye, and also desirable for gaining wisdom, she took some and ate it. She also gave some to her husband, who was with her, and he ate it. Then the eyes of both of them were opened, and they realized they were naked; so they sewed fig leaves together and made coverings for themselves. Then the man and his wife heard the sound of the LORD God as he was walking in the garden in the cool of the day, and they hid from the LORD God among the trees of the garden. But the LORD God called to the man, "Where are you?" He answered, "I heard you in the garden, and I was afraid because I was naked; so I hid." And he said, "Who told you that you were naked? Have you eaten from the tree that I commanded you not to eat from?" The man said, "The woman you put here***

***with me—she gave me some fruit from the tree, and I ate it.*** Genesis 3:2-12 (NIV)

- **The Influence of Third Party** - The parties in a marriage relationship are God, husband and wife. There is danger on the horizon the moment someone outside of these parties usurps influence. Adam and Eve allowed the Serpent to influence them and they landed in crisis. The Serpent, like other animals in the garden, was good until it influenced Adam and Eve. The in-laws, friends, neighbors, and co-workers are wonderful people sometimes with good intentions but they constitute third parties. They have no place in marriage.

- **Disobedience to God's Word** - Anything or person who makes dispute and questions the word of God will land him/her in crisis. There are wonderful TV talk or reality shows that push you outside the boundary of God's word. They make promises of good knowledge, wisdom, freedom and independence but they are just the beginning of a marital crisis.

  ***"...obedience is better than sacrifice."*** 1 Samuel 15:22
  ***"the fear of the Lord is the beginning of wisdom..."*** Psalm 111:10

- **Individualism of the Spouse** - Marriage is the union of a man and a woman by God. Marriage makes two become one and it turns "I, Me, Myself" to "We, Us, Ourselves". In marriage, husbands and wives harness their goals and objectives, do things together and move in the same direction. Crisis ensues the moment the wife's career is not the couple's career and the spouse's money is his or her money and not the couple's money. Conflict is at the corner the moment each partner shifts blame and seeks personal justification instead of covering up and taking responsibility for the other in the relationship.

- **Happiness Syndrome** - God's plan for everyone including couples is a good plan that will provide our desires according to His own will. The issue of many is that they want their desires met irrespective of God's will. Many husbands are ready to fight, abuse, and victimize their wives to fulfill their manhood without considering how God wants them to treat their wives. Eve had no concern about what God said, as long as the fruit was good to eat, beautiful and glamorous to look at, and gave her wisdom, money, fame and happiness. It is a marriage crisis when a man thinks that another woman can give him sexual pleasures better than his wife.

- **Leaving the church** - Leaving the presence of God is a dangerous subject and it is the beginning of crisis. There is nothing wrong in leaving one church for another, but it is a delayed crisis when the purpose is to hide something. It is a marriage crisis when a couple who used to enjoy the presence of God and fellowship of the saints are no more interested in church and fellowship based on some unfounded excuses. Adam and Eve compounded their crisis as they heard the voice of a stranger, left the place of sanctuary and worship and hid from God.

- **Accepting the World**: We live in the world but Christians do not belong to the world. It is a marital crisis when we become like the world instead of God. Following the world is a problem, the solution the world offers is not a solution, and when the solution seems to work, it works against God for a temporary period. Adam and Eve created a dilemma by eating the wrong fruit, got a temporary solution by covering themselves with fig leaves, and were eventually sent out of the beautiful Garden of Eden.

- **The Emergence of Nature:** Adam and Eve's crisis was compounded when the earth, the woman and the man were cursed. The pressure and complexity of life, the couple's roles and the existence of death became additional crises. The jobs, careers, businesses, and professions that should sustain and enhance marriage can turn to crisis. The misunderstanding or definition of gender roles is now an issue of conflict. The challenge of pregnancy or lack of it can be a crisis.

84. **What are the underlying principles about marital conflicts?**

Marital conflict is a disagreement and quarrel between a couple over issues. Couples may have conflict over sex, finances, communication, parents, in-laws, culture, career, church, children and vacation. The understanding of marital conflict should focus on the causes, types, effects, principles, number and the resolution of conflict. The underlying principles of conflict are:

- **Conflict is unavoidable** - There are inherent crises in all relationships, especially marital ones. Conflict is inevitable in marriage, and a successful marriage is not the absence of conflict but the presence of well-managed crisis. If the heaven did not escape crisis, the garden of Eden was upside down due to crisis, and Jesus our Savior had crisis with His disciples, how much more husbands and wives of today.

- **Conflict is a test of maturity** - Marital conflict reveals couples' personalities, character and attitudes, some of which are childish while others are commendable. Conflicts allow childish attitudes to be identified and corrected. Conflicts help us to see our spouse's point of view and perceptions. Through conflict a person may discover that he or she needs to work on anger and impatience. How will a person know they have the spirit of God to forgive unless he is offended?

- **Most Conflicts are resolvable** - Conflicts arise as a result of misunderstanding, miscommunication and misinterpretation of words, signals and perceptions. Conflict reveals a couple's and/or a spouse's needs, which may be personal, social, and financial. Conflicts are resolvable as needs are met, perceptions are understood, and different views are aligned.

- **Unmanaged Conflicts are dangerous** - Conflict in itself is not a problem; the problem is when it is not resolved or managed. Unmanaged conflicts may lead to greater problems such as stress, anxiety, infidelity, and divorce. Unmanaged conflicts can turn good to bad, kill initiatives and create bad decisions.

- **Conflict has underlying problems** - Conflicts don't just happen. There is cause or reason that creates them. For instance, there may be a conflict because a husband does not spend enough time with his family; the wife's needs are not met; there is not enough money in the bank; and the husband forgets the wife's birthday.

- **Conflicts apportion shared blame to the couple** - Neither spouse can exonerate themselves from involvement in a crisis. All parties involved in a conflict equally share the responsibility. The fact that one spouse contributes proportionally less blame compared to the other does not make either of them innocent. No spouse contributes proportionally zero blame to a marital conflict. Both spouses should accept responsibility and compromise where and when necessary to resolve conflict.

- **Conflict resolution is for peace and truth** - The mission statement of conflict resolution is to establish the truth and foster peace. Establishing truth is to be able to identify the underlying causes or problems of the conflict, and to be able to tell each spouse where he or she is wrong. Fostering peace is necessary to resolve the conflict and ensure that couples can move on as though the conflict did not happen. Striking a balance between peace and truth is a difficult job and it requires compromise, forgiveness, love and respect.

85. **What are the underlying principles of conflict resolution?**

Conflict resolution is a process of settling disputes, disagreements and differences to ensure truth and peace are the outcome. Truth is the aspect of attacking the problem and accepting the responsibilities of the problem. Peace is the aspect of restoring confidence, trust and happiness between the couple as though the conflict never happened. To resolve conflict, the following principles are important:

- **Do not ignore the Problem** - Do not sweep the problem under the carpet. Many think that the problem will disappear by not attending to it. No, it will not. Problems cannot be ignored if resolution is expected; walking away from it; keeping mute and not discussing it; pretending it does not exist or refusing to acknowledge it does not foster a resolution.

- **Do not underrate the problem** - Apart from not ignoring the problem, couples should not underestimate the problem. At this point the couple acknowledges the existence of the conflict but consider it trivial and not important enough to demand time to resolve it. A destructive fire does not start big but rather as a small spark. Galatians 5:9 (KJV) reads that *"A little leaven* *leavens the whole lump.* A small problem if not managed may lead to a great consequence. Anyone can underrate the problem by whining about it; yet make no sacrifice to address and resolve it.

- **Do not overrate yourself** - Some couples think they are too big for marital crisis. They ignore all of the warning signs. They will not only ignore and underestimate the problem, but they see themselves as being above the problem. They see themselves as too rich, famous, handsome, beautiful, intelligent, and spiritual to face certain kinds of marital conflict. Anyone can overestimate themselves when rank is pulled and status is hung on to. Statuses, such as husband, pastor, breadwinner, community leader, CEO, governor, or senator does not insulate or isolate a person from crisis.
- **Do not win at all cost** - Marital conflict resolution involves shared responsibility of husbands and wives. Tensions run so wild during conflict that apportionment of blame to spouses may create additional anger and resentment. Both spouses contribute to the conflict and should share in the blame and responsibility. The fact that one spouse caused only 10% of the conflict does not make anyone the better spouse if the other contributed 90% of the problem. A spouse's attempt to exonerate himself to win the argument at all cost is not helpful to the resolution of the conflict. The spouse's goal should not be to create a win-lose situation but rather a win-win situation. A spouse's attempt to win at all cost and to create a win-lose situation is unacceptable. When a spouse does not accept responsibility, he or she attempts to justify himself, and assign all the blame to the other spouse.
- **Do not attack your spouse's personality** - There is an underlying problem to every marriage crisis. The cause of

the conflict is the problem and not the symptoms or the people involved. Do not allow your emotions to betray your sensibility by attacking your spouse instead of the problem. Your spouse was wonderful before the conflict, he or she should remain wonderful during and after the conflict.

- **Do not miss the big picture of marriage** - Even in the fiery trials and the midst of conflict, the couple should not miss the big picture and the opportunity of glorying and pleasing God through their marriage. Conflict should make and improve couples instead of breaking them. In pleasing and glorifying God, the couple should seek the interest and welfare of their spouse and family instead of their personal interest. Be a good example for others to follow the will of God. Forgive, encourage and strengthen one another. The couple will miss the big picture if, and when, they keep score of errors and mistakes of their spouse.

- **Do not raise the white flag** - Conflicts are a natural part of a marriage relationship. The purpose of conflict is to make the persons better and not to break either of them or the marriage. A spouse should not end the marriage as a result of conflict. Most conflicts are resolvable and they are temporary problems that will soon pass away. Quitting means the problems cannot be resolved. It means you have no physical, mental or spiritual solutions to solve a temporary problem. Wait and work it out for the sake of future, family and faith. Marriage counselors and pastors are available to help. God's arms are opened wide to resolve the problems. To quit is to go to court and seek divorce.

## 86. How should Christians resolve marital conflicts?

Crisis is inevitable in marriage but couples are encouraged to handle crisis with maturity. It is not whether the couple will argue, disagree or have conflict with each other, but it is whether the couple will treat each other with love and respect when crisis actually happens. A spouse cannot control or prevent the existence of conflict, but a spouse can control or prevent the conflict from escalating through his or her response. To resolve conflicts, couples should follow or take note of these processes:

- **Understand the other party's feelings** - The couple should understand that during conflict one or both parties will possibly be hurt and become bitter and angry. The moment there is an argument or disagreement, it is important to know that both spouses will have different perspectives and viewpoints. Both spouses may have feelings of disappointment. The more one spouse expresses negative emotions, the more he or she faces counter negative emotions from the other spouse. Do not be naïve enough to think that the other spouse will let you run over them with your view points, shouts, feelings and emotions, except they are spiritually mature.

- **Reach out to make Amends** - Conflicts make emotions run wild. Because of self-justification, everyone is right in his or her own eyes and the other person is always wrong and the problem. Sometimes marital conflicts turn into a war between the husband and wife instead of a war between the couple and the problem. Amid this raging conflict, there must be a change of heart if the conflict will be resolved. One of the spouses should have a change of heart and reach out to the other spouse to resolve the conflict. The spouse who has a change of heart and reaches out is a leader and/or mature spouse. It is the responsibility of the husband, as the head of the home, to take the initiative of resolving marital conflict by reaching out to his wife. Reaching out is a test of leadership and maturity, and a man cannot claim the headship of his wife if he cannot humble himself, have a change of heart, and reach out to her. In a situation where the husband is not spiritually inclined, a mature wife will initiate the conflict resolution. In a clear-cut situation where the wife knows the conflict is all her fault, the appropriate action is for her to initiate the conflict resolution and to reach out to her husband.

- **Engage conversation about the conflict** - This may be difficult but the couple should communicate and have a conversation about the conflict. Difficult conversations require couples to identify the conflict, have the right perspective and adopt the right attitude toward resolution. This process allows the couple to come together and to resolve the conflict:
  - Agreeing on a specific time and place is good but is not necessary.
  - Each spouse should express their own view without attacking the other partner. They should also help identify the causal factors of the conflict. Spouses should listen attentively to each other's viewpoints. All problems should be listed to and addressed one by one.
  - To achieve the truth, each spouse should take responsibility and both spouses should accept their roles in creating the conflict. Apportioning blames will not help but each spouse should understand his/her contribution to the conflict.

- To achieve peace, recommended solutions should be offered and listed. Couples should start with an easy, simple, measurable and doable solution.
- Depending on the nature of the conflict, the couple may want to engage an arbitrator/mediator who is a predetermined person such as the couple's mentor, counselor or pastor. It is important not to take a marriage matter to anyone other than those permitted to intervene in marriage. Husbands should also assume their role as leaders and resolve conflict so that every small matter will not be taken to the arbitrator.

- **Ensure reconciliation and forgiveness** - Regardless of the difficulty or the degree of conflict, the couple should seek reconciliation. Reconciliation is the settlement or resolution of conflict, and it is achieved through repentance, forgiveness, restitution and celebration.

    - Couples should repent of what they did or failed to do before, during and after the conflict. For instance, a spouse may need to repent for his or her response to the errors, mistakes and conflicts initially caused by the other spouse.

      ***"Likewise, I say unto you, there is joy in the presence of the angels of God over one sinner that repents.*** Luke 15:10

    - Couples should sincerely confess, apologize and seek forgiveness from each other. Couples should also be willing to forgive each other to ensure reconciliation.

      ***"And be you kind one to another, tenderhearted, forgiving one another, even as God for Christ's sake has forgiven you.*** Ephesians 4:32

Forgiveness allows for restoration between spouses as well as healing for both. This action allows the couple to look forward and to seek the interest of the home. Vengeance is the opposite of forgiveness and it allows spouses to look backward to the hurt and pain that has been caused and motivates the couple to seek retaliation.

- Spouses should restitute to stop doing the wrong thing and by making up for their past failures. There are some past errors that cannot be corrected but the couple just has to let it go. Restitution helps to restore the trust that may have been lost because of the conflict.

  ***"And Zacchaeus stood, and said unto the Lord; Behold, Lord, the half of my goods I give to the poor; and if I have taken anything from any man by false accusation, I restore him fourfold.*** Luke 19:8 (KJV)

- Couples should celebrate one another and their marriage. The restoration of peace and joy is a sign of reconciliation.

  ***"Confess your faults one to another, and pray one for another, that you may be healed. The effectual fervent prayer of a righteous man avails much.*** James 5:16

87. **What should be done if a spouse does not believe or agree with the other's chosen career path?**

Career is what you do, become and make a living from. A Career path is what you plan to do or the new thing you are doing, or the new steps you are taking right now to get you to your career. Career includes job, education, profession, business, hobby, vocation, ministry or anything you are engaged in right now. A career path is the new job, second job, the new business, new opportunities, new degree, diplomas or whatsoever you are trying to obtain.

***"Seest thou a man diligent in his business? he shall stand before kings; he shall not stand before mean men.*** Proverbs 22:29

The reasons your spouse may not believe in your career path are:

- **Past Failure** - Track record, success rate, and experience are good indicators in winning support. For instance, if a husband has a track record of failure in his past endeavors, it will be difficult to win the wife's support to navigate into another venture.
- **Lack of agreement** - Amos 3:3 reads, *"Can two walk together except they agree.* A couple's agreement enhances success and unity of purpose. One venture agreement cannot be substituted for another venture. If one spouse embarks on a project, journey, business, education, or ministry without the approval of the other spouse, you will forfeit the belief and support of your spouse.
- **Lack of Skill** - Do you have the skill, knowledge and experience for what is planned to be done? Husband, don't hide under your assigned headship of the home and invest the family resources in ventures you have no clue or knowledge of. Beware of business scams, don't fall victim. Wife, nagging is not a substitute for appropriate skills.
- **Effect on family** - Family welfare and health are important considerations in the determination of a career path. Spouses may disagree or reject the career paths of their partners when it is detrimental to the family. For instance, a wife may reject a husband's new job appointment that requires family relocation or travel.

Likewise, a husband may not support his wife when her job schedule hinders their children's education.

- **Huge capital requirement** - Sometimes the career path may require an enormous investment of money that has to be saved, borrowed, or withdrawn from retirement savings. The investment of personnel may require the involvement of the other spouse when the spouse is not ready to be involved.

These are the things that can be done to gain the support of a spouse:

- **Recognize and address the issues:** Gaining the support of a spouse is easy if you can recognize and address their concerns. Don't assume that things will take care of themselves. A spouse's concerns need to be heard and adequately addressed. A spouse must be assured and reassured to gain the support needed to resolve problems and issues. A married man or woman must refrain from any venture that does not have the support of family, especially a spouse.

- **Know your vision and passion**: Every man and woman is created for a purpose, and the first assignment in life is to know one's purpose. When that purpose is known, every step and course of action taken should bring each person closer to their purpose. Any vision, ambition and career path should align with that purpose. Though this should be obvious to your spouse, you should lack no passion in communicating this to them. If your career path lines up with your purpose, a spouse should easily agree with you and also be supportive. But if the career path does not conform to your purpose, you may face a herculean task of trying to convince your spouse.

- **Career Path Analysis** - In determining a career path, a person should conduct a feasibility study and personal analysis of strengths, weaknesses, opportunities and threats of one's career. A person's strengths and opportunities will likely create enormous benefits and advantages that limit the threats and weaknesses of the person's new career. The purpose of a career feasibility study is to allow a person to examine the prospects of the career based on the forces of business. The career path analysis should reveal whether your career path is a viable venture or an albatross.

***"Suppose one of you wants to build a tower. Won't you first sit down and estimate the cost to see if you have enough money to complete it?*** Luke 14:28

No one can blame a spouse's refusal if your strengths do not match or support a chosen career path or if the career feasibility study is not sustainable. The fact that you are the husband is not enough to expose your spouse and family to a venture that you don't have the ability and capacity to accomplish.

- **Engage Career Advisors** - Marriage requires work and such work may include seeking the knowledge and wisdom of others. To be able to address the concerns of your spouse, sometimes it may be necessary to make consultations or seek the opinion of experts. These professionals, consultants and experts have a workable knowledge of and information relative to what they want to sell or share with people. A couple may need to engage such experts to obtain reliable information to allay concerns, doubts and fears about the career path.
- **Prayer** - In all marital affairs, there is a place for spirituality. A spouse that needs the support of the other spouse in their career path or other issues should engage the forces of prayer.

> ***"The king's heart is in the hand of the LORD, as the rivers of water: he turns it wherever he will.*** Proverbs 21:1

Prayer is communicating and seeking the help of God who knows all things and owns the heart of your spouse. He knows how to win your spouse's support and whether you need to follow a particular career path.

- **Marital Counseling** - Sometimes, the chosen career path may not be the main issue with regard to the lack of support from a spouse. Perhaps your spouse is looking for an opportunity to get your attention or to address some unrelated issues. Couples should have regular marriage counseling such as attending marriage seminars or lectures, couple's retreats, one-on-one with marriage counselors, and periodic visits to couple's marriage mentors.

  ***"Plans fail for lack of counsel, but with many advisers they succeed".*** Proverb 15:22

No couple should take their marriage relationship for granted. Whenever, there is lack of support or unresolved disputes, these matters should be raised at the marriage counseling session.

88. **How often do couples experience conflict?**

Marital conflict or crisis is a form of arguments and disagreements over issues. These issues can be anything such as food, traveling, job, school, church, children, and business. A conflict can be major or minor depending on its effects and consequences. Major conflicts have long lasting devastating effects, while the consequences of minor conflict are less damaging. To address this question, the issue of conflict focuses on the types, underlying principles, causes and effects, and resolutions. This question will focus on the types of conflict couples face in marriage.

- **Internal Conflicts** - These are personal issues and challenges that an individual brings into a marriage relationship. Each spouse has their own upbringing, past life and experiences that shape thoughts, characters and actions. A spouse raised in a family where housemaids and stewards did everything may find it difficult to handle homemaking responsibilities and could resort to conflict where the couple cannot afford the same service. A spouse raised in an abusive environment may also see shouting, yelling and hitting as a normal way of life. Internal or personal conflicts may include individual natural traits and personalities. Someone who is naturally happy may have less conflict with their spouse compared to someone who is muddy and angry.
- **Inherent Conflicts** - These are issues and challenges that exist between couple because of being in relationship. Every venture, pursuit and undertaking, with no exception of marriage, has its ups and downs, troubles and trophies, and conflicts and conquests. Couples may disagree and fight not because they want to but because there are inherent challenges and differences in a relationship more than that of a single person. Inherent conflicts arise sometimes because of the different perceptions, opinions and ideas of people in relationship.
- **External Conflicts** - These are issues and challenges that arise due to complexity and external stakeholders in the marriage relationship. The complexity of marriage involves the handling of issues such as sex, communication, finance and money, couple responsibilities, spousal abuse, culture and trust. External stakeholders are parents, in-laws, relatives, siblings,

friends, community, and church. External conflicts arise from disagreement or inability to harmonize the interests of the couple with the interests of the external stakeholders. It was because of this external conflict that Jesus said in Matthew 19:6 that "*...what God has join together, let no man put asunder.*

It is important for couples to learn how to resolve conflicts and to know the type of conflict they are facing. Individual spouses should look inwardly to determine the cause of the conflict. Internal conflict is usually caused by the domineering one and it has nothing to do with the other spouse. A spouse should be able to seek help to address their personal issues instead of attempting to shift the blame to the other spouse. Inherent conflict is created by both spouses and it should be treated as a shared responsibility instead of an event to shift all the blame to the other spouse.

The question of how frequent couples should have conflict is a question of the level of maturity and spirituality of each spouse, individually and collectively. While it may be difficult to completely rule out some marital conflicts, the understanding of types of conflicts and how to address them may serve to reduce the number of conflicts. For growing and immature couples, it may be normal to have more conflicts at the early stages of marriage rather than the later stages. For spiritually inclined couples, efforts should be made to reduce the frequency of marital conflicts.

89. **What should be done when a spouse experiences a crisis and withdraws from the marriage?**

A crisis may bring untold hardship, stress and pain. They can be physical, financial, psychological and spiritual. Some examples of physical crises are the loss of employment, lack of money, investment and business opportunity, expulsion from school, and revocation of business or professional license. Examples of financial crises may include but are not limited to the inability to pay house rent or mortgage, auto loan, children's tuition or school fees and household bills. Psychological crises may present themselves as illness, loss of a family member, failure to obtain credit, business opportunities or contracts, and delayed childbirth. Spiritual crises include but are not limited to backsliding, denouncement of faith or desertion of Christian fellowship.

In marriage, these types of crises are interrelated. A crisis may start as an internal or personal crisis but can create many inherent or external crises. A crisis that originated as inherent problems can escalate into internal and external crisis. This is because the problem of one spouse may be shared or transferred to the other spouse or become the problem of the couple. The context of this question assumes that the crisis is a personal crisis of one spouse that is negatively affecting the other spouse and the marriage. The question also reveals the devastating effects of this personal crisis, which may include the following:

- One or both spouses no longer care about his or her responsibility.
- One spouse is frustrated and has become unaccountable to the other.
- The spouses are no longer fulfilling the important commitments made before or after marriage. For instance, a spouse may change his or her career after marriage, thus bringing disappointment to the other.
- A spouse is depressed and may turn to the world, drugs and alcohol.

- A spouse has become isolated and engaging in activities against the moral or spiritual principles of the other spouse. An example of this is pornography.

When a spouse is going through personal or internal crisis to the point that he or she no longer participates in the marriage, the other spouse should adopt and engage these three suggestions:

- **Stay with God** - Life sometimes will throw us challenges but those challenges are common to man. Challenges of life should bring us closer to God rather than move us away from God. Even when our spouse denounces God or leaves the faith, we should stay with God. We should trust and serve God amid all of our marital crisis and challenges. God is still in control of all things and will see us through these crisis and challenges.

- **Stay with Marriage** - The first thing the world will suggest is to end the marriage. The world will advise that you are not your spouse's babysitter and that your spouse's problem is not your problem. But you are in marriage and expected to help and love one another. Spouses should pull one another up when one of the other falls down, and strengthen them when they are weak.

- **Seek help for Spouse** - It is only in marriage that the nakedness, weaknesses and crisis of a spouse should not bring shame. Marriage allows a couple to hold hands and walk side by side. Seek help for a spouse who has a crisis and needs assistance from the experts. Consult medical doctors if it is a physical ailment and a psychologist and therapists if problems are emotional. Consult a pastor if the need is spiritual. Consult your support group or circle of friends if it is loss of employment. God must be consulted for divine help in any of these situations. Pray, be patient and encourage one another. Whatever is the cause of crisis, seek an appropriate Christian intervention program.

90. **When should a spouse go to court?**

Court as part of the Judiciary branch of the government is responsible for interpreting the laws and adjudicating disputes. There is a need for the courts and judges in a society since disputes, conflicts and disagreements are bound to happen. Disputes or conflicts may be between politicians, business partners and their employees or customers or public, between students and instructors, between government and organizations, and between couples. Conflicts may be small, big or in-between. Most disputes are resolvable, while others need the intervention of the courts because they are too complicated for easy resolution.

We as Christians engage in many relationships with family, friends, community, organizations and governments; but we should recognize that the relationship with our spouse is unique and important. The relationship we have with our fellow believers, as members of the same spiritual family, is not the same as the relationship we have with non-believers who operate under different rules and principles. The relationship we have with our spouse supersedes the relationship with believers and non-believers. Because relationship can lead to disputes, Jesus Christ has given believers specific processes to adjudicate disputes.

***"Moreover, if thy brother shall trespass against thee, go and tell him his fault between thee and him alone: if he shall hear thee, thou hast gained thy brother. But if he will not hear thee, then take with thee one or two more, that in the mouth of two or three witnesses every***

> ***word may be established. And if he shall neglect to hear them, tell it unto the church: but if he neglects to hear the church, let him be unto thee as a heathen man and a publican.*** Matthew 18:15-17

The processes are: do not ignore the conflict, reach out to make amends, identify the source of conflict, do not win at all cost, forgive, do not miss the big picture, do not raise a white flag, and engage others and the church leadership to help resolve the conflict.

Christians are called to live a new life, worship God, evangelize non-believers, and be good models for the world. The church is called to be the answer to the world and settle disputes among the believers. A genuine Christian is not just a worshipper of God, but a part of the church and is expected to engage the church in settling marriage disputes. The Scriptures highlight reasons why Christians should not go to court.

> ***"If any of you has a dispute with another, do you dare to take it before the ungodly for judgment instead of before the Lord's people? Or do you not know that the Lord's people will judge the world? And if you are to judge the world, are you not competent to judge trivial cases? Do you not know that we will judge angels? How much more the things of this life! Therefore, if you have disputes about such matters, do you ask for a ruling from those whose way of life is scorned in the church? I say this to shame you. Is it possible that there is nobody among you wise enough to judge a dispute between believers? But instead, one brother takes another to court—and this in front of unbelievers! The very fact that you have lawsuits among you means you have been completely defeated already. Why not rather be wronged? Why not rather be cheated? Instead, you yourselves cheat and do wrong, and you do this to your brothers and sisters.*** 1 Corinthians 6:1-8 (NIV)

The reasons Christians should not take their spouse to court are:

- The saints will judge the world and the angels.
- The world and the church have different values, principles and priorities.
- The church has people who have better qualifications and wisdom than the worldly judges.
- The accused, offenders or defendants are our brothers and sisters in faith including our spouse.
- We are not better than the accused or offenders or defendants.
- We fail God and our mission when we think we can win the case rather than seeking to win over our offenders.

Couples go to court to file and engage in divorce battle. The argument that marriage issues are not trivial or small matter that should be brought to the church is just an excuse. The church is the solution to the problems of the world. Jesus came to establish the church and He is coming to rapture the church. As believers in Christ, we are part of the church.

There are times when Christians go to court. It is a win-win situation when couples resolve conflicts between themselves or with the help of the church. It is a win-lose or lose-win situation when a couple cannot resolve their differences. In this win-lose or lose-win situation, the matter may still end up in court after all attempts of resolutions have failed.

> ***"Settle matters quickly with your adversary who is taking you to court. Do it while you are still together on the way, or your adversary may hand you over to the judge, and the judge may hand you over to the officer, and you may be thrown into prison. Truly I tell you, you will not get out until you have paid the last penny.*** Matthew 5:25-26 (NIV)

Couples in court may need to hire attorneys, pay court fees and follow other judicial processes. The cases or disputes may be civil or criminal in nature. The court may use arbitration or bench or jury trials to adjudicate the disputes. The court may give judgment in favor of or against either party by sentencing one to a prison term, fines, or awarding punitive or statutory damages. Christian couples may go to court for any of the following actions:

- Litigation with an unbeliever.
- Litigating with a contract in respect of a business or property.
- Representing oneself as the defendant.
- Subpoenaed or hired to be a witness such as an eyewitness, professional or expert witness, or character witness.
- Litigating with a business organization as employers, vendors, contractors, or customer.
- Dealing with governments such as local, state, federal government, agencies and departments.
- A class-action law suit for negligence and fraud.

Chapter 12

# Separation, Divorce and Remarriage

*The Press* is more than a watchdog. It shapes and influences public opinion. The press, as news media, has its own ideology, agenda and political affiliation. Each news medium pushes and promotes its ideology by giving much news coverage to news items consistent with its ideology. The news media hires news anchors, contributors and correspondents to spin the same news and their opinion repeatedly until it resonates with the public. The news media follow the news consistent with public opinion and the views of the majority. The news media are run as business entities with goals of making profits. It is important for Christians to know that any idea, whether godly or ungodly, can be turned to favorable public opinion by the help of a powerful press. Christians should not take their principles, cues and instructions from public opinion and the press. For instance, the consistent sound of the beltway and mainstream media have turned adultery, fornication, same-sex marriage, divorce, abortion, and remarriage into a normal way of life. The press is not aligned with the principles of God, and, according to

1 Corinthians 1:25, *"For the foolishness of God is wiser than human wisdom, and the weakness of God is stronger than human strength".* Couples should not base their marriage on voices in the press.

91. **What are the consequences of divorce?**

The world view of the church is not only stagnant but in reverse gear. The church and the world views should be different. The irony is that the church is worse than the world, in that what is primitive in the world sense is perfected in the church. The church's malaise includes but is not limited to degradation of standard, shifting of boundaries, rejection of principle and a compromise of faith. I wonder if divorce was not one of the things that the scriptures said should not be mentioned among you. Today, Christians engage in divorce as though there is no consequence. The church trivializes the institution of marriage as if there is no implication. The effects of divorce can be highlighted under three main categories.

- **Family** - Marriage exists to create a family and to birth a generation. Family suffers when marriage ends. The early symptoms of a problematic marriage, before it climaxes in divorce, are fighting, arguments, humiliation, abuse, and infidelity. These outcomes sometimes have devastating impacts on the couple and their children. The impacts of divorce on the family are:
    - Disorganization. Divorce changes many things, which may include status, names, home address, and children's school.
    - Irresponsibility. Divorce compromises parental responsibilities to the children even when they have joint custody. There may be social, economic and psychological effects on the children. For instance, it may

make the children become irresponsible, practice a low standard of living, and display unexplained gross attitudes.

- Unhealthy legacy. It has been said that actions speak louder than words, so the parents are teaching their children that marriage does not work. Divorce becomes a legacy to the children and may be hard to change. Most grown up children from broken homes don't even want marriage, and those who marry don't want to fight for their marriage when there is a small crisis. This is one of the reasons there are many divorces in our churches today.

- **Future** - Marriage is a celebration of love and when marriage is dismissed, love is lost. Because love affects individual life, when it is lost through divorce, every aspect of family, including the future will be affected. The impact of divorce on one's future are:

    - It may lead to psychological challenges: Divorce creates physical stress, financial strain, psychological pressure and social humiliation on a couple. This is because the responsibility of two has become that of one. Divorce causes a loss or decrease in household income, loneliness; insecurity, and dejection.

    - It may affect employment, career and ministry: The continuous stress and challenges of divorce may create lack of focus and concentration, and may affect productivity at work and school. For those called into the ministry, divorce may impair their credential to fulfill their calling.

    - It may lead to the loss of a mentorship opportunity: Since a person cannot give what they don't have, a divorcee may not be able to defend the workability of marriage based on their own experience and lose the opportunity to mentor other young couples. Unfortunately, there are many divorcees who are mentoring young couples and spreading their own ideas on the non-workability of marriage. Also, many professional family counselors who have failed in marriage are in the counseling field. I wonder what they are imparting to their clients.

- **Faith** - Marriage is one of the things that the scriptures encourage believers in Christ to do for the glory of God.

  ***"And whatever you do, whether in word or deed, do it all in the name of the Lord Jesus, giving thanks to God the Father through him.*** Colossians 3:17

  Divorce, being a legal termination of the marriage covenant, cannot be to and for the glory of God. As believers, we have a duty and responsibility to represent and preach Christ on earth. The impact of divorce on faith are:

  - It causes believers to become covenant breakers. We appear wicked and ungodly when we divorce our spouse.

    ***"The man who hates and divorces his wife," says the LORD, the God of Israel, "does violence to the one he should protect," says the LORD Almighty. So be on your guard, and do not be unfaithful.*** Malachi 2:16

  - The faith in God is at risk. One of God's principles is differentiation. Believers are expected to be different.

    ***"I do not ask You to take them out of the world, but to keep them from the evil one. They are not of the world, even as I am not of the world.*** John 17:15-16

Unfortunately, we make our personal testimony flawed and lose the flavor of our sweetness through divorce. We make faith in God of no importance.

- Lost opportunity to build God's kingdom. Through divorce we agree with the world that marriage is not workable. We trash the virtues of love, faith, perseverance, and kindness which the kingdom teaches. No wonder we can no longer make sacrifices for our marriages and preach the gospel for the growth of the kingdom.

92. **What are the myths of divorce, and how should they be addressed?**

Divorce is the annulment of the marriage covenant. It trashes the promise, vow and agreement that a husband and wife have made with each other. Divorce has no appreciation of the memories, journeys and lives created by the marriage. Divorce focuses on individuality rather than two spouses. In divorce, the couple's relationship is dissolved, their properties are shared, and custody of the children is determined. Divorce means nothing to many probably because of their belief and its popularity and acceptability in our world today. These beliefs and popular practices constitute the myths of divorce, and they include:

- **Wrong Understanding of Marriage** - Marriage is sweet and provides a wonderful love story. The classic decoration, elegant wedding dress, array of flowers and beautiful atmosphere at the wedding ceremony sometimes give a deceitful impression about marriage. The idea that anything about marriage is a honeymoon is wrong. It is not always happily ever after. The idea that marriage is insulated from problems and other issues of life makes couples think that any marriage that is facing challenges should be dissolved and terminated. This explains the reason some marriages do not last but a few weeks after the honeymoon. The remedy is to understand the cycle of marriage which starts from Honeymoon or Wedding, to Reality of Marriage, to Old Wine, to New or No Wine, and back to Honeymoon or Wedding, and the cycle continues. The cycle of marriage is well explained in question #6 of my book titled *Before You Marry*.

- **God Allowed Divorce in the Bible** - Many nominal Christians succumb to divorce with a belief that God permitted it in the Bible especially in the Old Testament. They pointed to Abraham who divorced Haggai and Moses who married another wife and instructed others to divorce. They pointed to King David who had many wives as an indirect way of divorcement of old wives. They pointed to many pastors and bishops of today who have divorced and are still living their lives. The myths that the bible allowed divorce and other people do it is not from God. The same Bible said God hates divorce. Jesus said Moses allowed it because the hearts of people were hardened but in the beginning God did not permit it. The remedy to divorce is to get our hearts converted through the genuine salvation of Christ.

- **Divorce is the only solution to marriage problem** - Like any relationship, conflict is natural to the marital relationship. Most marriage conflicts are resolved amicably, but many couples see the existence of marital conflicts as the incompatibility of the couple, which can only be corrected with a split. Instead of couples engaging in prayer, amending their characters, adopting different strategies, undertaking spiritual and/or professional counseling, and seeking conflict resolution as part of the solution, they resort to divorce.

- **Divorce brings Maturity and Experience** - There is another myth or a blame game that couples are probably immature, inexperienced, youthful, and naïve and are prone to mistakes in their first marriage. The claim is that divorce gives them the opportunity to be wiser, matured and experienced for future marriages, and that the experience, skill and knowledge learned in the first marriage are available for the second marriage. This is far from the truth as the rate of second marriage divorce is worse than the rate of first marriage divorce. In the United States, the rate of divorce of first, second and third marriages are about 41%, 60% and 73% respectively. The remedy is to understand that marriage is and will continue to be a mystery from God. We must follow the word and principles, and have a godly heart to make marriage work.

- **Marriage is not for me** - Another myth or excuse is to hear someone say or conclude that something they passionately want is not for them after they have had it and lost it. Someone who zealously sought and yearned for love, found it and got married will later claim that marriage is not for them is an excuse for divorce. The remedy is that there is nothing wrong in not marrying or in saying marriage is not for you as long as you have not married. However, do not give this excuse after you failed in marriage.

- **I can still serve God faithfully and go to heaven** - Many Christians terminate the marriage covenant because of their belief that it won't hurt or affect their relationship with God. Yes, I agree that marriage, divorce and remarriage are not the criteria for salvation or heaven, but like any principle of God, it has its consequences. Between salvation and heaven, God expects us to shine as lights, live a sanctified and holy life, and follow His will to fulfill our destiny and glorify His name. When we break this, we diminish faith, hinder the gospel and may miss out as being true servants of God.

Most of these myths are reasonable and logical but they are against the will of God. God will provide assistance and grace if you are willing to sacrifice and make your marriage work.

93. **Should Christians remarry?**

Remarriage is having a second or third or fourth marriage after previous marriages have ended or been terminated. The reasons for remarriage may include:

- **Divorce** - A situation where the law or the court or the culture nullifies the marriage covenant. In this case, the couple is freed from the rights and obligation of marriage.

- **Separation** - A situation where a couple is still married but due to a loss of interest in each other or unresolved conflict live separately. A separated couple that lives in different countries may remarry in his or her resident country by not disclosing the previous marriage due to differing laws of different countries. This may be illegal but people still remarry for this reason.

- **Death of spouse** - Marriage automatically ends at the death of a spouse. The living spouse is freed from the marriage covenant.

- **Marriage Contract** - A situation where the couple agrees to marry for a certain good, purpose and period. The marriage is assumed dissolved at the delivery of the goods, fulfillment of the purpose, and the expiration of the period. A marriage contract may be made renewable every seven or ten years. A marriage contract may be based on one's immigration status. A marriage contract may be illegal but it is still a practice that leads to remarriage.

- **Polygamy** - A practice that allows a person to have more than one spouse. A husband may engage in second or third marriage to increase the number of wives to two or three. Likewise, a wife may remarry to increase the number of her husbands to more than one.

Marriage accrues economic, social and spiritual benefits. It cures loneliness, allows sex without guilt, and encourages two people to care for children. Because of these natural benefits, many people marry and remarry but Christians should approach remarriage in this manner:

- **Perfect Will** - It is the perfect will of God for a spouse to remarry after the death of their spouse. 1 Timothy 5:14 reads *"So I counsel younger widows to marry, to have children, to manage their homes and to give the enemy no opportunity for slander.* Marriage covenants end at death, and a living spouse can choose to remarry.

- **Permissive Will** - Remarriage due to divorce, separation, contract marriage and polygamy is under the permissive will of God. Marriage or remarriage is not a pre-requisite for heaven but salvation is. Christians that operate under the permissive will of God will surely face the consequence of His permissive will. Many churches do not want to associate with such a permissive will or share from the consequences. To this end, churches do the following:

    - Disqualify leaders who have remarried from being pastors or heads of their local churches. Many, who fall under this disciplinary action, start their own ministries. Other self-appointed persons or founders of their own churches who lack accountability and act as they please have gone into many marriages with varying explanations.

  - Refuse to conduct weddings for their members who are remarrying. When they choose to conduct the wedding, they prefer to conduct such weddings in their office or somewhere other than their sanctuary to encourage humility and serve as a deterrent for others.
  - Refuse sacrament and communion to members who have remarried.

- Perverse Will - Remarriage due to divorce, separation and polygamy is nothing to people who operate under the perverse will, and those people cannot be called Christians. The goal of perverse will is to dismantle the perfect will of God. If you have engaged in multiple marriages due to divorce and polygamy, you will need to examine your faith. The practice of a perverse will glorifies the devil and promotes worldliness.

  ***"Examine yourselves, whether ye be in the faith; prove your own selves. Know ye not your own selves, how that Jesus Christ is in you, except ye be reprobates?"*** 2 Corinthians 13:5

My recommendation is that Christians should strive to keep their marriage intact, but if for any reason they divorce and need to remarry, they should approach their new wedding with less fanfare and contrite hearts. The second wedding should not be done as if they are doing something that others should emulate.

### 94. Should a spouse seek divorce if a Christian spouse converts to another religion?

In life, expectations may differ from reality. The dream of every married man and woman is to have a marriage relationship devoid of conflicts and misunderstanding, a kind of fairytale relationship that has a happy ending. However, the reality of life is that not all relationships follow the rule of happily ever after. We live in a world of sin where the devil resides. It is a task to live righteously.

> ***"You will be hated by everyone because of me, but the one who stands firm to the end will be saved.*** Matthew 10:22 (NIV)

To determine whether to seek divorce or other redress to the above question, we will examine four scenarios.

The first is what to do when a loving and bible-believing couple goes astray from faith in Christ. There is nothing to be done since both spouses started in faith but decided to leave Christ. Neither of these spouses should have an issue with the behavior, character, disposition and action of the other spouse. For instance, a couple that married in church, attended church for a while and later decided to abandon church, for whatever reason should not complain at any time. They may end up as non-believing Christians or non-Christians.

> ***"Holding faith, and a good conscience; which some having put away concerning faith have made shipwreck.*** 1 Timothy 1:19

The second scenario is when one spouse backslides, stops attending church or stops practicing the Christian faith but does not convert to another religion. In this situation, the other spouse is not hindered from attending church or practicing his or her Christian faith. This action may raise serious concern to the believing spouse, but there is nothing they can do besides pray for and show love to the non-believing spouse. The Christian faith consists of three categories of believers - the Spirit-filled or hot-hearted, Senses-filled or warm hearted, and Satan-filled or cold-hearted believers.

> "*For it had been better for them not to have known the way of righteousness, than, after they have known it, to turn from the holy commandment delivered unto them.*
> 2 Peter 2:21 (KJV)

The third situation is when the couple started as non-Christians and one spouse becomes a Christian or believer. In this case, the believing spouse will need to pray, show love and be patient while believing God for the salvation of the non-believing spouse. The believing spouse will need to shine the light of the gospel to the non-believing spouse through his or her character and behavior.

> ***"Let your light so shine before men, that they may see your good works, and glorify your Father which is in heaven.*** Matthew 5:16 (KJV)

The fourth situation is when one spouse renounces faith and converts to another religion. The couple that started their marital journey as believers in Christ is having dual religious practices in the home. Dual religious homes could involve Christianity and Islam, Christianity and Hinduism, and Christianity and Judaism. This will result in numerous disagreements, conflicts and misunderstandings in the home. There will be differences in beliefs of how to raise children. There may be hindrances on the believing spouse and how to practice his or her faith. There may be unexpected and many more challenges. In this or any other scenario, divorce is not what the Holy Spirit recommends for believers in Christ. Here are some suggestions:

- A believing spouse should pray and love the non-believing spouse.

- A believing spouse should minister and win the non-believing spouse back to Christ.
- Depending on the situation, a believing spouse may separate but should not divorce their non-believing spouse.
- If a non-believing spouse initiates and seeks to divorce the believing spouse, they should accept the divorcement as the last option.
- A believing spouse who was divorced may remarry.

> ***"To the rest I say this (I, not the Lord): If any brother has a wife who is not a believer and she is willing to live with him, he must not divorce her. And if a woman has a husband who is not a believer and he is willing to live with her, she must not divorce him. For the unbelieving husband has been sanctified through his wife, and the unbelieving wife has been sanctified through her believing husband. Otherwise your children would be unclean, but as it is, they are holy. But if the unbeliever leaves, let it be so. The brother or the sister is not bound in such circumstances; God has called us to live in peace. How do you know, wife, whether you will save your husband? Or, how do you know, husband, whether you will save your wife?*** 1 Corinthians 7:12-16 (NIV)

95. **As a divorcee, is it possible to remarry my ex-spouse?**

The marriage covenant is often consecrated with the words "till death do us part." Unfortunately, the world has redefined the marriage covenant and bastardized the institution of marriage so much that a man can enter into two or more marriage covenants in his life time. In our world today, the average number of times a person marries is no longer one. The church is no different. The Christian that is supposed to be the light of the world is now getting his or her light from the world. It is gross to listen to the testimonies of so called saints in our churches claiming that they give glory to God for the success of their third or fifth wedding ceremonies or how wonderful their third or fifth husband is to them. The truth be said, such testimony does not give glory to God. The faith in Christ, as given to us is,

> ***"therefore, if any man is in Christ, he is a new creature: and old things are passed away; behold, all things are become new.*** 2 Corinthians 5:17 (KJV)

Today, the world provides soft rationales for divorce to include irreconcilable differences, amicable separation, conscious uncoupling, and many others. Couples are now going to "break-up moon" instead of "honeymoon". This is nothing but a bastardization of the marriage institution.

A divorcee that wants to remarry his or her ex-spouse will be doing the right thing. Naturally, this may look awkward since the law has terminated and buried the first marriage. Spiritually, it is the right thing to do because the marriage covenant was not broken in the first place and other marriage covenants entered into after the first marriage covenant are just complicating marriage covenants. A marriage covenant can only be broken at death by the standard of God.

> ***"When thou shalt vow a vow unto the LORD thy God, thou shalt not slack to pay it: for the LORD thy God will surely require it of thee; and it would be sin in thee.*** Deuteronomy 23:21 (KJV)

The bad news is that unfulfilled marriage covenants have consequences. Remarrying an ex-spouse will not only bring joy to heaven but it also cures the consequences of unfulfilled covenants. Heaven will be happy because:

- **It is a mark of repentance:** God is always happy when sinners become saints. God has no pleasure in the death of lawbreakers but wants them to repent and come to Him.

> ***"Likewise, I say unto you, there is joy in the presence of the angels of God over one sinner that repenteth."*** Luke 15:10 (KJV)

God also rejoices in the repentance of a backslider. Like the father of the prodigal son, heaven will celebrate the repentance of a divorcee who overlooks and endures the pain to reconcile with the ex-spouse and remarry them. The world may not appreciate it but God does.

- **It is a mark of restitution:** Because God is just and righteous He establishes restitution for anyone who had done ungodly things to people before they know Him. Restitution allows Christians to return things they obtain through cheating and fraud to any of their living victims.

> ***"And Zacchaeus stood, and said unto the Lord; Behold, Lord, the half of my goods I give to the poor; and if I have taken anything from any man by false accusation, I restore him fourfold."*** Luke 19:8 (KJV)

> ***"And must confess the sin they have committed. They must make full restitution for the wrong they have done, add a fifth of the value to it and give it all to the person they have wronged."*** Also, Number 5:7 (NIV)

Like Zacchaeus, any divorcee willing to restitute and please God will be blessed and approved of God. The world may scorn the person but God will be satisfied with that person.

- **It is a mark of godliness**: Remarrying the first ex-spouse may not be popular to the world but it is an act of righteousness. What is highly exalted among people may be an abomination to God.

> ***"Righteousness exalts a nation, but sin condemns any people."*** Proverb 14:34 (NIV)

Righteousness exalts an individual, family and nation. People will tell you, why bother since you have separated and divorced already, but you are following the path of God if you take a step of reconciliation. God is interested in exhibiting His glory through your return to godliness and holiness.

For a man or woman who remarried after the first divorce, it may be hard to remarry or rejoin with their first ex-spouse if they divorced their new spouse.

> ***"If a man marries a woman who becomes displeasing to him because he finds something indecent about her, and he writes her a certificate of divorce, gives it to her and sends her from his house, and if after she leaves his house she becomes the wife of another man, and her second husband dislikes her and writes her a certificate of divorce, gives it to her and sends her from his house, or if he dies, then her first husband, who divorced her, is not allowed to marry her again after she has been defiled. That would be detestable in the eyes of the LORD. Do not bring sin upon the land the LORD your God is giving you as an inheritance.*** Deuteronomy 24:1-4

This narrative explains the importance and danger of sex and marriage. A divorce certificate is not a cure to defilement, curses and consequences of a broken marriage covenant against faith, future and family. Remarrying an ex-spouse was impossible before the dispensation of grace but now it is possible because Christ said in the beginning it was not so.

96. **As a divorcee that seeks reconciliation and remarriage with an ex-spouse, how should one go about winning an ex-spouse back?**

It is the right thing to have a change of mind about divorce in order to reconcile and remarry the ex-spouse. God is pleased and approves of this as a mark of repentance, restitution, reconciliation and righteousness. It is important to understand that the world has no interest in reconciliation of family; if it does, it does it for business. The steps to follow to achieve remarriage of an ex-spouse have to come from God. Here are some suggestions:

- **Engage prayer**: This is important to win the heart of your ex-spouse especially if they are not interested anymore. With prayer, encouragement, acts of love and patience you may win a spouse's heart back. But both of you should be healed of past baggage and problems before you reach this point.

- **Engage your pastor who will**:

    - Counsel you and your ex-spouse separately.
    - Reconcile you and ex-spouse.
    - Reconcile you and your ex-spouse's families.
    - Pray for you and your ex-spouse to return and live as couple. The pastor will make a declaration or pronouncement of the two as a couple. There is no need for another church or traditional wedding.
    - Encourage you and your ex-spouse to have a court house wedding.

These steps are not as easy as listed. You might face numerous obstacles especially if your ex-spouse and his or her family are not interested in the remarriage. Your pastor is a major player and should assist with the help of the Holy Spirit and wisdom from God to counsel you on what to do every step of the way.

Chapter 13

# Marriage Autopsies and Biblical Couples

A *Mirror* shows the reflection and image of the object in front of it. A mirror allows one to examine oneself before other people examine them. It enables a person to make necessary adjustments and changes to their look. A mirror does not lie but gives back what stands in front of it. Matthew 5:14 reads that *"Ye are the light of the world. A city that is set on an hill cannot be hid.* Man's life is like a mirror that reflects an image to other people. Our life will either motivate or devastate other people. Our marriage will either glorify God or gratify the devil. Christians become examples for other people to follow. We become the scriptures that the world reads. Every person should look at themselves in the mirror and make necessary adjustments and corrections. Every person should examine others and learn from their mistakes. A wise person does not only learn from their own mistake but also from the mistakes of others. More importantly, couples should learn from the word of God and be an example of a good marriage to the young ones and the world.

97. **What are lessons learned from the marriage of Isaac and Rebecca?**

There are examples of many marriages in the Old Testament of the Holy Bible such as marriage between Abraham and Sarah, King Ahasuerus and Queen Esther, King Ahab and Queen Jezebel, Moses and Zipporah, and Samson and Delilah. But the marriage between Isaac and Rebecca was a unique marriage from which we can learn.

> ***"And Isaac went out to meditate in the field at the eventide: and he lifted up his eyes, and saw, and, behold, the camels were coming. And Rebekah lifted up her eyes, and when she saw Isaac, she lighted off the camel. For she had said unto the servant, What man is this that walketh in the field to meet us? And the servant had said, It is my master: therefore she took a vail, and covered herself. And the servant told Isaac all things that he had done. And Isaac brought her into his mother Sarah's tent, and took Rebekah, and she became his wife; and he loved her: and Isaac was comforted after his mother's death."*** Also, Genesis 25:21-23 read ***"And Isaac intreated the LORD for his wife, because she was barren: and the LORD was intreated of him, and Rebekah his wife conceived. And the children struggled together within her; and she said, If it be so, why am I thus? And she went to enquire of the LORD. And the LORD said unto her, Two nations are in thy womb, and two manner of people shall be separated from thy bowels; and the one people shall be stronger than the other people; and the elder shall serve the younger.*** Genesis 24:63-67 (KJV)

On one hand, it is revealed that:

- **Isaac loved Rebecca** - Isaac's love for Rebecca was a complete love of Eros, Phileo and Agape. Isaac loved Rebecca not only for her beauty and fair looks, but also in order to support her emotionally. He cherished and nurtured her. He forgave and encouraged her to be her best.

- **Isaac was comforted with Rebecca** - Rebecca's presence, voice, friendship, beauty, skills, strengths, and weaknesses were enough for Isaac. Rebecca was a bundle of joy and comfort to Isaac.
- **Isaac brought Rebecca to his heart** - Before Isaac got married, the person that filled his heart was Sarah, his mother, but after marriage, that love was his wife. This was not about the death of Sarah or about a physical house but it was about priority and influence in Isaac's life. His wife and mother had their different roles but he placed his wife in the inner chamber, a place of superior influence that Sarah used to occupy.
- **Isaac prayed for Rebecca** - Isaac was the only husband in the scripture that explicitly prayed for his wife when she faced problems, especially barrenness. Jacob complained instead of praying for Rachael. Instead of praying for Hannah, Elkanah doubled down and declared to her that he was worth more than 10 sons.
- **Isaac blessed his children** - Isaac prayed and blessed both Jacob and Esau.

The marriage showed that:

- **Rebecca was generous and kind** - She was modest in character and gentle in words. Her kindness brought her into marriage and kept her in it.
- **Rebecca knew and followed the Lord** - Rebecca consulted God when she had problems and she obeyed and followed through on what God told her. She did not allow her husband to thwart the plan of God for her family.
- **Rebecca complemented Isaac** - Rebecca was active before and after marriage. She corrected the error when Isaac, because of a gift or food, wanted to give the blessing of

leadership to Esau, and exposed the plot of Esau to kill Isaac.

- **Rebecca respected Isaac** - Rebecca did not nag, complain or criticize Isaac even when he was wrong. She obtained Isaac's approval before sending Jacob away.

The marriage life of Isaac and Rebecca reestablishes the fact that the foundation of marriage really matters. Their marriage was engineered by God as He answered the prayers of Abraham's servants. Isaac and Rebecca were worshippers of God as they consulted God, meditated and obeyed the word of God. Isaac and Rebecca maintained a monogamous marriage even in the face of barrenness.

98. **What are the lessons learned from the marriage of Joseph and Mary?**

Among the list of marriages in the New Testament, such as marriages between Zachariah and Elizabeth, Aquila and Priscilla, Ananias and Saphira, the marriage of Joseph and Mary is a classic model for believers in Christ. This was a marriage through which Christ came, was raised, nurtured and launched into ministry. Although God was His father, Mary and Joseph were His earthly parents. The marriage of Joseph and Mary was excellent because of some beautiful characteristics and qualities exhibited by the couple.

> ***"This is how the birth of Jesus the Messiah came about: His mother Mary was pledged to be married to Joseph, but before they came together, she was found to be pregnant through the Holy Spirit. Because Joseph her husband was faithful to the law, and yet did not want to expose her to public disgrace, he had in mind to divorce her quietly. But after he had considered this, an angel of the Lord appeared to him in a dream and said, "Joseph son of David, do not be afraid to take Mary***

***home as your wife, because what is conceived in her is from the Holy Spirit. She will give birth to a son, and you are to give him the name Jesus, because he will save his people from their sins." All this took place to fulfill what the Lord had said through the prophet: "The virgin will conceive and give birth to a son, and they will call him Immanuel" (which means "God with us"). When Joseph woke up, he did what the angel of the Lord had commanded him and took Mary home as his wife. But he did not consummate their marriage until she gave birth to a son. And he gave him the name Jesus."*** Matthew 1:18-25 (NIV)

On one hand, Joseph was:

- A Righteous Man - Joseph was upright before God and man. He was loyal, dependable and reliable in the sight of God. His righteousness made him the foster father of the savior of the world.
- A Worshipper of God - Joseph was a worshipper of God. He was not only a church goer but also a word doer. He took his family to the temple regularly. He knew and obeyed the voice of God through His Angel.
- A Protector of His Wife - He had a good heart. Even before the Angel spoke to him, he refused to put Mary into public shame. He did not wash his wife's dirty linen in or with public opinion, but decided to cover, protect and defend her. He contemplated divorce but did it not.
- A Friend of God - He made sacrifice for God. Not only did he marry someone impregnated by the Holy Spirit, he also did not touch Mary until the birth of Christ was completed.
- A lover - He loved and waited for Mary. He did not mistreat but rather cherished Mary.

- A Family Man – Joseph looked after his family. He was out searching for Jesus when he was missing. He raised all his children in the way of God including Jesus.

On her part, Mary was a devoted and righteous woman, a lovely wife, a worshipper of God, and a family woman.

The marriage of Joseph and Mary was built on the foundation of the word and will of God. Both were willing to honor and obey God at the expense of their individual interests. They preferred the opinions of God more than public opinion. They worshipped God regularly and fellowshipped with other believers in Christ. They jointly searched for Jesus Christ when He was assumed missing without placing blame or criticizing one another.

99. **What are lessons learned from the marriages of Christians that lasted under 10 years?**

In over eighteen years as a pastor, I have seen, heard and witnessed quite a few marriage relationships. In many of these marriages, I have been actively involved as a witness, counselor, main minister or part of the officiating team of ministers. Many of these marriages are successful, blissful and still thriving, while some of them have collapsed. This answer provides a short summary of four marriages that ended up in divorce. The names used in these examples are fictitious. The information provided is what was known to the author during interrogation, observation and counseling, and may not represent all the information about the case.

**Mr. David Banks & Mrs. Joan Banks' Marriage** – The marriage of Mr. David and Mrs. Joan started well with lots of fanfare and celebration at the wedding. They were both young and educated with promising futures. After the wedding, they moved away from people that knew them, including the two churches they attended before marriage. The former church of the bridegroom made several efforts to bring them back to the fellowship but they refused without reason. Like any other marriage, the Banks faced a challenge which could have easily been resolved, but there was no one to mediate for them. They forgot that everyone needs somebody, especially the children of God. The marriage did not survive for five years before it hit the rocks. The take-away here is that we should not neglect the gathering of the saints.

**Mr. Martin Sanders & Mrs. Lisa Sanders:** The couple was a pair of young Africans who started their relationship through social media. Both were mature physically and financially but were spiritually and psychologically immature. Mr. Martin was not mentally strong enough to wean himself from his mother's tutelage. Mrs. Lisa was not mentally strong enough to accept the criticism and advice from her own family even before marriage. The church wedding was cancelled at the last minute, due to flimsy excuses from the couple. Martin and Lisa went for a court wedding, moved to another city and had a baby. The first week, the mother in-law who came from Africa saw Mrs. Lisa and told her that she could not be her son's wife because she did not measure up socially with her son. Unfortunately, Mr. Martin, who was in his early thirties, was still a child at heart. Mr. Martin could not refuse his African mother, and therefore divorced his wife, Mrs. Lisa Sanders. The case reflects and showcases the challenge some of which are posed by parents and in-laws.

**Mr. Mark Green and Julie Green Marriage** - This is a marriage of two talented people who have strong support from their parents and the church. The Greens were loved as they were very active in the church. The problem of this marriage was linked to lack of trust and physical abuse. Mrs. Julie accused Mr. Mark of infidelity several times, which Mr. Mark denied.

The fact that Mr. Mark changed his career to a job that involved traveling and meeting people did not help their situation. Unfortunately, the marriage did not last a decade before Mr. Mark and Mrs. Julie went their separate ways despites family and pastoral interventions. The take away here is the danger of infidelity and spousal abuse.

**Mr. Terrence Wells & Mrs. Cynthia Wells Marriage:** The marriage between Mr. Terrence and Mrs. Cynthia was a beautiful union. Mr. Terrence was a young educated undocumented immigrant man from Africa and Mrs. Cynthia was a young, beautiful, educated African-American lady. The wedding was a classic one. The premarital counseling revealed many issues with the relationship such as cultural differences, behavior or character flaws, medical issue, and isolation from friends but none seemed to bother the couple as both confessed to be in love and have faith in God. About five years into the marriage, the man filed for divorce claiming he was fed up with dealing with the same issues that did not bother him initially. This case demonstrates that there is deception in the heart of people.

100. **What are the lessons learned from the marriages of Christians that lasted over 10 years?**

Genuine Christians mourn and grieve when their marriages are dissolved. But nominal Christians and unbelievers celebrate and feel relieved when their marriages collapse. The difference in the feelings and reactions of the two groups of confessors of faith is the condition of their hearts and their level of relationship with Christ. While many faithful and committed Christians will make sacrifices and do whatever it takes to salvage their marriage, many with ordinary interests and a worldly mindset will do nothing to rescue their marriage. Bad things happen to good people and Christians still fall into divorce for many reasons, but let the reason not be because of your failure to make the sacrifices and to do whatever it takes. This answer provides a short summary of four marriages that were terminated. The names used in these examples are fictitious. The information provided is what was known and interpreted by the author during interrogation, observation and counseling, and may not represent all the information about the case.

**Mr. Mathew Smith & Mrs. Karen Smith's Marriage:** Mr. Matthew Smith was an immigrant from Africa. He had lived for about 7 years in United States before returning to his country in Africa to marry his heartthrob and friend, Mrs. Karen Smith. Both were deeply in love and were blessed with a baby girl shortly after Mrs. Karen's arrival in US. Based on the wife's interest in business, Mr. Matthew secured all his savings and took out a small loan to open a business for his wife. While the business struggled in its early stages, Mr. Matthew continued to inject more capital from working overtime and a second job. To the amazement of the Mr. Matthew, Mrs. Karen was building a house in her name back in her country in Africa with the money from the business. Mr. Mathew's discovery of the secret was accidental. The marriage was over after he confronted his wife and she confirmed the secret. Pastoral intervention did nothing to appeal to Mr. Matthew as he felt betrayed. This case emphasizes the important of trust, transparency and the danger of keeping a secret from your spouse.

**Mr. Wilfred Song & Martha Song Marriage** - This was a marriage of two undocumented immigrants of African descent. The Songs were married with two children before they migrated to the US where they had their third child. The Songs were a respected couple in the church. Mr. Wilfred, considering the means of legalizing their immigration papers, discussed with his wife the possibility of marrying someone for immigration purposes. The wife refused because of their faith and Mr. Wilfred's history of sexual promiscuity. Mr. Song withdrew his membership from the church and became involved with different women. Mrs. Martha went to the church for a while but the behavior of Mr. Wilfred caused her embarrassment. The Songs have gone through a divorced and Mr. Wilfred has married another woman but is still waiting for the adjustment of his immigration status. This case highlights the challenges of immigration in marriage.

**Mr. Ray Steven & Mrs. Jane Steven's Marriage** - The marriage between Mr. Ray and Mrs. Jane seemed to be a perfect marriage until Mr. Ray started abusing Mrs. Jane. Sometimes, Mr. Ray would seize the car key and restrain Mrs. Jane from going out. He would not pay the mortgage and force Mrs. Jane to pay the mortgage with late payment penalties since the house was in her name. Mr. Ray would not allow her friends to visit them at home. He would kick and beat her during arguments. Mr. Ray would cheat on her sometimes when he travelled. He did not show up at the hospital during the birth of one of their children. This continued until Mrs. Jane completed and was certified in her professional career and she sought divorce. Mr. Ray was shocked when he saw the divorce papers. The professional counseling, therapy and his change of attitude were too late to stop the divorce. Community and pastoral interventions were too late to change Mrs. Jane's mind. This case shows that abuse is illegal, and infidelity is evil. It demonstrates the danger of taking your spouse and marriage for granted.

**Mr. Malone West & Sandra West:** This was a marriage of young immigrants of African descent. The marriage was promising, and it was full of joy and excitement. Mrs. Sandra's parents were very involved in the life of their daughter even before she married Mr. Malone. Prior to the West's marriage, Mrs. Sandra's parents had consulted the prophets who had told them that Mr. Malone was not fit for and might hinder the progress of their daughter. The fact that Mrs. Sandra was financially more buoyant than Mr. Malone inflated her parent's concern that Mr. Malone would drain Mrs. Sandra. Every time there was a disagreement, Mr. Malone would be haunted with the reminder that he was a cog in the wheel of his wife's progress. But Mrs. Sandra really loved her husband and was always at loggerhead with her family because of her husband. Mr. Malone isolated himself from his wife, friends and community. The involvement of his in-laws and other personal and spiritual issues led him to file for divorce despite the love of his wife. The case reveals the implications of Spiritism and in-law interference in marriage.

101. **What are the lessons from Jesus' attendance of a wedding ceremony?**

A wedding marks the commencement of a marriage relationship. Also, it is for the celebration of love and the mutual decision of two people who want to live the rest of their lives together. A wedding ceremony can be traditional, court, or church. There were many wedding ceremonies recorded in the Holy Bible which include the wedding of Jacob and Rachael, Ruth and Boaz, King Ahasuerus and Queen Esther, and many more. Jesus even gave a parable of a king that organized a wedding banquet for his son, and He attended a wedding ceremony with His family and disciples.

> "***On the third day a wedding took place at Cana in Galilee. Jesus' mother was there, and Jesus and his disciples had also been invited to the wedding. When***

> ***the wine was gone, Jesus' mother said to him, "They have no more wine." "Woman, why do you involve me?" Jesus replied. "My hour has not yet come." His mother said to the servants, "Do whatever he tells you." Nearby stood six stone water jars, the kind used by the Jews for ceremonial washing, each holding from twenty to thirty gallons. Jesus said to the servants, "Fill the jars with water"; so they filled them to the brim. Then he told them, "Now draw some out and take it to the master of the banquet." They did so, and the master of the banquet tasted the water that had been turned into wine. He did not realize where it had come from, though the servants who had drawn the water knew. Then he called the bridegroom aside and said, "Everyone brings out the choice wine first and then the cheaper wine after the guests have had too much to drink; but you have saved the best till now." What Jesus did here in Cana of Galilee was the first of the signs through which he revealed his glory; and his disciples believed in him"*** John 2:1-11 (NIV)

The answer to this question will address what can be learned with the presence of Jesus at the wedding of Cana of Galilee.

- **Marriage is important** - Christians need to recognize that marriage is important to God. The world, governments and celebrities may not appreciate it but God does. In the beginning, He made them male and female, but Jesus took time to honor the invitation to a wedding and there He performed the first miracle. The sustenance of marriage is the first miracle every couple should seek. Proverbs 18:22 reads *"He who finds a wife finds what is good and receives favor from the LORD."*

- **Family is a priority** - Marriage is the platform upon which a family is built. The day a man and a woman come together as husband and wife, a new family is born. You are now concerned with your spouse's interests. Even

Jesus who seemed not to be bothered and said, "my hour has not come" still yielded to His mother because He was part of a family. When you marry, you trade independence for interdependence and your family. Apart from God, marriage and family take priority over your work, business, interests, and friends. Job 1:1-3 reads that, *"In the land of Uz there lived a man whose name was Job. This man was blameless and upright; he feared God and shunned evil. He had seven sons and three daughters. And he owned seven thousand sheep, three thousand camels, five hundred yoke of oxen and five hundred donkeys, and had a large number of servants. He was the greatest man among all the people of the East.* Job's introduction was in the priority of his relationship with God, his family, including spouse, his work or business or wealth, and friends and communities.

- **Supremacy of the Word of God** - The word of God was paramount at this wedding ceremony. Mary told the servants *"Whatsoever He saith unto you, do it"*. In essence, do not argue about it. That is the key to the success or failure of marriage. In time of good or bad, problem or no problem, follow the word of God. The word of God is the creator's manual for living. It is the compass and Global Positioning System (GPS) for marital life. You cannot succeed in the journey of marriage without the Bible, the word of God. Isaiah 40:8 reads *"The grass withers and the flowers fall, but the word of our God endures forever"*

- **Communication is not negotiable** - Mary talked to Jesus about the issue because families must communicate. A couple should enjoy the voice and presence of each other. Don't go mute on your spouse. Don't allow anything to create a long term physical distance or separation between you and your spouse. Proverbs 12:14 reads *"From the fruit of their lips people are filled with good things, and the work of their hands brings them reward."*

- **Problems in life are unavoidable** - There will always be problems, even in marriage. The size of the problem may range from small to medium to large. The location of the problem is wherever people are found or whatever involves people such as church, school, marriage, business, friendship, or stores. Even with Jesus in attendance, there was a problem in this wedding. The problem may be personal, inherent or external, as explained earlier. Problems can originate from things such as food, wine, money, forgetfulness, or lateness. In this case, the wine had run out and Jesus told His mother "*woman, what have I to do with thee? Mine hour is not yet come.*" Marriage will bring disagreement, disappointments and problems but this is the time to encourage and show love to your spouse and is not the time to chastise or abuse. Colossians 3:19 reads *"Husbands, love your wives and do not be harsh with them."*

- **Unity is Essential** - Marriage calls for unification of two individuals into a single entity. Couples should embrace togetherness in all things as the world will strive to divide them. The master of ceremony at this wedding saw something strange about the new wine; instead of calling the couple, he called the bridegroom alone. The spouse should avoid individualism but rather be inclusive in all issues of marriage. The couple should operate as a single unit by speaking with one voice and making deals together. Genesis 11:6 (KJV) reads *"And the LORD said, Behold, the people is one, and they have all one language; and this they begin to do: and now nothing will be restrained from them, which they have imagined to do."*

*Matthew 19:5 (NIV) reads "And said, 'For this reason a man will leave his father and mother and be united to his wife, and the two will become one flesh'?"*

- **God is everything** - Life without the spirit is dead, likewise marriage without God is dead. God is the author and finisher of our life, faith, marriage, and work. In Him we move, live and have our being. A successful marriage will always be the one that not only has God as a party to it, but the center of it. Jesus was present at the wedding and His presence made the difference. He made the latter better than the former. The atheist and psychologist's ideas and views of the world have not been of much benefit to marriage. John 15:5 reads *"I am the vine, ye are the branches: He that abides in me, and I in him, the same brings forth much fruit: for without me ye can do nothing.*